AUSTRALIAN DESPERADOES

Also by Terry Smyth

Australian Confederates
Denny Day

AUSTRALIAN DESPERADOES

TERRY SMYTH

EBURY
PRESS

An Ebury Press book
Published by Penguin Random House Australia Pty Ltd
Level 3, 100 Pacific Highway, North Sydney NSW 2060
www.penguin.com.au

Penguin
Random House
Australia

First published by Ebury Press in 2017

Addresses for the Penguin Random House group of companies can be found at global.penguinrandomhouse.com/offices.

National Library of Australia
Cataloguing-in-Publication entry

Smyth, Terry, author.
Australian desperadoes: the incredible story of how Australian gangsters terrorised California/Terry Smyth.

ISBN: 978 0 14378 237 7 (paperback)

Australians – California – San Francisco – 19th century – History.
Gangsters – California – San Francisco – 19th century – History.
Organised crime – California – San Francisco – 19th century – History.
California – Gold discoveries.
San Francisco (California) – Social conditions – 19th century.

Cover photograph (man): AdobeStock
Cover design: Luke Causby/Blue Cork
Internal design and typesetting by Midland Typesetters, Australia
Printed in Australia by Griffin Press, an accredited ISO AS/NZS 14001:2004
Environmental Management System printer

Penguin Random House Australia uses papers that are natural, renewable and recyclable products and made from wood grown in sustainable forests. The logging and manufacturing processes are expected to conform to the environmental regulations of the country of origin.

*For the family downstairs, where all good
things happen – Kate, Ben, Sophie and Acky*

And for my sister Pauline

Contents

'There is in this city an organised band of villains
who are determined to destroy the city. We are standing
as it were upon a mine that any moment may explode,
scattering death and destruction.'
– *Daily Alta California*, 9 June 1851

'I have heard hundreds remark here that the day would soon come
when this country would be taken by the Sydney people.'
– Long Jim Stuart, leader of the Sydney Coves, 8 July 1851

Foreword

Not so long ago, I stood in Portsmouth Square, the old heart of San Francisco. It was in this former Mexican plaza that the first American flag was raised, where crowds cheered when California became the 31st state of the United States, and where lynch mobs once howled for blood. This was the place where the shout was heard that began the California Gold Rush. And it was here that so many of the events central to this story occurred.

Of course, Portsmouth Square today would not be recognisable to any of the characters in this story. Like the city that sprung up around it, the old plaza has had many incarnations, some inevitable, simply due to changing times, others of necessity after fire and earthquake.

Today, the former heart of the city is the heart of Chinatown. The plaza is now a park where children chatter in a playground, Chinese men sit reading or playing cards, homeless people sprawl on park benches and, where the old adobe customs house and town gaol once stood, pedestrians dodge traffic at the entrance to an underground car park.

Standing there in the old city square, my thoughts turned to the town where I was born and raised – Newcastle, New South Wales – and to the curious connection between the two cities.

In the days of sail, both were bustling ports, equally notorious for shanghai gangs, and in my youth I once met an old salt who claimed he had been coshed in a dockside pub in Newcastle and woke up aboard a clipper ship, on his way around the Horn to Frisco. It took him ten years, he told me, to drink his way back home.

After the 1906 San Francisco earthquake, in which some 3000 people were killed and most of the city destroyed, rubble from the streets was used as ballast for sailing ships. Ships that docked at Newcastle dumped their ballast at Stockton, on the north side of Newcastle harbour, greatly expanding the foreshore, which is still known as the Ballast Ground.

To walk on the Ballast Ground at Stockton is to walk upon what is left of old San Francisco, and, occasionally, remarkable finds are made. I recall a notable discovery by a man named Jack Dawson, who found among the ballast a box marked 'Tiffany & Co'. Inside were six ornate glass goblets, all miraculously intact, having survived the quake, the voyage and the dumping at Stockton. I understand the goblets are still with Dawson's family.

In Portsmouth Square, the only reminders of old San Francisco are a plaque commemorating the first raising of the American flag, in 1846, and a monument to the Scottish writer Robert Louis Stevenson, who visited San Francisco for a few months in 1879, and rented a room somewhere near the square.

Asked what might be Portsmouth Square's claim to fame, today's San Franciscans will most likely tell you that a scene from the 1971 Clint Eastwood movie *Dirty Harry* was shot there. Few, if any, will know of things that happened there in the 1850s, when California was the real Wild West and San Francisco was its dark heart. But that's understandable. Most people will not know this story because it was buried like the ballast, and because there are no heroes in this story.

– Terry Smyth, January 2017

Introduction

Dos Eldorados

Once there were two fabled lands of riches beyond the dreams of avarice. One was called California – named after a mythical queen of the Amazons – and was believed to be somewhere in the Americas. The other, which the Bible called Ophir, and from where King Solomon's fleet 'brought back 420 talents [about 16 tons] of gold'[1] was thought to lie somewhere in the South Pacific.

These lands of gold had fired the European imagination since antiquity, and, by the sixteenth century, with much of the world yet to be discovered, were widely believed to exist. Europe's great powers, competing for maritime supremacy, sent their ships to the ends of the earth, following fanciful maps and carrying goods for trade and arms for conquest.

So convinced were the Spanish that Ophir was to be found, ripe for plunder, on the coast of *Terra Australis Incognita* – the unknown southern land – that in 1546 a conquistador of Chile, Pedro Sancho de la Hoz, was appointed governor of the undiscovered country: a land rich in gold and silver, said to lie south-west of the Strait of Magellan – the narrow channel separating mainland South America from Tierra del Fuego.

As with the destruction of the Aztec empire in Mexico and the Incas in Peru, the planned conquest of Ophir to satisfy Spain's lust for gold was justified by an assumed duty to convert the heathens of undiscovered lands to Catholicism. To that end, Juan de Silva, King Phillip III's confessor, wrote to Pope Urban VIII in 1623, requesting 'that the mission to the natives of the Austral Lands be confided to the spiritual care of the Franciscan friars, who would undertake their "conquest" by spiritual and peaceful means'.[2]

However, expeditions sent to find and conquer the southern land of gold foundered in the wild storms of the Roaring Forties or were driven offcourse by the powerful Peru Current and forced to turn back. Nature made sure the natives of fabled Ophir would never see the glint of conquistador armour or the grey robes of missionary priests.

Amazons had always been out there, just beyond the edge of the known world. The ancient Greeks told of a race of warrior women – Herodotus wrote of them in his *Histories*, Homer in his *Iliad*. In the Middle Ages, Crusaders returned with tales of fierce female warriors who fought with Muslim armies. Christopher Columbus returned to Spain with a second-hand tale of an island in the New World inhabited only by women. The conqueror of Mexico, Hernan Cortes, and other conquistadores relayed similar tales, and in all such stories the land of the Amazons was always rich in gold, silver and precious stones.

So, in the early sixteenth century, when Spanish explorers heard rumours of an island of Amazons off the north-west coast of Mexico, they named it after the island in a popular romance novel of the day. The book, *Las Sergas de Esplandian* (*The Adventures of Esplandian*), by Garci Rodriguez Ordonez de Montalvo, was a particular favourite of Cortes, and in an era of exploration, when fact and fiction were often indistinguishable, could well have fostered his belief in the existence of a golden isle of women.

Montalvo wrote:

'Know ye that at the right hand of the Indies there is an island called California, very close to that part of the Terrestrial Paradise, which was inhabited by black women without a single man among them, and they lived in the manner of Amazons. They were robust of body with strong passionate hearts and great virtue. The island itself is one of the wildest in the world on account of the bold and craggy rocks. Their arms are all of gold, as is the harnesses of the wild beasts which, after taming, they ride [flying beasts called griffins – part lion, part eagle]. In all the island there is no other metal.

'They live in well-excavated caves. They have ships in which they go to raid other places, and the men they capture they carry off with them, later to be killed as will be told. At other times, being at peace with their opponents, they consort with them freely and have carnal relations with them, from which it results that many of them become pregnant. If they give birth to a female they keep her, but if to a male they kill him. The reason for this, as is known, is that they are firmly resolved to keep the males at so small a number that without trouble they can control them with all their lands, saving those thought necessary to perpetuate the race.

'Over this island of California rules a queen, Calafia, statuesque in proportions, more beautiful than all the rest, in the flower of her womanhood, eager to perform great deeds, valiant and spirited, and ambitious to excel all those who have ruled before her.'[3]

Calafia – black, brave and beautiful – is convinced by a captured Muslim warrior named Radiaro to come to the aid of a Muslim army defending Constantinople, under siege by Christian crusaders. She sets sail with her army of Amazon warriors, with their golden weapons and griffins, and joins the defenders of Constantinople.

Captured in battle when the Crusaders sack the city, Calafia converts to Christianity, marries a Spanish knight named Talangue, and sails back to California with her army and her husband to establish a Christian monarchy where men rule, women know their place, and they all live happily ever after. Apparently.

By the mid-eighteenth century, the name California was generally applied – although unofficially at first – to the northernmost outpost of the Spanish Empire's American possessions. It was not an island, as had been supposed, but a peninsula, and yielded neither gold nor jewels nor black warrior women.

In November 1769, on arriving overland from Mexico at a shallow bay north-east of the Californian peninsula, a Spanish expedition led by Don Gaspar de Portola claimed the territory for King Charles III. On the bay shore, the explorers built a fort and a Franciscan mission, which they named Mission San Francisco de Assis, and, in a cove on the inland side of the peninsula, south of the bay entrance, a settlement named after a plant common to the area – Yerba Buena ('Good Herb', *clinopodium douglasii*, an aromatic herb of the mint family). In time, the pueblo of Yerba

Buena would adopt a contracted version of the name of the mission – San Francisco.

Six months after the Spanish claimed San Francisco Bay, a British expedition led by Lieutenant James Cook sailed into a shallow bay on the east coast of New Holland – a lost continent no longer – and claimed the entire east coast in the name of King George III. In recognition of the bay's unique flora, Cook called it Botany Bay, a name that would become synonymous with the exile of Britain's convicts to penal colonies in the land Cook called New South Wales.

The California of fable became a reality almost 80 years later when, on Monday 24 January 1848, a carpenter named James Marshall, while building a sawmill near Coloma, on the American River, noticed some shiny specks in a water channel below the mill.

'I picked up one or two pieces and examined them attentively,' Marshall wrote, 'and having some general knowledge of minerals, I could not call to mind more than two which in any way resembled this: sulphuret of iron, very bright and brittle; and gold, bright yet malleable.'[4]

He collected a few more specimens and showed them to a Mr Scott, a fellow carpenter.

'What is it?' Scott asked.

'Gold,' Marshall replied.

'Oh no,' said Scott. 'That can't be!'[5]

But it was. And when word got out, and a merchant named Sam Brannan ran through Portsmouth Square, in San Francisco, waving his hat in one hand and a bottle of gold dust in the other, yelling, 'Gold! Gold! Gold from the American River!', the rush was on.[6]

Three years later, in Australia, a prospector named Edward Hargraves, lately returned from the California goldfields with little to show for his efforts, was riding with a companion, John Lister, through the Macquarie River country, in central-western New South Wales. When the pair stopped to water their horses, Hargraves, who had noted the similarity of the land to the gold-bearing regions of California, took his pick and pan into a creek bed and washed out five specks of gold.

It was Wednesday 12 February 1851. 'This is a memorable day in the history of New South Wales,' he told Lister. 'I shall be a baronet, you shall be knighted, and my old horse will be stuffed, put in a glass case and sent to the British Museum.'[7]

Appropriately for the place where the ancient fantasy became fact, Hargraves named the goldfield Ophir, and for the second fabled land of riches, the rush was on.

In those few fevered years between 1848 and 1851, thousands of Australians left home and hearth for California, hoping to strike it rich on the goldfields. The exodus was not entirely made up of gold-seekers, however. There were some who joined the exodus across the Pacific with criminal intent. In San Francisco, through mayhem and murder, a gang of Australian desperadoes terrorised the town. They called themselves the Sydney Coves, and this is the story of their rise and fall.

Chapter 1

A kind of mania

The tiny, tattered fishing village of Brighton was fated to change forever when a certain Dr Richard Russell turned his mind to the curious fact that the oceans were so full of salt that salt makers, 'before they deposit their brine, boil it till it will suspend an egg'.[1]

From that prosaic observation, Dr Russell deduced:

'That great body of water, therefore, which we call the sea, and which is rolled with such violence by tempests round the world, passing over all the submarine plants, fish, salts, minerals, and in short, whatsoever else is found betwixt shore and shore, must probably wash over some parts of the whole, and be impregnated, or saturated with the transpiration, if I may so term it, of all the bodies it passes over: the finest parts of which are perpetually flying off in steams and attempting to escape to the outward air, till they are entangled by the sea and make part of its composition; whilst the salts also are every moment imparting some of their substances to enrich it, and keep it from putrefaction.

'By these means, this fluid contracts a greater soapiness, or unctuosity, than common water, and by the whole collection of it being pervaded by the sulphureous steams of bodies which pass through it, seems to constitute that fluid we call sea water, which was intended by the great author of all things to be the common guardian against putrefaction and the corruption of bodies.'[2]

Russell's claims that bathing in the sea, and even drinking sea water, were good for the health, popularised in his 1753 book, *A Dissertation Concerning the Use of Sea Water in Diseases of the Glands Etc.*, inspired increasing numbers of England's upper and middle classes to dip their toes in coastal waters and sample a sip of the briny deep. The good doctor particularly recommended the waters at Brighton, in Sussex, where, by a happy coincidence, he had set up a medical practice in a beachside house – the largest and grandest house in the village. The influx of well-heeled visitors – steady for several years – became a stampede after 1783, when George, Prince of Wales, paid a visit to the town, which by then boasted fashionable hotels and rows of houses far grander than Dr Russell's. The prince – 'Prinny' to his entourage of dissolute friends – was a rake, drinker and gambler of no mean repute; as careless with the truth as he was with money and his affections. To announce the prince's arrival, a gun at the shore battery fired a salute. Unfortunately, the cannon exploded and killed the gunner, but the death did not dampen the delight at royal patronage, or the fireworks display that evening.

Prinny stayed in Brighton for 11 days, during which time he rode to hounds, attended a ball and the theatre, and outraged the locals with his carousing. And while there is no mention of him ever going near the water, such was the scramble to go where the royals go and do as the royals do that sea bathing quickly evolved from a mere fad to a kind of mania. With the heir to the throne as its patron, Brighton boomed. The erstwhile fishing village, now a coastal resort, was *the* place to go, not just for your health's sake but for the sake of your social standing.

Picture a boy of 16, identifiable as a local by his smock shirt, and as poor by the state of it, standing on the shingle beach at Brighton, his ears ringing from the splashes, shouts and laughter of tourists wading in the sea, unseen behind their bathing machines. The boy keeps his distance from the machines – a row of covered carts rolled into the water. He knows only too well that the carts, like the people frolicking in the shallows, are from another world.

It is 1834, and the boy is of a generation Brighton's boom times forgot. He's too young to remember when the Steine, now covered in rich men's houses, was covered in fishing nets from one end to the other, before barriers were erected to keep the fishermen out. But he is old enough to remember the riots when Sussex farm labourers were thrown out of work by the introduction of agricultural machinery. He knows of the people found dead of starvation on the streets of Brighton, blissfully ignored by the passing parade of toffs on their way to the pavilion, the pier or the beach.

The boy is one of Brighton's resident poor, who these days almost outnumber the prostitutes and beggars on the streets, pestering wealthy citizens and visitors for a coin or two in the name of Christian charity.

For many, home is one room that serves as bedroom, sitting room and kitchen for up to 30 men, women and children. For those lucky enough to find employment serving the needs of the fashionable resort, cheap housing is available, knocked up in a hurry on the remaining wasteland, with no effective sanitation. In a town famed for its curative waters, few of the streets where the poor live have sewers. Raw sewage is deposited into cesspits carved into the bedrock, which, being porous chalk, cannot prevent the effluent oozing through the walls of houses and polluting the drinking water wells. Each year, in the poor streets of Brighton, some 800 people die of contagious diseases.

For the boy on the beach, as for so many Brightonians born to disadvantage, the future is an abstraction hardly worth thinking about. There is only today, and today the chance to climb out of the cesspit involves crime. He clutches in his hand a Bank of England one-pound note. He's well aware that it's counterfeit, one of thousands of poor-quality, easily forged notes that have been circulating throughout the country for years. The penalty for forgery used to be death, but had recently been amended to transportation to New South Wales for life. So the boy, deciding that it's in for a penny, in for a pound, swallows hard and heads for the high street.

The boy's name is James Stuart.

Chapter 2

'What a great misfortune'

It has been raining heavily all afternoon at Sutter's Fort, in the Mexican territory of Alta California (Upper California). It is early January, 1848, and at his residence in the fort on the American River, after his customary siesta, wealthy Swiss-born settler Johann Sutter is writing a letter when his business partner James Marshall bursts into the room.

Marshall, who is building a sawmill for Sutter some 90 kilometres upriver, near Coloma, is dripping wet and clearly agitated, and Sutter, assuming something serious has occurred, instinctively looks to make sure his rifle is close at hand.

Recalling the event almost a decade later, in an article for *Hutchings' California Magazine*, Sutter writes: 'He told me then that he had some important and interesting news which he wished to communicate secretly to me, and wished me to go with him to a place where we would not be disturbed, and where no listeners could come and hear what we had to say.

'I went with him to my private rooms. He requested that I lock the door. I complied, but I told him at the same time that nobody was in the house except the clerk, who was in his office in a different part of the house. After requesting of me something which he wanted, which my servants brought and then left the room, I forgot to lock the doors, and it happened that the door was opened by the clerk just at the moment when Marshall took a rag from his pocket, showing me the yellow metal; he had about two ounces of it; but how quick [Marshall] put the metal in his pocket again can hardly be described.'[1]

With the clerk gone and the door safely locked, Marshall again shows Sutter the specimens. 'He told me he had expressed his opinion to the labourers at the mill that this might be gold,' Sutter writes, 'but some of them were laughing at him and called him a crazy man, and could not believe such a thing.'[2]

After testing the metal, Sutter declares it to be gold of at least 23 carats. 'After this, [Marshall] had no more rest nor patience, and wanted me to start with him immediately for Coloma,' Sutter writes, 'but I told him I could not leave as it was late in the evening and nearly supper time, and that it would be better for him to remain with me till the next morning, and I would travel with him.

'But this would not do. He asked me only "Will you come tomorrow morning?" I told him yes, and off he started for Coloma in the heaviest rain, although already very wet, taking nothing to eat.'[3]

After a restless night mulling over the consequences – good and bad – of a gold strike on his land, Sutter sets off next morning for Coloma. It's still wet, cold and miserable.

Sutter writes: 'About halfway on the road I saw at a distance a human being crawling out from the brushwood.'[4]

It's Marshall, still agitated and even more sodden and bedraggled. He tells Sutter that he rode all the way to Coloma last night, changed horses and rode back to meet him. The partners ride on together, and reach Coloma with the weather clearing at last. There, Sutter finds gold in the mill race, just as Marshall had told him.

Why James Marshall was in such a hurry to get back to Coloma remains a mystery. Perhaps he was fearful of losing his claim to fame. Eyewitnesses would later declare that it was not Marshall who found the first gold but 16-year-old John Wimmer, the son of Marshall's assistant, Peter Wimmer, and his wife Jennie, the camp cook. So the story goes, John found a nugget while playing in the mill race, and showed it to his father and to James Marshall. Both men assumed it was probably only fool's gold, but Jennie, who had worked on goldfields elsewhere, was not so sure. It being washing day, she was making soap in a kettle, and so placed the specimen in the boiling kettle. On removing it untarnished, she assured the men that it was the real thing.

Sutter hints at this when, on relating how he had a ring made from the piece of gold Marshall gave him, with his family crest on the face of the ring and, engraved on the inside, 'The first gold, discovered in January 1848', he adds:

'Now if Mrs Wimmer possesses a piece which has been found earlier than mine Mr Marshall can tell, as it was probably received from him. I think Mr Marshall could have hardly known himself which was exactly the first little piece, among the whole.'[5]

There is no love lost between Sutter and Marshall. They are business partners but certainly not friends. Marshall, a carpenter with a nervous disposition and several failed business ventures behind him, has never built a mill. Sutter, who contracted him for the project because no millwright was available, is increasingly concerned that he is not up to the task. The sawmill, from which Sutter intends to raft timber downriver to the port at Yerba Buena – or San Francisco, as some have lately taken to calling it – is part of his grand plan to develop his own private fiefdom. He has named it New Helvetia, which already boasts farms, vineyards, orchards, stores and a tannery near the fort, and is soon to include a flour mill, built with timber from the sawmill.

Sutter, who fled Switzerland deep in debt and one step ahead of the police, abandoning a wife and children, had been granted the land in 1839 by the Mexican governor of Alta California. Alta California, which had been a territory of Mexico since 1821, when Mexico gained independence from Spain, was poor, sparsely populated, and remote from an unstable and out-of-touch government in Mexico City. And with Oregon to the north, Nevada to the east and Arizona to the south-east, the territory was a prime target for American expansion from coast to coast, inspired by the doctrine of Manifest Destiny.

Sutter, who claimed to be a former captain in the Swiss Guards, volunteered his services to the governor, Juan Bautista Alvarado, as the ideal man to establish a colony in the Central Valley as a buffer zone to deter Americans and other foreigners from settling in Mexican territory.

The truth was that Sutter had not been a captain of the Guards but a shopkeeper and part-time sublieutenant in the reserves, but with his military bearing and trimmed whiskers he certainly looked the part. Suitably impressed, Alvarado granted him title to 200 square kilometres of land on the northern frontier of the territory, and appointed him captain of militia, although Sutter preferred to be addressed as 'General'.

By 1846 it had become apparent that nothing and no one could keep Americans out of California, and certainly not the 'General' at Sutter's Fort. With war between Mexico and the United States on the horizon, Sutter reasoned that he could continue to prosper by waving the Stars and Stripes as enthusiastically as he had waved the Mexican tricolor.

Now, in January of 1848, after two years of war and some 44,000 casualties on both sides, American troops have occupied most of Mexico's northern holdings, and the map of the North American continent is about to be redrawn. Sutter, a Mexican citizen, is fearful that if Alta California is ceded to the United States he might lose title to his property, and see his dreams of an agricultural and industrial empire trodden underfoot by hordes of gold seekers. With that in mind, he calls for all his mill workers to assemble.

Sutter: 'I told them that I would consider it a great favour if they would keep this discovery secret only for six weeks, so that I could finish my large flour mill at Brighton, which had cost me already about $24,000 to $25,000. The people up there promised to keep it secret so long.

'On my way home, instead of feeling happy and contented, I was very unhappy, and could not see that it would benefit me much, and I was perfectly right in thinking so, as it came just as precisely as I expected.'[6]

Sutter has written to the US military governor of California, Colonel Richard Mason, requesting title to the land above his fort, where his sawmill is under his construction and where gold was discovered. The reply is not to his liking. While signed by Colonel Mason, it was written by Mason's aide-de-camp, Lieutenant William Tecumseh Sherman.

Sherman, who will later make history as a Union general in the Civil War, recalls in his memoirs, 'I wrote off a letter, reciting that California was yet a Mexican province, simply held by us as a conquest. Therefore it was impossible for the Governor to promise him a title to the land.'[7]

To compound Sutter's woes, Sutter's Mill camp cook Jennie Wimmer reveals the secret of the gold strike to a teamster delivering supplies from Sutter's Fort, and gives him a small amount of gold as a gift. On his return to the fort, the teamster strolls into Brannan's Shirt Tail Store, asks for a bottle of brandy and offers to pay for it in gold dust. The storekeeper, Charlie Smith, asks the teamster where he got the gold, the teamster tells Smith, who tells his business partner Sam Brannan, who famously runs through the streets of San Francisco yelling, 'Gold! Gold! Gold from the American River!'[8]

Johann Sutter, his worst fears realised, writes: 'So soon as the secret was out my labourers began to leave me, in small parties first, but then all left, from the clerk to the cook, and I was in great distress.'[9]

Meanwhile, on 2 February, under the Treaty of Guadalupe Hidalgo, which ends the war, Mexico cedes to the United States a vast territory comprising the future states of California, Nevada, Utah, New Mexico, Arizona, Colorado, Wyoming, Oklahoma, Kansas and Texas.

'Then the people commenced rushing up from San Francisco and other parts of California,' Sutter writes. 'In the former village [of San Francisco] only five men were left to take care of the women and children. The single men locked their doors and left for Sutter's Fort, and from there to the Eldorado.

'What a great misfortune was this sudden discovery for me! It has just broken up and ruined my hard, restless and industrious labours, connected with many dangers of life, as I had many narrow escapes before I became properly established.'[10]

By August of 1848, after the New York press tells the world of the discovery of gold in California, Sutter's farms and orchards are overrun with prospectors and squatters. His crops have been trampled, his fences broken and his cattle stolen. His workshops and stores sit idle and his sawmill is abandoned. In his tannery the hides lie rotting in the vats, and at his unfinished flour mill even the millstones have been stolen. In the years to follow, United States courts will continue to deny him title to his Mexican land grants, leaving him bankrupt, and he will spend the rest of his days trying in vain to gain compensation from the United States government.

'By this sudden discovery of gold all my great plans were destroyed,' he writes. 'Had I succeeded for a few years before the gold was discovered I would have been the richest citizen on the Pacific shore, but it had to be different. Instead of being rich, I am ruined.'[11]

James Marshall's fate will be similarly cruel. With the mill venture lost to the gold rush, he will plant a vineyard that fails, then invest in a goldmine that produces no gold, and will die alone and penniless.

Chapter 3

The veneration of Saint Barbara

The skipper of the schooner *Plymouth*, Captain George Gould, walks into the office of the *Sydney Morning Herald* with a bundle of Californian newspapers and letters under his arm. Captain Gould, whose ship arrived in Sydney from the Sandwich Islands (now Hawaii) on Wednesday 20 December 1848, is himself a herald – the bearer of Australia's first news of the California gold rush.

On Saturday 23 December, the *Herald* reprints extracts from the reports and letters, which reached Hawaii in July on the freighter *Euphemia*. The news is six months old, not due to delays in sea mail but because California's newspapers have all closed.

'We have received, per *Euphemia*, dates from California to the 20th of June,' the *Herald* tells its readers. 'Our files of California papers up to the date of their death have come to hand. The yellow fever has taken hold of all the members of the craft there, from the editors to the imps, and carried them off to the gold mines. The only item of interest is the news from the gold diggings – other matters receive no attention.

'The whole country is in a state of turmoil, and everybody is flying to the gold region to reap a fortune. All the seaport towns are deserted. Out of a population of nearly one thousand, San Francisco only contains about 50 or 60 souls, and these would leave were it possible. The news of the gold discoveries has spread with lightning speed, and the minister, merchant, artisan, mechanic, farmer, labourer, and loafer have all gone to seek their fortune.

'Farms and crops are deserted, and all branches of business are at a stand. Up to the latest dates there was some two thousand men, women, and children, on the ground digging, and the roads were thronged with multitudes more pressing forward to obtain a portion of the glittering treasure.'[1]

The published reports from California include letters from unidentified individuals. One, dated 29 May, states: 'The gold occurs in an alluvium, and is disseminated over a region of 50 or more miles in length. The people who are there digging obtain on an average from $10 to $50 per day washing by hand – some obtain $100 per day, but not continually.

'It is on wild land, and of course everybody goes and digs that pleases. All who have been to examine either remain to dig or have returned with their families to make preparations. As a consequence, all branches of business except gold digging are at a dead stand. The crops will in all probability be extensively neglected, and food will doubtless have to be imported to prevent scarcity.

'What the result of all this will be no-one can tell. That it will prove disastrous to the permanent welfare of the country I have no doubt. It certainly will not promote industry, sobriety, or good morals.'[2]

A letter dated 5 June echoes the warning: 'Woe to the morals of the country, and woe to the mouths that some months hence will want food.'[3]

The *Herald* relays the *California Star* editorial of 3 June. A week before it ceased publication when its staff – including the editor – ran off to the diggings, the *Star* predicted that the epidemic of gold fever would cause the social order to collapse.

'For the next nine months, or until legislative action in the seat of government, or what is more probable, the enactment and enforcement of law in this country, the gold mines in the north will gather together as wild a class of unchristianised fellows as ever escaped the thraldom of honest law, and broke loose upon barbarism. Until restricted by measures for the preservation of order, the security of person, and property protected, we may hear of continual mischief among the miners in its fearful excess, and rows and robberies without intermission.

'It is an exciting work – that of gold gathering – and it will be morally impossible for so large a body, composed of such opposite natures, to avoid collision and tumult. Reports reach us by every arrival from the section of country to which all eyes are turned, of every day's increased addition to the number already actively employed. If any of our readers suspect our views high coloured, and our opinion in this matter ponderous and exaggerated, we cannot but believe another month will amply satisfy such that we have not presented an overdrawn picture.

'The fact is, such a dangerous class as that referred to are now formed. It is well known that the country has been harassed by organised and practised horse-thieving marauders – that deserters from army and navy have contributed to swell the list of outlawed desperadoes, and it is pretty certain that most of these bad characters are moving northward, where their presence will be speedily and severely felt. Desertions from the garrisons of the country are every day taking place. Liquor – a vile, maddening mixture – has been introduced in large quantities among the labourers, to breed brawl and contention, and, the word of sages is, it will soon tell its tale!'[4]

By late the following January, the news has spread throughout the Australian colonies. Most Australians have never heard of California, and few have even the faintest notion of what lies ahead, yet thousands clamour to board anything that will float to make the perilous journey to the Pacific Coast of North America, many attracted by cheap fares in steerage.

In January 1849, seven ships sail for San Francisco from Sydney, and one from Hobart. Many more will follow. First to see the Golden Gate – the entrance to San Francisco Bay – on 2 April after 71 days at sea, is the barque *Eleanor Lancaster*, carrying 52 passengers at £30 for a cabin and £10 for steerage. She is the first in from Australia but she is far from alone. There are more than 400 ships anchored in the cove – from England, from New York, from New Orleans, from New Zealand, from Panama – all disgorging pilgrims on a quest for a miracle of Saint Barbara, virgin martyr and patron saint of miners.

For the Australians, there is an unfamiliar site on the docks – Chinese men with shaven heads and queues, in blue cotton shirts, baggy trousers, wooden-soled shoes and broad bamboo hats. For decades, hard times in China had driven people to migrate to South-East Asia, but many had returned when conditions at home improved.

In recent years, however, a combination of economic decline and political corruption under the Manchu dynasty, rebellions, feuding warlords and a series of natural disasters, including drought and famine, triggered a flood of migrants not only to neighbouring countries but also to Peru, Mexico, Cuba, Hawaii,

Canada and – when word reached China of the gold strike at Sutter's Mill – to California.

To the Chinese joining the rush, California is Gum Shan (Gold Mountain), and within two years these early arrivals at San Francisco, which they call Dai Fow (Big City), will be followed by some 25,000 more.

The first Australians ashore find themselves in a curious place – a quiet village turned into a rowdy, rough-cut city overnight. It is a city where nobody lives, it seems, because everyone they meet here is a stranger passing through or a merchant come to sell his wares and move on. And with about a thousand prospectors arriving every week, San Francisco is showing the strain; feeling the growing pains. The Australians set up a squatters' camp on Rincon Hill, a sandy peninsula on the southern shore of Yerba Buena Cove. The hill is military land, however, and the army orders the squatters out. They move to the north side of the cove, to an area that will come to be known as Sydney Valley.

In need of supplies, the Australian forty-niners find it impossible to fend off the vultures vying to pick their bones and their pockets. Shovels and spades cost around $10. Flour is $60 a barrel, coffee $2 a pound, eggs $3 a dozen, and hotel rooms are being offered for lease at a staggering $18,000 a year.

Once fully equipped and thoroughly fleeced, the aim is to rush to the diggings by any means possible. The fortunate few can afford to travel by boat up the Sacramento River as far as Sutter's Fort, but for most the journey to Sutter's Mill is a wearisome 225-kilometre trek on foot through unforgiving country.

The transcontinental journey is even more arduous, and desperately slow, and there are rumours of parties gone missing or attacked by Apaches.

Some coming from New York avoid sailing around the Horn or taking the hazardous overland route by disembarking at the port of Chagres, on the isthmus of Panama, trekking through the jungle across the isthmus, then taking ship for San Francisco, a journey of 37 days.

In England, the satirical magazine *Punch* offers the following sobering advice to those tempted to join the exodus:

'*What class ought to go to the diggings?* Persons who have nothing to lose except their lives.

'*Things you should not take with you to the diggings.* A love of comforts, a taste for civilisation, a respect for other people's throats, and a value for your own.

'*Things you will find useful at the diggings.* A revolving pistol, some knowledge of treating gunshot wounds, a toleration of strange bedfellows.

'*The sort of society you will meet with at the diggings.* Those for whom the United States are not big enough; those for whom England is too hot; those who came to clean out the gold, and those who came to clean out the gold finders.

'*What is the best thing to do when you get to the diggings?* Go back home.

'*How gold may be best extracted.* By supplying, at exorbitant prices, the wants of those who gather it.

'*What will be the ultimate effect of the discovery of the diggings?* To raise prices, to ruin fools, to demoralise a new country first, and settle it afterwards.'[5]

Few in England are deterred by such warnings. This year has presented the English with a choice of two epidemics: cholera or gold fever. They can stay at home and wait for the disease sweeping the country to bring them hollow eyes, black lips and certain death, or take ship for California – a four-month voyage around Cape Horn – to fossick for a flash of yellow. For many – and especially for Londoners, who live in fear of miasmas from the open sewer that is the Thames – the choice is clear. And besides, according to reports from the diggings, it seems success is all but guaranteed. The word is that people are kicking up nuggets in the dirt like pigs rooting for ground nuts, some getting as much as eight to 10 ounces a day.

On 10 November 1849, Queen Victoria proclaims the fifteenth of that month a day of thanksgiving for the end of the cholera epidemic that caused more than 55,000 deaths in England and Wales that year. Many of her subjects have already departed for fairer climes, however. On 1 November, 100 British ships are counted in the harbour of San Francisco, adding to the city's growth in population from about 500 to an estimated 15,000 in less than a year.

The public mood is similarly irrepressible in Australia, where the *Sydney Morning Herald*, fearing mass migration to California could send the fragile colonial economy spiralling into depression, reprints the *Punch* article, and the *Colonial Times and Tasmanian*, under the headline 'Bad News, Bad News', warns:

'The golden statements in reference to [California] are declared to be false, and independent of the place being inundated with goods, gold has become scarce, and obtained with great difficulty.

'If any of the friends of those who will give the undersigned security of their passage money, they may have a return passage, which may be the means of saving many of the unfortunates from great misery, and even death.

'Application to be made within seven days from the present date. Apply to John Thomas Waterhouse, Packet Office, New Wharf.'[6]

The warning is reinforced with an outright lie: 'Any but American citizens found digging or trespassing will be fined and imprisoned, and any gold found upon them will be forfeited to the state. Suitable rewards will "most probably" be offered for their apprehension, and any American citizen be rewarded for apprehending the same.'[7]

Directly below this dire warning is an advertisement for the barque *Duchess of Clarence*, departing soon from Hobart Town for San Francisco via Hawaii, and 'admirably suited for passengers, for the accommodation of whom she will be fitted up right fore and aft'.[8]

Finger-waggling warnings of doom and ruin prove equally ineffective. Already, songs celebrating the gold rush are wildly popular. A favourite with the diggers, as well as with people back home entranced by the romance of the rush, is Stephen Foster's 'Oh, Susanna!'

> I come from Alabama with my banjo on my knee.
> I'm going to Louisiana, my true love for to see.
> It rained all night the day I left, the weather it was dry
> The sun so hot I froze to death, Susanna, don't you cry.
>
> Oh! Susanna, oh don't you cry for me,
> For I come from Alabama with my banjo on my knee.[9]

'Oh, Susanna!' is a minstrel song, written before the gold rush. 'Oh, California!', a parody written in 1848 by Jonathan Nichols, a passenger on a ship bound for San Francisco, has become the unofficial forty-niners anthem, and is even more popular than the original.

> I sailed from Salem City with my washbowl on my knee.
> I'm going to California the gold dust there to see.

It rained all night the day I left, the weather it was dry.
The sun so hot I froze to death, oh brothers, don't you cry.

Oh, California, that's the land for me.
I'm going to San Francisco with my washbowl on my knee.

I soon shall be in Frisco and there I'll look around
And when I find the gold lumps there I'll pick them off the ground.
I'll scape the mountains clean, my boys, I'll drain the rivers dry,
A pocket full of rocks bring home, oh brothers don't you cry.[10]

There is even a popular play, *Cockneys in California*, a one-act farce by Joseph Stirling Coyne, concerning the misadventures on the goldfields of innocents abroad. All's well that ends well, thanks to a large gold nugget found just in the nick of time, and in a grand finale the entire cast dances to a lively tune, oddly titled 'Everybody's Independent and Grand National Californian Fandango'.[11]

Of the 52 passengers on the *Eleanor Lancaster*, fortune will favour one in particular, but not in the form of a gold strike. Alexander Sinclair Murray, a Sydney lawyer's clerk who migrated to Australia from Scotland at age 15, has not come to California to dig but to trade. He hires a longboat and begins trading goods on the Sacramento River, and before long buys a bigger boat, then, in time, a 175-ton brig, then a schooner, then a steamboat, then another and another. By the 1860s Alexander Murray will be running steamboats not only in the Pacific Northwest of America but in New Zealand and Australia, out of Sydney and on the Murray River.

A fellow passenger, William Jackson Barry, will be even more successful, if only in his own mind. According to conflicting versions of his life story, Barry was born in 1819 or 1820 in Dublin or in the village of Melbourn, in Cambridgeshire, or neither of the above. He claims to be the son of a Cambridge veterinarian, and travelled to Australia while on a world tour with a wealthy relative. Another version has it that he was a convict transported to Australia at the tender age of nine aboard the ship *Red River* or *Red Rover*. Records show there were no convict ships with those names, however.

In yet another version, Barry was a convict assigned as a servant to a Sydney butcher before running off to join a gang of bushrangers, taking part in highway robberies and at least one bank hold-up before signing on as a seaman aboard a whaling ship under the alias Jimmy Ducks. As Ducks, he proves so skilful a sailor that he is made captain, is shipwrecked but miraculously survives, joins the navy – he doesn't specify which navy – and sails to India and to China, where he fights at the Battle of Canton during the First Opium War in 1841.

In Western Australia, he marries Hannah French, a wealthy whaler's daughter who sadly dies in childbirth. Grief stricken, Barry returned to Sydney where he opens a butcher's shop before catching gold fever and taking ship for California.

If Barry found gold in California or even got his hands dirty he makes no mention. He will claim to have made several fortunes there by unspecified means but to have lost them all to bandits, a bank swindle and another shipwreck. What is known is that he remarried in California, to Adelia Buckley, and together they had six children.

Styling himself 'Captain' Jackson Barry, the erstwhile butcher and failed businessman finds his niche as an author and lecturer. Touring Australia, New Zealand and England, he makes a modest living spinning ripping yarns of his outlaw days; of wild adventures on the seven seas; of feuds on lawless goldfields; of desperate battles with Aboriginal warriors and Native American braves; and daring escapes from cannibals in the South Seas. All Barry's adventures feature himself as the lantern-jawed hero, and while it is evident that none of these tales of derring-do are true, he is tolerated by audiences for his flamboyance. Barry is clearly a fraud and a liar comparable with Baron Munchausen, the eighteenth-century German nobleman who delighted the aristocracy with risibly embroidered tales of his military exploits, yet he is an engaging, likeable and colourful character. There are times when his audiences pelt him with rotten eggs and fruit, but more often they reward him with rapt attention punctuated by bursts of laughter.

Captain Jackson Barry is a figure of fun. Perhaps he's well aware of that but simply doesn't mind. After a lecture by Barry in Dunedin, New Zealand, the *Saturday Advertiser* newspaper publishes a review in verse by the poet Thomas Bracken:

Who wrote a book of wondrous tales
And stories about hulks and jails?
Who floated on the backs of whales?
Why, Captain Jackson Barry.

Who, when he reached Old England's strand
Was taken kindly by the hand
By dukes and knights and nobles grand?
Why, Captain Jackson Barry.[12]

By 1892, Barry, at 73, is still on the circuit, and each lecture adds further embellishments to his tales. In New Zealand that year, a

Southland Times report on a lecture to a small audience in a village hall reports that he spoke for two hours on 'how he left England for Australia in 1828; gave a graphic picture of Sydney as it appeared when he reached it early in 1829; described his encounters with blacks and bushrangers; his meeting with John Batman [the founder of Melbourne] when he came to Port Phillip from Tasmania, and with William Buckley, the wild white man who had lived over 30 years with the natives; told how he came to New Zealand in a whaler in 1836, taking occasion to disclaim the feat attributed to him by the poet Bracken of having ridden 300 miles on the back of a whale, although he admitted having clung to a dead one for eight or 10 hours; and described how he was captured by cannibal Maoris and learned their languages from living dictionaries.

'He next related how he escaped and returned to Sydney; how he prospered as a whaler and returned to New Zealand in 1842; how the gold fever attracted him to California in 1849; how he returned to Victoria in the fifties; and how, in 1860, he revisited New Zealand with a lot of horses. He tried a lot of occupations but 1862 found him a butcher and Mayor of Cromwell [a town in the Central Otago region, founded during the Otago gold rush].

'Captain Barry next gave some particulars of his trip to England in 1879, when he landed with 17 shillings and sixpence, gave lectures, made money, hobnobbed with the nobility and interviewed the Queen.'

Barry concluded his talk by commenting, to gales of laughter, 'They've been knighting a lot of numbskulls of late, and don't be surprised, although I am 73, if Captain William Jackson Barry comes back Sir William Jackson Barry.'[13]

William Jackson Barry died in Christchurch, New Zealand, in 1907, at Sunnyside Mental Asylum. At his funeral, members of the congregation recited Thomas Bracken's poem about him riding a whale. Whether or not the irony was intentional is anybody's guess.

The ship that brought the first Australian forty-niners to California will be denied Saint Barbara's blessing. On her arrival at San Francisco, the crew of the *Elizabeth Lancaster* jump ship and run off to the goldfields. For a while she plies the Sacramento River as a floating brothel and gambling den before crossing the Pacific back to Australia in 1850, to become a coastal trader.

In 1856, on departing Newcastle for Melbourne with a cargo of coal, she is wrecked in a fierce gale. With their vessel driven onto a submerged sandbank, the crew cling to the rigging all night as the ship breaks apart beneath them. All seems lost until, as an anonymous poet tells us:

An awful sea was running and not one in all that crew
Was one who thought those boats could be brought those
boiling breakers through.
But then a little fair-haired man pushed and panted as he ran
And urged us all the waves to scan and to our mates be true.
'Now lads,' he shouted shrill and clear, 'Who'll venture it
with me?
Each minute lost a life will cost in such a tumbling sea.[14]

No lives are lost thanks to the courage of that 'little fair-haired man', a sailor named William Skilton, who braves the raging seas in a small boat three times to row the captain and crew safely ashore.

Aside from the industrious Alexander Sinclair and the preposterous William Barry, the original Australian forty-niners who came on that ill-fated ship will leave no trace in history; no indelible mark on the saga of San Francisco. But other Australians are soon to follow whose marks will draw blood and leave terrible scars.

Chapter 4

From the ends of the Earth

It is noon on Sunday 14 April 1850. As the Pacific Mail steam-ship *Tennessee* dips into San Francisco Bay, passengers crowding the deck let out three cheers – three rousing shouts of exhilaration on arriving at last, and of relief at having escaped the perils of the deep.

One of the passengers on the 20-day journey from New York is a man named James Stuart – tall and handsome, with dark curly hair and whiskers – who joined the ship at Panama, along with a friend from Sydney, James Burns – known as Jimmy from Town – whom Stuart smuggled aboard.

Jim Stuart has heard such cheering before. He heard it in England years ago when he and his fellow convicts shuffled out of a prison hulk into the sunlight. For what had seemed an eternity, after being sentenced to transportation for forgery, he had been on a voyage to nowhere – on an old naval warship, no longer seaworthy, used to hold prisoners until a ship was available to take them to the bottom of the world.

On the overcrowded hulks, ravaged by cholera and dysentery, the dead lay among the living for days on end, crammed into three decks containing up to a thousand men. The prisoners, shackled and packed close together at night, were unable to move as rats ran over them. The stench was intolerable; the shackles tore their ankles to shreds; in the summer they sweltered, and in the winter they froze.

So, when at last they were herded onto a convict ship – even though they had no notion of what fate awaited them – it's little wonder that as the sails filled and the ship, with timbers creaking, shuddered and lunged into the channel, they cheered till their throats were sore.

Stuart, then 18, was one of 260 convicts – men and boys – who boarded the barque *Henry Porcher*, bound for Sydney. His career as a forger had been short-lived, amounting to a single – first and last – attempt to pass a counterfeit banknote. The forgery was spotted at once; he was arrested, tried and sentenced to transportation for life.

After several months rotting alive on the aptly named prison hulk *Fortitude*, on which success was survival, he found himself below decks in close company with felons from all parts of England and with all manner of backgrounds and dispositions. Some were career criminals – burglars, pimps, pickpockets and others to whom time in Newgate Prison or on the hulks was a rite of passage. One, Thomas 'Long Tom' Forrester, was destined to be a notorious bushranger who would end his days swinging from a rope. Most, however, were petty thieves; victims of circumstance; those whose offences were, like Stuart's, crimes of poverty and desperation.

One of the prisoners, Thomas Hitchen, alias Higgin, was a notably colourful character not for the nature of his crime – he was just one sheep snatcher among many – but for his tattoos. These included a male figure and the inscription 'When you see this, remember me and bear me in your mind' on his torso; a man and a woman, a flowerpot, two birds and the words 'True love' on his right arm; an anchor on the back of his left hand; and, on his left arm, a man standing on an anchor, a fish, a bird on a branch, the date 1831, and a woman with a basket.[1]

For a few, the acts for which they were being sent to the ends of the Earth could hardly be called crimes at all. One such was 15-year-old Evan Cape, sentenced to seven years' transportation for snatching another boy's cap as a prank and running off with it.

Some of the prisoners from the hulk *Fortitude* brought disease with them. Within a few days of departure, cases of diarrhoea were spreading, and the ship's surgeon, Thomas Galloway, feared an outbreak of scurvy or even cholera was likely. Hoping to prevent an epidemic, Galloway made sure the decks were swabbed daily and that the prisoners' holds were well ventilated and fumigated each morning.

In his account of the voyage, Galloway wrote, 'Within the tropics, the boys and as many of the men as circumstances would permit were daily compelled to wash and bathe their persons or have buckets of water thrown over them between the hours of five and eight in the morning.

'During the cold weather, as we advanced to the southward, the prisoners were frequently exercised by marching or running around the deck. Dancing was also encouraged and every means used to keep their circulation in activity whilst on deck for air. This latter measure I think was highly advantageous as the scorbutic seizures, except in a few of the most indolently disposed, more readily yielded to the treatment adopted than in my former voyages when the weather during the latter part of the passage but seldom admitted of such means being put in practice.'[2]

Despite the surgeon's best efforts, eight convicts and one soldier died during the 119-day voyage – three of cholera, two of dysentery, two of phthisis (pulmonary tuberculosis), one of diarrhoea, and one of scrofula (lymphatic tuberculosis). Of those who died, the oldest was aged 60 but most were in their twenties, and the youngest just 17.

Meanwhile, some 40 convicts, soldiers and soldiers' wives were put on the ship's sick list, mostly with diarrhoea, but some with cholera. Those struck down included James Stuart, listed as having been ill with diarrhoea for four days.

On New Year's Day, 1835, when the *Henry Porcher* sailed into Sydney Harbour, the prisoners let out three hearty cheers. As the ship rode at anchor in the cove, boats came alongside to ferry the convicts ashore. Some, due to the severity of their crime or because of troublesome behaviour during the voyage, were clapped into leg-irons and sent to work on chain gangs. The rest were marched from the quay to the barracks: past the disdainful glances of free settlers and emancipists, a sign of growing opposition to convict transportation in the colony; past looks of pity or disinterest from convicts in their broad-arrow uniforms; past a marketplace with a whipping post, stocks, and pillories where hapless men and women, held fast by the neck and wrists, were being pelted with rotten fruit and eggs by a gleeful crowd.

At the barracks, the convicts were housed in wards – allocated according to the convict ship on which they arrived – there to await their assignments. Meanwhile, discipline was maintained by solitary confinement but more often by the lash.

James Backhouse, a Quaker missionary who visited the barracks, wrote, 'One of the officers, who had been here only about 15 months, said upwards of one thousand men had been flogged in the course of that period. He stated his opinion to be that how much soever men may dread flagellation, when they have not been subjected to it, they are generally degraded in their own esteem and become reckless after its infliction.'[3]

While the prisoners in the barracks suffered at the hands of men who apparently believed brutality was character-building, the more fortunate residents of Sydney were celebrating the birth of a new year in which, the *Australian* newspaper predicted, 'we should see hope and pleasure, sunshine and splendour'.[4]

The newspaper boasted that a colony born of 'a scheme to which had in its origin a selfish desire to be quit of a portion of our countrymen whose existence in the land of their birth could no longer be tolerated', had blossomed into a land of promise, 'emerging, like a dragonfly from the putrid waters, from the depths, the darkest abyss of human degradation'.[5]

The harvests of maize, wheat, oats and barley had been abundant and of good quality, despite the threat of a caterpillar plague, and the vineyards had produced a promising vintage. The wool crop had been better than expected, the harbour was bristling with ships, and property prices in the town were rising steadily. 'In Sydney, buildings spring up with mushroom rapidity, and in very many parts of the town there are edifices of which Regent Street need not be ashamed, and before which, those of our English country towns would hide their diminished heads.

'These things speak for themselves,' the *Australian* opined. 'It is manifest that our condition is improving in a ratio much greater than can be boasted by any other country under the sun.'[6]

As the voice of vested interests in the continuation of the convict transportation, the *Australian* declares, 'In this prosperity all classes partake. The convict population are comfortable and well tended. They are quiet and peaceful, and we have reason to believe that the majority of settlers would sooner have this class of person as labourers than those of the free who have hitherto emigrated. They are found to be well-conducted and orderly when under proper care and subject to proper treatment.'[7]

On the seamy side of Sydney Town it was business as usual. Sarah Barnes, a colourful local character better known as Kitty Clover, was before the bench yet again, charged with luring a drunken sailor to her room and robbing him of a watch and £2 in silver.

In her defence, Kitty swore that the sailor was sober when he came to her house, although he was far from sober when he left, and that he had given her the watch and silver as a Christmas gift.

The sailor, asked if this were true, said, 'Well, your Honour, it might have been. Damn me if I recollect, however, if she's a mind to give me the watch and other things she took from me, I've no objection to settle the matter quietly.'

The defendant agreed, the judge dismissed the case, and Kitty and the sailor left the courtroom together, arm in arm.[8]

Teasing imaginations in a colony starved for news from abroad, the *Sydney Monitor* reported: 'A large balloon having a car in the form of a ship, to contain 17 persons, is about to take its flight from Paris to London.'[9]

The balloon, called the *Eagle*, had been promoted as 'the first aerial ship, and which is to be manned by a crew of 17 persons' in a timber-framed cabin surrounded by netting to prevent the crew from falling out.[10] The plan was to fly the airship between

London and Paris, then to make similar return trips to Brussels, Amsterdam, Berlin, Madrid and other European capitals.

The impending flight of the *Eagle* – 48 metres long, 15 metres high and 12 metres wide – sparked much speculation in Britain and Europe that a revolution in trade and travel was nigh, and inspired many fanciful predictions on the future of aerial transport, including balloons propelled through the air by dolphin-like fins, oars, paddle-wheels, flocks of geese or pigeons, and by 30 eagles, three abreast.

The *Eagle*, propelled by four movable cane-and-fabric wings and two rudders, made its maiden flight in the Champ de Mars before some 50,000 Parisians who had paid one franc each to witness history in the making. Excitement mounted as the balloon inflated, but then it broke from its moorings, rose up a short distance, burst into flames and fell to Earth. The crowd, incensed, pounced on the wreckage and tore it to pieces. The *Eagle* had landed.

The *Tennessee* eases into the dock, lines are lashed to bollards and passengers gently jostle, as if there were a prize for first down the gangplank. James Stuart, waiting to disembark, shows the marks of a hard life, his fine features marred by a scar on his right cheek, and a damaged middle finger on his right hand. Where and how he sustained those injuries he will never say.

In Australia, Stuart's good behaviour earned him a ticket of leave – a parole document granting convicts freedom to live and work in a specified district of a colony before their sentence has expired or they have been pardoned. Ticket-of-leave convicts can hire out their labour or work for themselves, and can buy property. They must attend church on Sundays, and cannot travel beyond their designated districts without their masters' permission.

Granted his freedom after serving six years of his sentence, he made his way to the colony of South Australia, then to South America, ending up in Panama, where he took ship for California. Perhaps he made an honest living during those years, or perhaps, after spending his youth in the company of hardened criminals, learning tricks of the trade and brutalised by the system, he lived outside the law. Of that, too, he will never say, but in the man stepping ashore today, it's likely that little remains of the boy sent to perdition for passing a fake pound note.

Chapter 5

Oranges and leg-irons

The barque *Lady Kennaway*, built in Calcutta in 1817 to carry tea to Britain, is now carrying convicts to Australia, which the aristocratic woman she is named after, Lady Charlotte Kennaway, would surely consider a fall from grace.

As the ship departs England in October 1836, bound for New South Wales, she carries within her creaking planks detachments of the 80th and 50th regiments, some with wives and children, a mutinous crew, notorious for jumping ship in foreign ports, and 300 convicts – men and boys – from hulks at Woolwich. One of those convicts is a young man from Manchester, convicted of burglary and sentenced to transportation for life. His name is Samuel Whitaker, and the path of his life will closely follow that of a young man sentenced to the same fate two years earlier – James Stuart.

The *Lady Kennaway* is at sea barely a month when more than a dozen of the convicts fall ill with scurvy. The ship's surgeon, James Wilson, fearing he might soon have an epidemic on his hands, sends a message to the ship's master, Captain Robert Davidson, requesting that he 'carry the ship under your command in to the harbour of Bahia [in north-eastern Brazil], it being the one nearest. Mooring her at some considerable distance from the shore, complete her in water and then take on board such refreshments as may be there directed for arresting the progress of the said complaints.'[1]

The captain agrees, and when the ship arrives in Sydney after a voyage of 123 days, Surgeon Wilson is pleased to report: 'The guard and convicts were given fresh meat and vegetables with three oranges while in port, and on sailing we took on board six live bullocks, with a proportion of vegetables for use at sea and some soft bread and oranges for use of the sick.'[2]

The crew, it seems, are not offered the new menu.

'We were six days in harbour,' Wilson concludes, 'and to the happy effects which the refreshments procured at Bahia had upon the general health, not only of the six, whose number was reduced from 13 to six, but which extended its influence all over, would I mainly attribute the much higher state of health in which the convicts were landed in Sydney than that they were embarked in England.'[3] Apart from the two who died, of course.

True to form, on docking in Sydney, the crew of the *Lady Kennaway* jump ship. Under the headline, '*Lady Kennaway* again', the *Sydney Gazette* reports:

'The ship's company of the *Lady Kennaway* were brought before the police on Tuesday, charged for about the dozenth time with desertion. Those men will not work, they ground a complaint against the Captain on the score of starvation, and that when they applied to him for more food, he drilled them by their being kept upon deck without cause, and not allowed a watch below. They were sentenced to lose all wages due, and clothes they might have on board.

'Surely there is to be found in this port some captain of sufficient nerve, who, after exhausting every punishment which the law allows to curb refractory seamen, will resort to that alone which can keep such spirits in subjection, namely, corporal punishment. They need have no fear of the verdict of a jury here, and the punishment being inflicted here. There is no remedy in England; it is different certainly if the punishment was inflicted on the high seas.

'There are numerous instances in this colony of such cases being brought before the Supreme Court, in which both plaintiffs and the petty foggy portion of the profession who backed them have been scouted by an honest jury. The Captain of the *Richmond* whaler has led the way – he is an American. Let Britons then show that they are not devoid of that necessary spirit so requisite to keep in due order the defenders of the wooden walls of Old England.'

The editor adds a note: 'Our correspondent must surely be mistaken respecting these men being subjected to no further punishment by the laxity of the Colonial Act if they should again abscond. If he is correct in this respect, we would ourselves run the risk of punishing this crew with moderate corporal punishment.'[4]

Like James Stuart before him, Sam Whitaker is marched to Hyde Park Barracks to await assignment. Convicts could be assigned as servants in Sydney, as farmhands and shepherds in the country, or, if deemed troublesome – or if just plain unlucky – to chain gangs building roads and other back-breaking work.

A revealing picture of life on a chain gang is found in the journal of another *Lady Kennaway* convict, Charles Adolphus King.

Like Sam Whitaker, King, a fellow Mancunian, was convicted of burglary. At just 17 years old he was sentenced to 14 years' penal servitude, and while assigned as a shepherd was caught sheltering an escaped convict and sent to work in chains on a road party.

In his 1840 booklet, *The Life, Hardships and Dreadful Sufferings of Charles Adolphus King*, he describes a typical day in the lives of convicts on a chain gang.

'Long before the stars had left the skies they were roused to work, and after partaking of a miserable breakfast of hominy [porridge-like food], they went to work under a guard of soldiers. The clanking of their chains was most dismal. Every gang had a pair of triangles, and, for the most trivial offence, or an act of disobedience, they were brought before a military man, the case was stated to him, and the convict was immediately tied up and flogged, and then sent to work again under the heat of a burning sun, and this might be repeated two or three times a day for the least offence.

'At night, they all lay down together in one apartment, with only a little bark as a bed, and should a word be spoken, or the least noise heard, the offender was ordered up by the sentinel on duty, and he was either handcuffed or his hands tied behind him, and compelled to stand in the place till morning, and sent as usual to his work again.'[5]

King absconded from the chain gang, smuggled himself on board an American whaler in Sydney harbour, and in 1839 returned to England – by way of New Zealand and Canada – and was promptly arrested and charged with returning from transportation. In court, King spoke of his experiences as a convict in New South Wales, and of his adventures after escaping. When his story – a romanticised and possibly fictional account, with many acts of daring, high drama and close shaves, including surviving being speared in the back by a Maori warrior – was published in the press, the public petitioned Queen Victoria for clemency.

Her Majesty was not one to be rushed, but eventually, after serving four years in solitary confinement, King was granted a free pardon. He set about making a modest living on the lecture circuit, dressed theatrically in chains and convict garb, delivering lectures on 'The Horrors of Transportation and Convict Life'.[6] It has been suggested that King was the model for the character of Abel Magwitch in Charles Dickens' *Great Expectations*.

Unlike Charles King, Sam Whitaker, like most convicts, will never write his own history, favourably embroidered or not. What little is known of his convict experience is that he was assigned to the Hunter Valley, probably as a farm labourer, where he was granted a ticket of leave for good behaviour, but that in 1847 it was cancelled after he was charged with giving false evidence. The case concerned is unknown, but it was not uncommon for a convict whose ticket of leave had been revoked to be sentenced to work on a chain gang for a time.

At last, on 1 February 1849, 13 years after he stepped ashore in Sydney, Sam Whitaker is granted a conditional pardon, meaning he is free as long as he doesn't go back to where he came from. But he has no such intention. So far, since news of the Californian gold strike reached Australia, only about 100 people have left Sydney for the Golden Gate. Whitaker, destined to be among the first Australian forty-niners, but whose ambitions do not include wielding a shovel, bids farewell to the life of a lag and takes ship for San Francisco.

Chapter 6

A red-letter day

Oh, how we love a parade! It is Tuesday 29 October 1850, and San Franciscans are celebrating California becoming the 31st state of the Union.

This day, proclaims the *Daily Alta California*, is 'the day set apart as one which should re-echo the glad welcome of California into the Union of her 30 sister states, and which our citizens, with one mind of joyful expectation and warm patriotism, had looked forward to with very great interest, was ushered in with a federal salute from the Plaza by a detachment of Company M, 3rd US Artillery under the command of Lieutenant H. G. Gibson. The pieces were handled in fine style.

'A crowd had assembled on the square and the loud-mouthed cannon found a ready echo in the voices of the multitude as the American flag was run up to the tall tapering staff and floated above their heads and the "dogs of war" beneath its striped bunting.

'The shipping in the harbour unanimously followed the request in the program and their own feelings by displaying the flags and ensigns of their particular nations, some of them being very beautifully dressed from the royal truck [the cap at the top of the mast of a topsail] to the flying jib-boom ends with gay and flaunting flags, ensigns, jacks and signals.

'Soon the city was all alive with the hum of busy preparation and happy voices, the street thronged with a cheerful and excited multitude, and galloping marshals and aids on splendid horses, marching and counter-marching of military, fire and civic companies and societies – all gave a lively and gratifying appearance, and told very plainly that the public was in earnest, and the occasion one which had touched every heart and fired every mind.'[1]

The band strikes up and the parade moves off, from Montgomery Street and up Sacramento Street, led by the Chief Marshall, resplendent in blue sash and white scarf with gold trim. Close behind is a company of mounted men carrying a blue satin banner with 31 silver stars and, in letters of gold, 'California – E Pluribus Unum' ('Out of many, one' – the motto of the United States).[2]

Members of the Society of California Pioneers carry a banner showing a digger striking a rock, and a piece of the rock flying off to reveal the seal of the new state. The pioneers are followed by a marching band, the California Guards in their new uniforms, the Washington Guards, veterans of the Mexican War, and sailors from a visiting US warship.

'The foreign consuls, resident in San Francisco, were followed by a company of Englishmen, bearing the cross of Saint George,' the *Alta California* reports. 'In this division we noticed a considerable number of Germans, Italians and Spaniards.

'The Celestials [Chinese] had a banner of crimson satin, on which were some Chinese characters and the inscription "China

Boys". They numbered about 50 and were arrayed in their richest stuffs, and commanded by their chief, Norman Ah Sing.'[3]

Now come the mayor, aldermen and other city officials under a banner proclaiming 'San Francisco, the Emporium of the Pacific'. A carriage led by six white horses carries 30 small boys in white shirts – each representing a state of the Union – and one 'beautiful little girl, dressed in white, with a head-dress of roses,' under a banner declaring 'California – the Union, it must be preserved.'[4]

Marching into the Plaza is the city police force, formed only a year ago, and firemen with Kickerbocker Number Five and other horse-drawn fire engines decked out in bunting and roses, and one engine with an eagle perched atop its ladder, much to the delight of the crowd.

Bringing up the rear, Freemasons, Oddfellows, United Americans and other societies in their regalia, more marching bands, more little boys and girls in white satin, and more banners: 'A Treasure Found'; 'The Belle of the Pacific'; 'Religion, Liberty and Law'.[5]

With all the marchers assembled in Portsmouth Square, a band plays *Hail Columbia*, a clergyman offers a prayer imploring the Almighty to 'grant us such wisdom from on high that we may never allow our freedom to degenerate into licentiousness, nor our religion into intolerance and bigotry.

'May brotherly love and Christian fellowship be the distinguishing characteristics of the citizens of California, and may her rulers and magistrates be so governed by Thy will, and guided by Thy Holy Spirit, that they may have grace faithfully to administer the laws, to execute justice and to maintain truth.'[6]

All intone 'Amen', the band inexplicably belts out *La Marseillaise*, and Judge Nathaniel Bennett, the state's newly minted Supreme Court Justice, launches into a long and rambling oration that compares the statehood of California with the rise of the Roman Empire. 'The world has never witnessed anything equal or similar to our career hitherto,' he tells the crowd, to applause and cheers. 'Scarcely two years ago, California was an unoccupied wild. With the exception of a presidio, a mission, a pueblo or a lonely ranch scattered here and there, at tiresome distances, there was nothing to show that the uniform stillness had ever been broken by the footsteps of civilised man. The agricultural richness of her valleys remained unimproved, and the wealth of a world lay entombed in the bosom of her solitary mountains, and on the banks of her unexplored streams.'[7]

Before the American conquest of California there were no more than 20 houses in San Francisco. Now, there are more than 30 framed houses, 22 shanties and 26 adobe dwellings, with streets laid out in a grid. Lots no one would buy a year ago are fetching $10,000 and more, and parts of town yet to be surveyed are dotted with tents. Along the shore, dwellings have sprung up on piles above the water, while abandoned vessels, whose crews have deserted to head for the goldfields, have been hauled inland and used as homes, warehouses and offices.

The hub of the ramshackle city is the former Mexican plaza, renamed Portsmouth Square, with, in its north-west corner, an adobe customs house used as the city's administrative centre, and in its south-west corner a bar and billiard saloon.

To any Yuki people among the crowd today, Judge Bennett's paean to Manifest Destiny is a wordless, booming sound – the beating of the wings of 'Au-pal', the eagle of death; harbinger of doom.[8]

Downtrodden by 'the footsteps of civilised man', the indigenous people of California are victims of *vacuum domicilium* – 'vacant lands' – the American version of *terra nullius* – 'nobody's land' – the doctrine used by the British to justify the invasion of Aboriginal Australia.

With the discovery of gold at Sutter's Mill, the Yuki are being pushed from their traditional hunting grounds by a tidal wave of gold-seekers. In the years to come, the gold will peter out and the diggers will leave, but the settlers who follow in their wake will stay forever.

The Yuki, outraged by murder, rape and slavery at the hands of the whites, will make war on the invaders, and for that will be hunted almost to extinction. By the 1860s, the Yuki population of perhaps 20,000 will be reduced to less than 300, and by the twenty-first century their language will be spoken by only a handful of people.

Chapter 7

Oliver is in town

Some say he looks like Jesus Christ, except that Christ never carried a brace of pistols in his belt, or a bowie knife.

Jim Stuart's reputation has preceded him. On the goldfields at Foster's Bar, up on the Yuba River, it was noticed that while he never got his hands dirty digging for gold he always had plenty on hand for gambling. At the diggings, when word went around of highway robbery, horse stealing, burglary and other villainy, his name was invariably mentioned. And when caught red-handed with cash stolen from a gambling den, arrested and brought to trial, with a lynch mob baying for his blood, he broke out of jail and got clean away.

By 1853 there will be more than 200 lynchings in California, and gold prospectors will spend more than $6 million on guns and knives. The rate of homicide on the goldfields is 500 per 100,000, and lynch law is the rule rather than the exception. Even by frontier standards the level of violence and anarchy on the goldfields is excessive, but San Francisco is even worse.

'I was in San Francisco in 1851, when two hotels got to running each other,' writes a returned Australian forty-niner to the *Colac Herald* in 1885, recalling his roaring days. 'I forget their names, but that doesn't make any difference.

'Number one started with a brass band concert on the balcony every evening, and it drew big crowds, including about all of number two's guests. Pretty soon, however, number one began to lose its guests by the score without any apparent cause. The proprietor increased his brass band and polished up his bar, but without effect.

'It didn't take him long to find out that number two was having nightly cocking mains [cockfights] and dogfights for the exclusive benefit of guests. Then number one got back part of its guests by introducing private prize fights and slugging matches.

'It may sound preposterous, but it's a fact that when miners and others wanted to settle personal differences they used to go to the proprietor of number one, who paid them well for a fight, the money going to the winner. Of course, these exhibitions were given in private quarters, and none but guests and their friends were admitted.

'Number two saw number one's prize fights and slugging matches, and went one better. They knocked out one end of their dining room and built on it a stage and a greenroom and all other accessories, and had variety performances at breakfast, dinner and supper. This turned the tide in favour of number two, until one day a desperado went into number one and shot the bartender. This made number one famous, and placed it far ahead of number two in the estimation of the public.

'The proprietor, however, saw his opportunity, and prepared a coup d'etat. He headed a gang which went out and captured the murderer, and strung him up on the dining-room stage at supper, and all the guests were accorded the privilege of firing their revolvers at his dangling body.

'One shot accidentally went through the head of a waiter, and the entertainment far exceeded the proprietor's most sanguine expectations.'[1]

The part of town known as Sydney Valley or Sydney Town – and later as the Barbary Coast – is described by Herbert Asbury, chronicler of America's underworld and author of *The Gangs of New York*, as 'the haunt of the low and vile of every kind. The petty thief, the house burglar, the tramp, the whoremonger, lewd women, cutthroats, murderers, all are found here. Dance halls and concert saloons where bleary-eyed men and faded women drink vile liquor, smoke offensive tobacco, engage in vulgar conduct, sing obscene songs and say and do everything to heap upon themselves more degradation, are numerous. Low gambling houses, thronged with riot-loving rowdies, in all stages of intoxication, are there. Licentiousness, debauchery, pollution, loathsome disease, insanity from dissipation, misery, poverty, wealth, profanity, blasphemy and death, are there. And Hell, yawning to receive the putrid mass, is there also.'[2]

In his memoir, Malachi Fallon, San Francisco's first chief of police, and suspected corrupt cop, recalls:

'San Francisco's population was then made up of rough young men with adventurous spirits, excited by the discovery of gold. They needed a strong and experienced hand to keep them in control. Many of them were of the cowboy class, while the worst were deserting whalemen coming from all parts of the world. They were not men of evil principles but they felt the excitement of the time and enjoyed the lack of restraint in a town where there was no social organisation or adequate legal control. Outside of this looseness of moral forces at the time, they were good fellows.'[3]

Fallon's police force, founded in 1849 and comprised of Fallon himself, a deputy chief, three sergeants and 30 constables, does not impress visiting Frenchman Albert Bernard de Russailh. After a visit in 1851, de Russailh observes that the men of San Francisco 'have all the characteristics of savages and think only of death and slaughter. They always carry revolvers and they draw them at the least provocation, and threaten to blow your head off. I often wonder if this great people will revert altogether to barbarism.

'As for the police, I have only one thing to say. The police force is largely made up of ex-bandits, and naturally the members are interested above all in saving their old friends from punishment. Policemen here are quite as much to be feared as the robbers. If they know you have money, they will be the first to knock you on the head. You pay them well to watch over your house, and they set it on fire.

'In short, I think that all the people concerned with justice or the police are in league with the criminals. The city is in a hopeless chaos, and many years must pass before order can be established. In a country where so many races are mingled, a severe and inflexible justice is desirable, which would govern with an iron hand.'[4]

So here he is in San Francisco, the man the authorities call English Jim. Safe in the no-go zone known as Sydney Valley – where Australians run most of the brothels, gambling dens, illegal bars and boarding houses notorious as thieves' kitchens – he is free to mingle with the expatriate colonials who give the place its name.

Sydney Valley is a three-block stretch of Pacific Street, between Montgomery and Stockton streets at the base of Telegraph Hill (in present-day Chinatown), from near Portsmouth Square to the docks at Buena Vista Cove. The *San Francisco Herald* describes the district as the quintessential den of iniquity. 'There are certain spots in our city infested by the most abandoned men and women. The upper part of Pacific Street, after dark, is crowded by thieves, gamblers, low women, drunken sailors, and similar characters,' the *Herald* reports. 'Unsuspecting sailors and miners are entrapped by the dexterous thieves and swindlers that are always on the lookout, into these dens, where they are filled with liquor, drugged if necessary, until insensibility coming upon them, they fall an easy victim to their tempters.

'When the habitués of this quarter have a reason to believe a man has money, they will follow him for days, and employ every device to get him into their clutches. These dance-groggeries are outrageous nuisances and nurseries of crime.'[5]

As the population of the district expands, Sydney Valley is adjoined by blocks known as Devil's Acre, Battle Row, Cat Alley and The Slaughterhouse. To describe the nefarious inhabitants of the district, a new word is coined. Derived from 'Huddle 'im!' – the catch-cry of gangsters closing in on a victim – the word is 'hoodlum'.[6]

The street gang soon to be known as the Sydney Coves is a loose association of colonial villains that in time will include James Burns alias Jimmy from Town, Sam Whitaker, William Windred, Ben Lewis, Johnny Edwards, George Smith, John Jenkins, George Adams, Teddy McCormick, Thomas Belcher Kay, Matthew Hopwood alias Big Brummy, Jim Briggs, Dutch Charley, Bob McKinney alias McKenzie, Billy Hughes, Jim Brown alias Bowen, and John Morris Morgan, also known as Old Jack.

Irish-born Jimmy from Town is a talented burglar and enthusiastic pimp. Short-tempered and abrasive, he is sometimes a disruptive element in the gang, but as a close friend of Stuart's he enjoys a favoured position, and will prove invaluable in planning robberies and gaol breaks.

George Adams, known as Jack Dandy, is an English-born ex-convict from Sydney. A millwright turned professional criminal, he is skilled at designing and making housebreaking tools and keys.

Sam Whitaker, neat in dress and upright of bearing, is an accomplished thief transported in his youth to New South Wales for life but later granted a conditional pardon – the condition being that the recipient could travel to anywhere in the world except to Britain or its colonies.

Whitaker arrived in San Francisco in 1849 and, with fellow ex-convict Teddy McCormick, opened a lodging house in Sydney Valley. Theirs is the Port Phillip House which, like all lodging houses in the valley, offers not only room and board but hard liquor, gambling and girls.

Whitaker began a torrid affair with Mary Ann Hogan, an Australian lodging-housekeeper and receiver of stolen goods, while her husband Michael was away at the diggings. On returning to find Sam Whitaker in bed with his wife, Michael Hogan kicked him out, but it seems everyone in San Francisco – that is, everyone but Michael Hogan – knows the tryst between Sam and Mary Ann continues.

Soon, the word on the Sydney Valley grapevine will be that the lovely Mary Ann is dispensing her favours to Jim Stuart as well. Each man will later boast that she secretly keeps a photograph of him, and Whitaker will claim that Stuart, in a jealous rage, once threatened to shoot him.

Thomas Belcher Kay, also known as Singing Billy and Count Peri, and whose real name may or may not be Thomas Gibson, is an escaped convict from Van Diemen's Land. By lining the right pockets, he has managed to get himself appointed Port Warden. As overseer of comings and goings on the bay, Kay is privy to information on ships in the harbour and dockland businesses that are prime targets for robbery.

He runs a gymnasium in Sydney Valley, and can often be found in the district's brothels, where he runs a sting with some of the whores. They spike a customer's drink, he relieves the drugged client of his gold, and he and the girls split the takings.

William Windred, convicted of having robbed his own aunt, served four years in Van Diemen's Land before coming to California. He is a contentious figure, as we will later discover.

The first thing to know about Dutch Charley – a formidable ally of the Australians – is that he's not Dutch. Charles Patrick Duane was born in Tipperary, Ireland, in 1827, and emigrated to New York with his family as a child. In his youth, being large, strong and handy with his fists, Duane forged a reputation as a bare-knuckle prize-fighter, and had acquired the nickname of a German fighter he defeated, Dutch Charley. By his twenties, Duane was famous in New York City not only for his prowess in the ring but as an enforcer for corrupt Tammany Hall politicians who controlled the city. He soon made himself a terror to opponents of his political masters, and was feared even by the notorious street gangs of New York.

Since joining the exodus to California, Charley has found gainful employment not on the goldfields but in San Francisco, as enforcer for David Colbreth Broderick, a fellow New Yorker and son of Irish immigrants.

Broderick, a stone mason who had failed to win political office in New York, moved to California where he successfully ran for membership of the California State Senate, having financed his election campaign by a cunning fraud. Gold dust was then worth about $16 an ounce, and, there being no government mint, private companies struck gold coins of several denominations. Broderick set up a business smelting and assaying gold, minting gold coins that contained less gold than their face value.

Within a year he will be president of the state senate, acting state governor, and boss of a vicious and corrupt regime in control of San Francisco. Dutch Charley, for the part his fists and guns played in Broderick's rise to power, will be rewarded with an appointment as the city's fire chief.

John Jenkins is a runaway lifer from Van Diemen's Land. A giant of a man, with red hair and beard, he owns the Uncle Sam lodging house, bar and brothel, which he rented to a married couple from Van Diemen's Land, named Connolly. A few days after signing the lease, Mr Connolly died suddenly, and his wife, a notorious harpy and gossip, became Jenkins' mistress. Her husband's death was mysterious and timely, and the word around the valley is that she poisoned him.

Matthew Hopwood, known as Big Brummy because of his size and his birthplace of Birmingham, England, was transported to New South Wales for life for robbery, in 1836, at the age of 21. He was one of a dozen men from the convict ship *Bengal Merchant* assigned to the Australian Agricultural Company, which had been granted a million acres in the colony to provide England with wool and crops by exploiting convict labour.

Hopwood was assigned to the company's holdings at Port Stephens, 100 miles north of Sydney by sea. His good conduct there earned him a ticket of leave in 1845, but it was cancelled in 1849 when he was caught gambling. There is no record of

Hopwood being granted parole a second time, or a pardon, so it's possible he was one of a number of escaped convicts who somehow made their way to California.

John Goff, while not an active member of the gang, is a useful collaborator. Goff, keeper of the Panama House lodging house, had been transported to New South Wales for life for burglary, and moved to California on receiving a conditional pardon. His Panama House is a regular meeting place for criminals and corrupt police.

Sydney Valley abounds with notorious lodging houses with innocuous names – the Cottage of Content, the Bird in Hand, the Live and Let Live, the Heart in Hand, the Uncle Sam, the Welcome, and Rose Cottage.

The district also boasts more than its share of colourful characters – Billy Sweet Cheese, Bungaree Jack, Moe the Jew, Tommy Round Head, the Peruvian Angel, the Slasher, King the Barber, James 'Fighting Man' Kelly, Vyce the Bear Hunter, Barnes the Tinman, and Palmer the Birdstuffer.

Some are ex-convicts and all are of a larcenous inclination, but what they lack is a leader, and it seems they have found one in James Stuart, the man they will come to call Long Jim.

To the American ear, the colonial accent sounds like London cockney, Boston Yankee or a hybrid of both, and their speech is peppered with convict slang, known as 'flash language'. A cove, for instance, is a small, sheltered bay, but in flash language a cove is also a man. And if a cove were to tell an American that as a kinchen on a lag ship he knew what it was like to wear the bands, he would mean that as a young lad on a prison hulk he knew what it was like to go hungry.

If a cove complains that he has done all his blunt flying the mags, he means he lost all his money gambling. If he says it's a bad night for the scamp when Oliver is in town, he means that highway robbery is risky on a moonlit night. And should he announce his intention to get swished to the mollisher he dorses with, anyone mouthy enough to call that mollisher a mott better be ready to flash their sticks or bolt. In other words, if he says he intends to marry his mistress, anyone foolish enough to call that woman a whore had better be ready to draw his pistols or run for his life.

Chapter 8

No luck with pick and shovel

In the spring of 1850, Simpson Davison is standing on the dock of the bay, marvelling at how much San Francisco has changed during the few months he and his partner Edward Hargraves were upcountry at the diggings, failing to strike it rich.

The previous winter, Davison and Hargraves – two Australian graziers turned gold-seekers – had arrived in San Francisco on the barque *Elizabeth Archer*. She was carrying 140 passengers – the better-off in the ship's seven cabins, and the rest in steerage. Davison, 29, the son of a prominent banker, and owner of several cattle and sheep stations west of the Great Divide, was wealthy and successful, with a talent for braggadocio.

His cabin mate Edward Hargraves, 33, the son of a British army officer, was neither wealthy nor successful. Hargraves, who at the age of 14 went to sea as a cabin boy, had experienced more lows than highs in his various business ventures, yet his self-assurance put Davison's in the shade. Convinced he was destined for fortune and fame somehow, somewhere, Hargraves had sold all his cattle to scrape up the price of a cabin ticket on the *Elizabeth Archer*.

Back when his ship dipped into the bay, San Francisco as Davison first saw it was a city of shanties, tents and masts. In the harbour were hundreds of ships, many of them deserted, their crews having jumped ship to head for the goldfields. Ashore, rows of huts reached the top of Telegraph Hill. The wharves were cluttered with merchants' makeshift booths selling everything from fruit to fish to underwear, and hucksters' tables where innocents abroad could try their luck at the pea-and-thimble game. Bullock carts hauled sacks of goods along the muddy waterfront streets, and on a hillside a block back from the harbour were hotels, stores and restaurants, many with canvas roofs, unfinished yet open for business.

Now, to Davison's eye it seems the ships lining the shore stretch at least twice the distance he had noted on his arrival, hundreds more ride at anchor in the bay, and the fingers of new piers poke out from the foreshore.

The hub of the city has changed, too, but not for the better. Two recent fires – deliberately lit – ravaged the city centre, wiping out shanty rows, houses, hotels and offices alike. The aim of the arsonists was chaos, and amid the chaos they robbed and looted with apparent impunity.

Of 70 suspects arrested after the latest fire, 48 were from Sydney, and Davison learns that the accusing finger has been pointed at the part of town around the base of Telegraph Hill. An Australian enclave, the area is known as Sydney Valley. It is a rabbit warren of clapboard and canvas gambling dens, brothels, illegal grog shops and shabby boarding houses haunted by 'coarse rogues from Sydney'.[1]

Davison has learnt that Sydney Valley, off-limits to the city's ineffectual and corrupt police force, is the headquarters of a gang of Australian criminals whose notoriety grows by the day. The gangsters, in their distinctive broad-brimmed straw hats, called cabbage-tree hats, and always carrying guns and knives, are known as the Sydney Coves or the Stuart Gang. The law-abiding citizens of San Francisco, who fear and loathe these swaggering colonials, derisively call them the Sydney Ducks, after the plain 'duck cotton' clothing many of them wear. But anyone who dared call a Cove a Sydney Duck to his face would most likely end up a dead duck.

Back home, the hated Australian arrivals have their defenders. 'Great excitement prevails respecting the arrival of persons from these colonies, all of whom are supposed to be convicts,' snorts the *Sydney Morning Herald*.

'The *Alta California*, in an article on the subject, pleads hard for an enactment to prevent their landing. "Thousands of Jack Sheppards [a notorious English thief and gaol-breaker], living, moving, murdering cut-throats," according to our contemporary, have arrived from the penal colonies, and are committing depredations and depraving the morals of the community.'[2]

While Australians in general are no longer welcome in San Francisco, some have managed to find honest work in the city, notably in the mercantile and building trades, and have even joined citizens' groups that meet ships from Australia on arrival to vet the passengers. Those deemed unsavoury characters are deported back to Australia.

Other Australians taking ship for home have found little or no gold at the diggings, or arrived to find they could not afford the $50 mining licence fee imposed on foreign diggers.

Simpson Davison, despite having had no luck with pick and shovel, does not join the ranks of the disappointed and destitute. He still has plenty of money in his pockets, and he spends some of it on trade goods to sell at the goldfields, and a small ship to ply the Sacramento River to deliver the goods.

Meanwhile, Davison's old prospecting partner Edward Hargraves has turned up in San Francisco, flat broke and at a loose end. Davison, perhaps more out of pity than need, offers Hargraves a share of the profits if he will help sail the ship. Hargraves, who was a sailor in his youth – or claims to have been – accepts the offer.

While preparing to set sail, both men stay at the home of a mutual friend from Australia. It's here that on the same day, 5 March 1850, both write letters home. Remarking on similarities between the Californian goldfields and areas around Bathurst, in central western New South Wales, Hargraves writes to Sydney merchant Samuel Peek:

'I am very forcibly impressed that I have been in a gold region in New South Wales, within 300 miles of Sydney, and unless you know how to find it you might live for a century in the region and know nothing of their existence.'[3]

Davison will later claim that his letter, to a sheep farmer friend, made the same observation, but the letter, unlike Hargraves', was destroyed, and so the credit for starting the 1851 Australian gold rush – along with a £10,000 reward and a government sinecure – will go to Edward Hargraves.

Simpson Davison will later recall that when, at the diggings, he and Hargraves announced they would be leaving California, confident of finding gold in Australia, an American digger scoffed, 'There's no gold in the country you're going to, and if there is that darned queen of yours wouldn't let you dig it.'[4]

Hargraves retorted, 'There's as much gold in the country I'm going to as there is in California, and her gracious majesty, God bless her, will appoint me one of her gold commissioners, then I shall get my friend Davison here a like appointment.'[5]

As it turns out, the queen will keep her end of the bargain. Hargraves will not, and Simpson Davison will fade into obscurity.

Edward Hammond Hargraves will win a place in history for the discovery of gold in Australia, yet the credit should fairly have been awarded almost 30 years earlier to a convict who, while working on a chain gang near Bathurst, dug up a gold nugget. The convict, whose name, sadly, history does not record, dutifully reported the find to his overseer, who accused him of creating the nugget from melted-down stolen gold ornaments – an accusation based upon no evidence whatsoever – and had him flogged. No doubt, the overseer kept the nugget.

The clock is about to tick over into the year 1851, and the eyes of the world are on America. Jewellery made in New York from Californian gold is the latest must-have for the well-heeled across the Atlantic and the Pacific. American innovations in photography have produced images of incomparable clarity and brilliance, and Samuel Colt's latest invention has sired the era of the gunslinger.

The .36 calibre Colt Navy revolver, a cap-and-ball six-shooter, is much lighter than dragoon revolvers still in general use, which were designed to be carried in saddle holsters. The Colt Navy revolver, suitable for carrying in a belt holster, is set to become the iconic weapon of the American west and other frontier societies. In the United States, famous Colt Navy users will include Wild Bill Hickok, Doc Holliday, Robert E. Lee and the Texas Rangers. In Africa, it will be favoured by the explorer Richard

Burton, and in Australia by bushrangers Ned Kelly and Frank Gardiner.

The Sydney Coves, too, favour Colt revolvers, although their leader, Long Jim Stuart, prefers to carry a brace of .44 calibre double-barrel pistols.

Chapter 9

Sainted women and painted ladies

The miners came in forty-nine,
The whores in fifty-one.
They rolled around the barroom floor,
Then came the Native Son.
[Anonymous, Old San Francisco doggerel]

On the Californian goldfields, one young man was not ashamed to admit that when, one evening, he came closer to a woman than he had been in six months, he damn near fainted.

In 1851, less than eight per cent of the population of California was female, and many of those women were so-called 'bad' women – also known as painted ladies, fallen women, ladies of the night, soiled doves or just plain whores. So rare were respectable, so-called 'good' women that when the first such female arrived in the mining town of Columbia, in the Sierra Nevada foothills, she was greeted by a brass band and a parade.

When word of the gold strike spread across the world, the

first prostitutes to arrive hailed from Mexico, Chile and Nicaragua. Of the Nicaraguan ladies, Mark Twain wrote in his *Travels with Mr Brown*: 'They are virtuous according to their lights, but I guess their lights are a little dim.'[1]

In San Francisco, prostitutes from Latin America hung out their red lights in the streets at the foot of Telegraph Hill, in Sydney Valley. In time, they were joined by soiled doves from France, Peru and Australia, and many doves found themselves working for the Coves. It is claimed that San Francisco now has more brothels than the rest of the United States combined, and that madams and pimps there often become extremely wealthy and – within the wild frontier culture – almost respectable citizens.

Not all the women of the brothels, bars, gambling dens and streets were prostitutes in their countries of origin. Miners often arrange for unmarried female relatives to come to the goldfields where they quickly find husbands, but life for a married woman on the goldfields is fraught with danger. A woman newly widowed or abandoned by her husband can find herself destitute if she does not find a new partner immediately. If she cannot, or will not, she might be lucky enough to find work as a seamstress, nurse, cook or laundress. Otherwise, often her only means of survival is prostitution, with its constant risks of rape, disease, pregnancy and assault, as well as debts to madams and pimps she can never repay.

In August 1851, in a letter to a friend back home, Enos Christman, a Pennsylvania printer's apprentice, writes from the Sonora goldfield:

'Sonora is a fast place and no mistake. Such motley a collection as we have here can be found nowhere but in California.

'Sonora has a population hailing from every hole and corner of the globe – Kanakas, Peruvians, Negroes, Spaniards, Mexicans,

Chileans, Chinese, British convicts from New South Wales known as the "Sydney Birds", Englishmen, Frenchmen, Dutch, Paddies, and not a small sprinkling of Yankees.

'We have more gamblers, more drunkards, more ugly, bad women, and larger lumps of gold, and more of them, than any other place of similar dimensions within Uncle Sam's dominions.

'The Sabbath is regarded as a holiday, granting men and women a more extensive licence to practice vice than any other day of the week.

'I feel that I am a rover, a wanderer on the face of the earth, in a land flowing, not with milk and honey, but with flapjacks and gold dust, far from home and kindred, and surrounded by the offscourings and scum of society from all parts of the inhabitable globe. All selfish, each for himself, and his Satanic Majesty for all.

'I have scarcely met with half a dozen respectable women, or men with their families, since I left the Atlantic states. The women of other nations, where few there are, are nearly all lewd harlots who are drunk half the time or sitting behind the gambling table dealing monte. To see a woman who can read and write is a curiosity. Indeed, the majority of our females are a disgrace to woman. All, all ruined!

'This sorry state of things, I hope, will not last much longer, for every steamer which arrives in San Francisco brings many families of wives and children, and as soon as we get a few of them among us, a new order of things will commence.'[2]

Enos Christman's expected flotilla of feminine propriety will arrive later rather than sooner. For a few years now, many in California have shared his belief in the civilising influence of woman; that in their absence men revert to barbarism.

In San Francisco, in 1849, the *Alta California* intoned, 'Woman, to society, is like a cement to the building of stone'[3], and one woman intent on providing that cement was the writer and feminist Eliza Farnham. As leader of the California Association of American Women, she called for 'intelligent, virtuous and efficient' women to accompany her from New York to San Francisco as mail-order brides, convinced that 'the presence of women would be one of the surest checks upon many of the evils that are apprehended there'.[4]

Applicants were asked to provide testimonials from their clergymen as to their character, and $250 for passage to San Francisco and other expenses.

More than 200 women responded to Farnham's call. And on receiving news in April of 1851 that the ship of brides – the aptly named *Angelique* – has set sail from New York, bound for the Golden Gate, some suspect the enterprise could be a ruse to bring in yet more prostitutes, but the male population in general is wildly supportive. The *Alta California* enthuses, 'Eliza Farnham and her girls are coming, and the dawning of brighter days for our golden land is even now perceptible.'[5]

When the *Angelique* docks in the bay, however, the crowds of would-be suitors lining the shore are sorely disappointed. Of the 200 women who responded to the call, only two step ashore. The rest, it seems, got cold feet and stayed home.

Still, for the lonesome digger, there is always the *Model Artistes* show at the Athenaeum Theatre on Commercial Street. The theatre, opened in May 1851 by a showman and quack scientist styling himself 'Doctor' Robert Collyer, features a troupe of beautiful artists' models from New South Wales, who pose nude and near nude on stage as living statues. The performance, which sparked riots in New York and in Mobile, Alabama, and was banned in Cincinnati, plays to packed houses in San Francisco. Unsurprisingly, the audiences are almost entirely male.

A year after it opens, Collyer's theatre will burn to the ground in the worst of the fires blamed on the Sydney Coves.

It has occurred to some women that California's gender imbalance might work in their favour. One such is Dorothy Scraggs, who places the following ad in a Marysville newspaper:

'A HUSBAND WANTED

'By a lady who can wash, cook, scour, sew, milk, spin, weave, hoe (can't plough), cut wood, make fires, feed the pigs, raise chickens, rock the cradle, saw a plank, drive nails etc. Could once dance, can ride a horse, donkey or oxen, besides a great many things too numerous to be named here.

'Now for her terms: Her age is none of your business. She is neither handsome nor a fright, yet an old man need not apply, nor any who have not a little more education than she has, and a great deal more gold, for there must be $20,000 settled on her before she will bind herself to perform all the above.

'Address to Dorothy Scraggs, with real name. P.O. Marysville.'[6]

It's to be hoped the redoubtable Dorothy got her man.

Chapter 10

Latter-Day Sam

The farm boy from Painesville, Ohio, has done rather well for himself. Admittedly, along the way there were lapses of judgement, dubious deals and the occasional dismal failure – in land speculation, publishing and other ventures – but here in California he has fallen on his feet. Samuel Brannan, destined to become California's first millionaire, is the very model of a self-made man, albeit with more than a little help from his brethren in the Mormon Church – the Church of Latter-Day Saints.

Brannan had arrived in California, in July 1846, in dramatic style. As a prominent church elder, he had sailed from New York on the ship *Brooklyn*, leading an expedition intent on establishing an independent Mormon colony in the Mexican province – by force, if necessary.

Had the *Brooklyn* sailed into San Francisco Bay three weeks earlier the Mormons might have succeeded, but at the sight of a US warship in the bay and the Stars and Stripes fluttering over the pueblo of Yerba Buena, they knew their grand plan had been scuttled.

Still, many stayed and settled, including Sam Brannan, but although Brannan had been appointed leader of the Mormon Church in California, he was mistrusted by many of his co-religionists. All Mormons were obliged to contribute tithes – ten per cent of their earnings – to the church. Brannan, who collected the tithes, was suspected of pocketing the money. That would explain, some reasoned, how he so quickly managed to establish a newspaper, two flour mills, grazing land and livestock, as well as building a fine house in Yerba Buena.

By 1848 Brannan's interests included a mercantile store near Sutter's Fort, called Brannan's Shirt Tail Store. It was here that Brannan's business partner, Charlie Smith, learned of the gold strike at Sutter's Mill, hence Brannan's famous cry of 'Gold from the American River!' that sparked the rush.

News of the discovery was slow to reach US Army headquarters at Monterey, California's old Spanish and Mexican capitol, on the central coast. There was no regular mail service; mail had to come by ship, around Cape Horn, and there was no overland delivery until 1848.

'I well remember the first overland mail,' writes Lieutenant William Tecumseh Sherman, then stationed at Monterey. 'It was delivered by Kit Carson in saddlebags from Taos in New Mexico.'[1]

Kit Carson – scout, trapper, soldier and explorer – was a legend in his own lifetime, and Sherman was anxious to meet the famous frontiersman 'who had achieved such feats of daring among the wild animals of the Rocky Mountains and the still wilder Indians of the plains'.[2]

On encountering Carson at a tavern, he was surprised to find 'a small, stoop-shouldered man, with reddish hair, freckled face, soft blue eyes, and nothing to indicate extraordinary courage or daring. He spoke but little, and answered questions in monosyllables'.[3]

Sherman writes: 'Stories reached us of miraculous discoveries, and spread throughout the land. Everyone was talking of "Gold! Gold!" until it assumed the character of a fever. Some of our soldiers began to desert; citizens were fitting out trains of wagons and pack mules to go to the mines. We heard of men earning fifty, five hundred, and thousands of dollars per day, and for a time it seemed as though somebody would reach solid gold. Some of this gold began to come to Yerba Buena in trade, and to disturb the value of merchandise, particularly of mules, horses, tin pans and articles used in mining.

'I of course could not escape the infection, and at last convinced Colonel Mason that it was our duty to go up and see with our own eyes, that we might report the truth to our government.'[4]

When Colonel Mason and Lieutenant Sherman visited the goldfields, Sherman noted that the diggers included about 300 Mormons, led by Sam Brannan, 'on hand as the high priest, collecting tithes'.[5]

William Squires Clark, a respected Mormon elder, was in the camp, 'talking to Colonel Mason about matters and things generally, when he inquired, "Governor, what business has Sam Brannan to collect the tithes here?"' Clark admitted that Brannan was head of the Mormon Church in California, and he was simply questioning as to Brannan's right, as high priest, to compel the Mormons to pay him the regular tithes.

'Colonel Mason answered, "Brannan has a perfect right to collect the tax, if you Mormons are fool enough to pay it."

'"Then," said Clark, "I for one won't pay it any longer!"'

'I understood, afterwards,' Sherman writes, 'that from that time the payment of the tithes ceased, but that Brannan had already collected enough money to hire Sutter's hospital and to open a store there, in which he made more money than any merchant in California during that summer and fall. The understanding was that the money collected by him as tithes was the foundation for his fortune, which is still very large in San Francisco.'[6]

Brannan's response to accusations that he had stolen the Lord's money was that he would repay the money if he got a receipt signed by the Lord.

By 1850, Sam Brannan is the richest man in San Francisco. He is a major landowner and leading merchant, and his interests now include banks, railroads and telegraph companies. His influence in civic and state affairs is considerable, and that, along with a short and violent temper, makes him a dangerous man to cross.

That temper has been tested of late by a series of daring and violent crimes, and of the failure of the police and judiciary to bring the perpetrators to book.

On the morning of 27 October 1850, when San Franciscans open their morning newspapers, it's expected that the biggest story of the day will be the upcoming opening of the Jenny Lind Theatre. 'This is the name given to an elegant, spacious saloon fitted up in the newly completed Parker House, on the eastern side of Portsmouth Square,' the *Alta California* tells its readers. 'It has a neat and pretty stage and an auditorium fitted up with commodious settees, capable of holding probably 500 persons with all ease. The walls and ceilings are handsomely painted in fresco. The proprietors contemplate opening tomorrow evening with a musical olio and feats of legerdemain.'[7]

But that story is not the splash. It's this:

'On Friday night, five men went on board the brig *James Caskie*, off Clarke's Point, and demanded of the captain his money. The captain refusing, they beat him senseless, and until his wife, who feared they would kill her husband, delivered to the robbers the money, about $900. A man who was on board at the time was made prisoner by the robbers. They were all masked and otherwise disguised.'[8]

Through the remaining months of 1850, and into the new year, San Franciscans read of robberies, assaults and suspicious fires on almost a daily basis. A pattern is emerging.

Then, on Wednesday 19 February 1851, San Franciscans read of an outrage the *Alta California* decries as 'one of the most barefaced, cool and audacious robberies of which the annals of any country give a history'.

'Last evening, about eight o'clock, Mr Charles J. Jansen was in his store on Montgomery Street, two doors from Washington, when two men entered and wished to be shown some blankets.

'Mr Jansen, who was, when they entered, in a partially reclining position on his counter, rose to serve them, when one of them drew from his pocket a slung shot [a long cord with a weight at one end, at the centre of a knot], with which he struck Mr Jansen three times over the right temple, knocking him senseless on the floor. When Mr Jansen recovered his senses he found that his desk, containing about $2,000, had been opened and the money taken.

'Mr Jansen's wound, which was immediately dressed by Dr Temple, is not considered dangerous, as the skull is not fractured, although it is a wonder that he was not killed.

'Thus, almost in broad daylight, the store of a peaceable citizen is entered and a robbery, almost a murder committed. In such a state of things who is safe? Is there no remedy? No means by which the perpetrators of these outrages may be ferreted out and brought to justice? If once caught, if the law cannot punish them, an indignant community will.'[9]

Increasingly, fingers are being pointed at Sydney Valley. The word is that certain Australian residents of that notorious district have lately graduated from vice and petty larceny to organised crime. Sam Brannan has a remedy in mind – an armed force of citizens willing to take justice into their own hands. Vigilantes.

Chapter 11

Kangaroo courts

Sam Brannan's notion of a citizen's organisation dedicated to restoring public order by taking the law into its own hands is hardly a radical idea. In 1849, in San Francisco, when veterans of the Mexican–American War – mostly former members of New York street gangs – formed a gang called the Hounds and took to harassing Mexicans and extorting protection money, some 250 citizens formed a militia and drove the Hounds from the city.

And lately, an increasing tendency towards vigilantism has been apparent throughout California, particularly on the goldfields, where claim jumping is a continuing problem and informal tribunals have proved more effective than legally constituted courts. Such tribunals are known as mustang courts or kangaroo courts, a term which, perhaps surprisingly, did not originate in Australia.

This is undeniably rough justice. Suspected offenders are tried by their peers without delay, presumption of innocence and due process are largely ignored and retribution is swift and savage.

Any interference by the proper authorities is resented and violently resisted, and it is not unusual for an officer of the law attempting to rescue a man condemned to be executed to be himself threatened with death. There have been instances of sheriffs being shot while trying to rescue a prisoner; of sheriffs who bravely faced down the mob and carried off a rescue; but, more often, of sheriffs who agreed with the verdict of the kangaroo court and left the prisoner to the mercy of the mob.

There has been at least one instance of a state governor who rebuked a county sheriff for failing to prevent a lynching in a mining town, only to be told by the sheriff to mind his own business. After all, a sheriff is an elected official responsible to the voters, not to the governor, and he ignores the will of the people at his peril. As the *San Francisco Daily Herald* puts it: 'The sheriffs throughout the country have been more true to the interests of the people, and more honest in the discharge of their duty than any other class of official. We know of but two instances in the state in which the sheriff has come under the ban of public censure.'[1]

Presumably, neither sheriff was re-elected.

As the exodus from Australian towns to the California diggings continues apace, concerns are voiced that Australia might go the way of California, where lynch law rules.

The Australian press, which has for so long and with so little success attempted to discourage the exodus, tries a new tactic – comparing the relatively safe and orderly conditions on the Australian goldfields with the lawlessness and chaos of California.

Australians, especially those with relatives on the California diggings, are concerned to read of outrages such as the case of

Fred Rouse, an Englishman charged with murder. Before he could be tried, Rouse was dragged from a Sacramento court by a lynch mob and hanged. Then there was the lynching by vigilantes of two suspected horse thieves, James Baxter and Charles Simmons. The alleged rustlers, according to American historian Jay Monaghan, 'spoke with an accent that made their captors suspect them of being Australians under assumed names'.[2]

An article from the *Sacramento Transcript*, reprinted in Australian newspapers, reports that Baxter and Simmons were caught red-handed driving some 15 stolen horses across the Cosumnes River, in northern California, and 'hanged at a few minutes notice'.

The report explains: 'The people along the Cosumnes River, who occupy the different ranchos, and have large bands of horses and mules, have suffered so much within the last few months that they have become perfectly desperate, and will treat with no clemency whatever thieves who are clearly convicted.'

Ranchers Gage and Almond, on being tipped off by a teamster that men had been spotted 'attempting to cross the river with stock, and were having a hell of a time,' rode out at night to confront the rustlers.

'What horses are those you have?' the ranchers demanded. The men replied that the horses were their own, that they had bought them at Dry Creek, and were taking them to the American Fork.

'Are they all yours?' Gage asked.

'Yes, all but one.'

'When did you leave Dry Creek?'

'Late this afternoon.'

'God damn you, you have stolen these horses!' yelled Gage, who had recognised the horses' brands as his own. Baxter and Simmons were taken prisoner and escorted back to the Gage and Almond ranch.

The *Transcript* continues: 'The prisoners were then arraigned, and a motion made to give them a trial by jury, but the proposition was hooted down by the incensed crowd. A motion was then made that they be hanged at once, which was carried by acclamation.

'They were called upon to make a confession, being told they had but half an hour to prepare for the solemn change that awaited them. They gave their names as James Baxter, of Maine, and Charles Simmons, of Massachusetts. The names, however, may have been assumed.'

When told time was up, they begged, 'For God's sake, let us live a little longer!', and were granted five more minutes of life, during which time one was heard to whisper to the other, 'Let's tell them all about it.'

'No, no, hush!' the other replied.

The report concludes: 'Lariats were brought, nooses made, and the guilty wretches hanged. This took place at 12 o'clock last night, and their bodies were still suspended this morning when our informant left, although persons were engaged in digging two graves. This is truly a lamentable affair, and one which clearly shows the excited state of the public mind.'[3]

Were the condemned men Australian? They claimed to be New Englanders, and while there are similarities between the Yankee drawl and the Australian drawl, the men's origins remain unknown.

Putting a positive spin on this tragic tale, the *Sydney Morning Herald* crowed: 'Our fellow subjects at home would mark the superiority of our Eldorado over all others in point of civilisation, industry, social order, and all that Englishmen deem essential to the calm engagements of domestic life.'[4]

Chapter 12

Who killed Charlie Moore?

On the road to the Yuba River, in broad daylight on Saturday 7 December 1850, someone shot Charlie Moore dead. Many believe that someone was Long Jim Stuart, who, while on the run with horse thieves, and broke after losing at cards, happened upon Moore, shot him in the back and robbed him.

Moore, a miner, was riding with two partners from their claim near Winslow's Bar to William Dobbins' ranch, on the Yuba. The *Marysville Herald* reported, 'When about four miles from their destination, they separated; Mr Moore came on one road and his partners another.

'He had $2,300 belonging to himself and partners. His partners arrived at Dobbins' ranch and waited there for him. After a short time, a Spaniard came to the ranch and said there was a man who had been shot lying dead above. Mr Moore's partners immediately went in the direction indicated by the Spaniard, supposing that Mr Moore was the murdered man. They did not succeed, however, in finding him that day.

'The next day, Sunday, they took the Spaniard with them and found Mr Moore lying in a small ravine, dead, with three slug wounds upon him, one of which penetrated his spine, and another had entered under the shoulder and pierced the left lung. The murderers had rifled the body of the money.

'Suspicion attaches to three individuals, who are on their way below, to take passage to the Atlantic states. We understand that a party has left in pursuit of them.'[1]

The following March, after testimony had been taken from witnesses, the *Marysville Herald* fills in the gaps in the story. When the search for Moore resumed, 'they were joined by a Chilean who stated that the day before, while engaged in repacking a mule, about a mile from Dobbins' ranch, they heard the report of a gun, and on going some 200 yards further they saw a man about the same distance beyond them, running away.

'Soon after, they found a man lying down with a cloak thrown over him, and a mule nearby, whom they supposed had been thrown off. On examination, they found that he was wounded, and soon saw him breathe his last.

'The Chilean led them to the spot, where blood was discovered but no body of the murdered man. Here they separated for a thorough search and soon found his body in a ravine, among some bushes, with the cloak thrown over it. The tracks of three men were seen, two of them bearing the appearance of fine boot tracks, having small heels, the other an ordinary coarse boot. In the vicinity they discovered a camp in the midst of a thick chaparral [dense, thorny bushes] which entirely hid those within it from passers by, and at the same time commanded a view of the road for a mile. In this camp was found a hatchet, some lead, sardines, dried tongue, light bread and some other things.'[2]

The body, identified as that of Charles Moore, was taken to the ranch and examined by a doctor. The victim had a knife wound to the head and had been shot three times in the back with a shotgun.

'Mr Dobbins testifies that on the day before the murder occurred, three men stopped near his house, dismounted, and appeared to be in consultation. After a while, two of them came into the ranch and enquired about provisions etc. They purchased some shot, two bars of lead, two dried beef tongues, a German double-barrel shotgun, some light bread and other articles. The lead, dried tongue and light bread Mr Dobbins identified as being the same sold to these men. The boots worn by them corresponded to the tracks discovered.'[3]

According to Dobbins, one of the men matched the description of Long Jim Stuart, alias English Jim, suspected of leading the brutal assault and robbery of the captain of the *James Caskie*, and who was believed to be hiding out in the Yuba River area. Thomas Broadwater, Moore's partner, obtained a warrant for Stuart's arrest and immediately set out in pursuit. On arriving in Sacramento, Broadwater learned that a man called James Stuart had been arrested for burglary and was on board the prison ship.

The *Transcript* reports: 'Yesterday two gentlemen arrived from Yuba County having a warrant for the arrest of James Stuart, or "English Jim", an individual charged with the murder of Charles Moore on the Yuba River and robbing him of $2,500. These gentlemen visited the prison ship and recognised the murderer in the man arrested on Thursday night.'[4]

With their leader facing the noose, the Sydney Coves are in dire need of a mouthpiece for the mob. On 16 December 1850, under the headline 'Singular offer if true', the *Transcript* reported: 'A lawyer, in extensive practice in Boston, has been offered $12,000 per year for two years, the payment guaranteed by security on real estate in New York to go to California and exercise his talent in defending an association of burglars and thieves. The condition of the offer was that any money received by him for defending others, or for services rendered to others than members of the gang, should be credited to them as part payment of the salary. He peremptorily declined the offer.'[5]

Two days later, Stuart escaped from the prison ship. 'During Tuesday night last, four prisoners escaped from on board the prison brig, which lies in the river,' the *Transcript* reported. 'It appears that they cut through the floor in the hold of the vessel, and then proceeded cautiously to the portholes in the bow, from whence they escaped into the small oar boat attached to the brig.

'It is said that the prisoners cut through the floor with a small penknife, which must certainly be regarded as somewhat extraordinary.'[6]

Not so extraordinary perhaps, judging by this revelation from District Attorney Milton Latham. Rushing to the defence of the sheriff of Sacramento County, Major McCulloch, and the warden of the prison brig, who have been blamed for the poor security on the vessel, Latham wrote: 'I feel it my duty to make a statement in reference to the escape of prisoners from the brig on Tuesday night. I have no hesitancy in saying that no blame can be attached to them. The brig, as a prison, is entirely insecure. Major McCulloch has made efforts to have it made strong and safe. In this he has failed, for no-one in the city is willing to render his services for a compensation in county scrip.

'Upon examination, I found the floor planks about one-third of an inch thick, and the chains and locks capable of being broken by mere manual force. It is unreasonable to suppose that the sheriff would repair the brig at a personal expense of a thousand dollars. Unless immediate action is taken, our community will have no safeguard against the acts of desperadoes and villains.'[7]

And the biggest, baddest desperado of them all, the outlaw Jim Stuart, was still on the loose.

Chapter 13

Fanning the flames

The *San Francisco Daily Herald* is in no doubt that the fire on the previous Saturday night was deliberately lit. 'The building in which it originated was found to be on fire in three places, and there is every reason to believe combustible materials were used in fanning the flame. The design of the incendiaries was obviously to make a rush, in the confusion, on the office of the Pacific Mail Steamship Company and seize the treasure left there for shipment by the *California*.

'One store near the scene of conflagration was entered by a gang of ruffians and stripped of all it contained under pretence of removing the articles from danger, and of course the owners have been unable to find them since. Various robberies were committed, and many arrests were made at the commencement of the conflagration, and we are in hopes the activity of the police will enable them to detect the ruffians who planned and put this nefarious design into execution.

'On Monday we warned the authorities of the existence of a

gang of desperadoes banded together for the purpose of plundering the community, and we predicted that an attempt would be made to fire the city in order to profit by the confusion for the execution of their marauding purposes.

'The citizens now see that if they ever hope to put down this organisation of thieves and vagabonds they must depend upon themselves. A volunteer patrol should be formed, and, above all, a stern example should be made of the first wretch who is known to be guilty of incendiarism or robbery. We do not advocate the rash and vengeful infliction of summary punishment on any person against whom the proof is not positive of his connection with those crimes, but although opposed to capital punishment in old communities where the execution of the law is so perfectly systematised that justice seldom fails of its victim, nevertheless believe that some startling and extraordinary correction is necessary in San Francisco to arrest the alarming increase of crimes against property and life, and to save the remainder of the city from destruction.'[1]

The *Sacramento Transcript* reports that the Mayor of San Francisco has posted a reward of $1000 for information leading to the arrest of the arsonist who set fire to the Cook Brothers and Company store, and that 25 men were arrested for looting during the blaze.

'We could scarcely restrain the exclamation of "Good!",' says the *Transcript*, on learning that 'on Saturday night, during the fire, a gentleman met a ruffian in the act of carrying away a box upon his shoulders. Upon enquiry as to what he was going to do with it, the fellow replied that the box was his own – he was going to save it.

'But it happened to be the property of the party who addressed him, and upon refusing to put it down, a knife was plunged into the thief, who was immediately taken away by his accomplices, and nothing has been heard of him since.

'We conceive this to be rather a summary remedy, while at the same time we have no sympathies for those miscreants who embrace the occasion of a fire to rob others of their property.'[2]

The same issue reports the number of acres planted with grapes in New South Wales between 1843 and 1849, and the quantity of wine and brandy produced in that period. The information, says the *Transcript*, shows 'the growing importance of that far-off land. Our own relations with it must continue to become more and more intimate, and thus we have a deep interest in everything pertaining to that colony which sustains at this moment a relation with England similar to that of our American states previous to the Revolution.'[3]

Chapter 14

'Fie upon your laws!'

Charles Jansen is alone in his manchester and haberdashery emporium on Montgomery Street when a bearded man in a wide-brimmed hat enters and says he wants to buy a dozen blankets. The man seems slightly intoxicated.

As Jansen is showing the man some blankets, another man, wearing a cloak, enters the dimly lit store. 'I first saw him about 10 feet from the door,' Jansen later recalls. 'He stopped about halfway up the store and asked the price of canvas.'[1]

As Jansen stoops to pick up a length of canvas, one of the men shouts 'Now!' and Jensen is struck on the head and falls to the floor. After being hit two or three more times and kicked in the chest he loses consciousness.

On waking sometime later he struggles to his feet, discovers he has been robbed of about $1700 in gold, staggers outside and screams for help. People who rush to his aid tell him they spotted the notorious Jim Stuart and another of the Sydney Coves gang hurrying towards the waterfront.

On Saturday, about noon, with Marshal Malachi Fallon and a strong police escort, two men charged with robbery and attempted murder are marched down the street to Charles Jansen's house. The men, arrested in Sydney Valley soon after the crime, are William Windred and Thomas Berdue.

Jansen, still suffering from the savage beating he received, confronts them at his bedside. The newspapers report: 'Mr Jansen identified both the prisoners, to the best of his knowledge and belief, but not quite positively as to either, especially as to Windred.'[2]

When William Windred is brought before Jansen, wearing a cabbage-tree hat and a cloak, the merchant says he bears a resemblance to the taller of the two men – the second man who entered his store – but cannot positively swear to it. He admits that because the 16-metre-long store was lit by a single candle, he could not be certain.

When Thomas Berdue is brought before him, Jansen identifies him as the first man to enter the store. The likeness is perfect, the merchant says. 'I could not imagine a closer resemblance.'[3]

Thomas Berdue is tall and well built. He has curly hair with a small bald spot on the crown, a scar on his right cheek, and a deformed middle finger on his left hand – a description remarkably similar to that of Long Jim Stuart.

As the prisoners, on leaving Jansen's house, are being escorted through Portsmouth Square, a swelling crowd follows them. Some shout 'Lynch them! Hang them!', pushing and shoving in an attempt to get their hands on Berdue, assuming he is the hated leader of the Sydney Coves. The police fend them off, however, and the prisoners are returned to the police station in safety.

At 2 pm, in a courtroom packed to overflowing with hostile onlookers, Windred and Berdue appear before Judge Shepherd.

After Jansen's deposition has been read to the court, the accused men's attorney, Hall McAllister, has barely begun to state the case for the defence when the judge adjourns the case until the following Monday. An application for bail is made but immediately withdrawn.

Meanwhile, the crowd in the courtroom has become increasingly threatening, and as the court officers are about to remove the prisoners someone cries, 'Now's your time!' and a mob rushes in from outside. The officers surround the prisoners, fists fly as they struggle to repel the attackers, and in the general melee Windred's face is a study in terror.

Suddenly, a militia troop, which fortuitously has just returned from parade, bursts into the courtroom, rifles cocked and ready. The troopers fix bayonets and surround the prisoners, and the mob backs off.

Order in the court has been restored, but outside the crowd continues to grow and is becoming more and more belligerent. At 5 pm, Sam Brannan appears to address the crowd. In a fiery speech, damning the prisoners to hellfire, Brannan whips the mob into a murderous frenzy. They are baying for blood now, and a lynching seems inevitable until Marshal Fallon steps forward and delivers a speech which, according to a press report, does him 'infinite credit for his manly courage, good sense, and fidelity to his duty as public officer, to the prisoners'.[4]

The marshal reminds the mob that he is an officer of the law, that the prisoners are in his charge, and that any attempt to remove them from his hands will be forcefully resisted. The crowd, unsure whether or not Fallon will back up his words with action, becomes more amenable to reason, and after passionate appeals by Mayor John Geary and other worthies, agrees to a compromise to an immediate lynching. The agreement is that the prisoners would be held in custody overnight. Meanwhile, a committee of prominent citizens – which included Sam Brannan, unsurprisingly, but not the mayor or the city marshal – would examine the charges against the prisoners and report to the assembled populace at 10 am the next morning. Apparently satisfied, the crowd gradually disperses.

At the committee meeting, proposals that Windred and Berdue be granted a fair trial are howled down. An apoplectic Sam Brannan says he knows for certain these men are murderers and thieves, and that a trial would be pointless. 'I will see them hang by the neck or I will die!' he declares. 'The law and the courts have never hung a man in California yet!'[5] The way he sees it, the people, led by the likes of himself, have the right to be judge, jury and executioner.

In the wake of the attack on Charles Jansen, a handbill is circulated on the streets of San Francisco:

'Citizens of San Francisco, the series of murders and robberies that have been committed in this city, without the least redress from the laws, seems to leave us entirely in a state of anarchy. "When thieves are left without control to rob and kill, then doth the honest traveller fear each bush a thief!" Law, it appears, is but a nonentity to be scoffed at; redress can be had for aggression but through the never failing remedy so admirably laid down in the code of Judge Lynch. Not that we should admire this process for redress, but that it seems to be inevitably necessary.

'Are we to be robbed and assassinated in our domiciles, and the law to let our aggressors perambulate the streets merely because they have furnished straw bail [that is, bail for which the sureties are fictitious]? If so, let each man be his own executioner. Fie upon your laws! They have no force.

'All those who would rid our city of its robbers and murderers, will assemble on Sunday, at two o'clock, on the Plaza.'[6]

On Sunday, when Brannan's committee, joined by Mayor Geary and other city officials, meet outside the courthouse to address the people, they find a restless, noisy crowd filling the streets from north to south. When the mayor urges the people to observe the law and allow the accused men a fair trial before a legal tribunal, his words are drowned out by shouts of abuse. Judge Levi Parsons and others supporting the rule of law receive the same treatment. With the mood clearly ugly and bound to get uglier, the committee men beat a hasty retreat, and a short time later return with a proclamation, copies of which are distributed among the crowd.

The proclamation, signed by Sam Brannan and three others, asserts 'that the prisoners, Stuart and Windred, are both deserving of immediate punishment, as there is no question of their guiltiness of crime.

'The safety of life and property, as well as the name and credit of the city, demand prompt action on behalf of the people.'[7]

When the proclamation – essentially a licence for lynch law – is read aloud, most probably by Sam Brannan, the crowd surges towards the lock-up where the prisoners are being held. There are cries of 'Fetch them out!' and 'Hang them!'[8]

Then a curious thing happens. An unidentified man, smoking a fat cigar, takes the stogie from between his teeth, and, in a voice that somehow cuts above the hubbub, urges the mob to consider that the call to hang the prisoners there and then was made by a minority of the committee. The least they could do, he says, is to wait for the report of the entire committee, particularly since there were serious doubts as to the guilt of one of the prisoners.

He implores them to be patient, to act like Americans and to 'do the thing up brown' – an old American expression meaning to do something perfectly or thoroughly; to get it just right.[9]

The effect is immediate and dramatic. Not only do the people calm down, they cheer the unknown speaker, who then melts into the crowd.

The people determine to await the report of the entire committee, as the mystery man suggested, and, amid something approaching a carnival atmosphere, that report, when it arrives, is greeted with rapturous applause. The report suggests that the people choose 13 citizens to act as judge and jury to try the prisoners. Nominations are put to the vote, a prosecutor and defence counsel are appointed, and, at 2 pm, in a sad irony, the two Australians face a kangaroo court.

The prisoner presumed to be Jim Stuart is tried first. The evidence being concluded – in record time – the jury retires to consider its verdict. By 9 pm the jury is still out, trying the patience of the citizens crowding the courtroom, and of the crush of people in the corridor, pressing so heavily against the courtroom doors that they have shattered the glass. At last, the jury sends a message to the court that they are waiting for the defence counsel, Judge David Shattuck, to address the court. The judge, however, is nowhere to be found. Some say he received death threats for agreeing to defend the Coves and has gone home.

Eventually, Shattuck turns up and addresses the public. He asks the crowd if they are willing to give the prisoners a fair chance for their lives. The crowd jeers, and someone shouts, 'What chance did they give others?'

Shattuck tells the crowd that when they agreed to give the men a trial he had supposed they meant it, and not to murder them, which they could have done without a committee. To that, someone cries, 'A Sydney man would murder anybody for four bits!'

From this point the proceedings degenerate into a pantomime of catcalls and continual interruptions. 'Bring in the jury!' the crowd chants, but when the jury returns they ask the judge to be dismissed because they cannot agree on a verdict.

The press reports, 'In the midst of much confusion the court discharged the jury, and there being many cries for the vote, one of the jurors said they stood nine for conviction and three for acquittal, some gentlemen having grave doubts as to the question of identity.' With that, the court adjourns to resume on Monday.

While high farce was being played out in the courthouse there had been plenty of drama on the streets, where restive crowds decided not to wait on a judge and jury to decide the Australians' fate. When a man calling himself Captain Jim Howard announced that he intended to 'storm the city hall and tear them out and hang them', some 50 men rallied to his call. Outside the courthouse, a pistol was fired and the men rushed at the doors but failed to break them down.

At the station house, Marshal Fallon, Sheriff Hays and their deputies blocked the entrance.

'Here they come!' someone yelled, and Fallon barked, 'Stand firm, men!'[10] But the lynch mob, not inclined to confront armed officers, had turned back. Within minutes, the mob had broken up and the streets were quiet.

In Australia, where the case has intrigued and shocked the public, the press reports: 'The trial of Stuart, alias Thomas Berdue, indicted for an assault with intent to kill, committed on the 10th of February at 8 o'clock pm, on Charles J. Jansen, was conducted on Saturday evening, after occupying the District Court for two days.

'The defence set up for the prisoner was an alibi, and several witnesses swore positively that they were in Stuart's company the whole of the evening of the assault, until nine or 10 o'clock. But the jury did not believe them.'[11]

The alibi, sworn by two Australians – Robert Patterson, a Sydney Valley boarding-house keeper, and George Cooper Turner, a colourful racing identity – was refuted by, of all people, Michael and Mary Ann Hogan, owners of the boarding house where the defendants lodged. The Hogans testified that they had seen both men that night at a time when they were supposedly with Patterson and Turner, and that both were dressed in dark clothing as described by Jansen. Berdue, thought to be Stuart, was found guilty and sentenced to 14 years' imprisonment, the maximum the law would allow. Windred, in turn, was found guilty and sentenced to ten years in jail.

The report concludes: 'Stuart was very much overcome and with tears protested his innocence of this and all other charges of robbery and murder. Throughout the trial a great number of spectators were present. We believe that the decision of the jury will be approved almost unanimously by those who heard the testimony in the case.'[12]

What the Australian press cannot yet report – because news from California is so slow in reaching Australia – is that neither man will serve a day of his sentence. Windred has escaped from the police station, never to be seen on American shores again. And Berdue, sent upriver to Marysville to be tried for the murder of Charles Moore, another of Stuart's alleged crimes, is set to make legal history.

Whereas Sam Whitaker will later take the credit for breaking Windred out of jail, and a fanciful version of events will claim

Windred tunnelled his way to freedom, the more likely scenario is that Belcher Kay, being port warden and well acquainted with corrupt police, could easily have smuggled a key to Windred, who simply walked out the door. It was certainly in Kay's best interests to help Windred escape, given that Windred knew of Kay's involvement in the Jansen robbery and might be persuaded to tell all.

Chapter 15

'One vast sheet of flame'

The glow from the firestorm can be seen from Monterey, 140 kilometres to the south. For the sixth time in a year and a half, San Francisco is burning.

In less than ten hours, the fire that began late on the night of Saturday 3 May 1851, in a paint and upholstery store above a hotel on Portsmouth Square, has spread across 18 blocks, fanned by high winds, consuming more than 2000 buildings and destroying three-quarters of the town. At least nine people have died, including a fireman and four citizens trapped in a supposedly fireproof iron-shuttered building.

This conflagration – much worse than the fire that preceded it – is described in graphic detail in an eyewitness account by an English ship's captain, Frank Marryat.

'At eleven in the evening, the fire bell again startled us, but on this occasion the first glance at the lurid glare and heavy mass of smoke that rolled towards the bay evidenced that the fire had already a firm grip on the city.

'The wind was unusually high, and the flames spread in a broad sheet over the town. All efforts to arrest them were useless. Houses were blown up and torn down in attempts to cut off communication, but the engines were driven back step by step, while some brave firemen fell victim to their determined opposition.

'As the wind increased to a gale, the fire became beyond control. The brick buildings on Montgomery crumbled before it, and before it was arrested, over 1,000 houses, many of which were filled with merchandise, were left in ashes. Many lives were lost, and the amount of property destroyed was estimated at two and a half million pounds sterling.

'No conception can be formed of the grandeur of the scene, for at one time the burning district was covered by one vast sheet of flame that extended half a mile in length.'[1]

As with previous fires, arson is suspected, as a cover for wholesale looting. As ever, suspicion falls upon the Sydney Coves, and when looted goods worth about $10,000 are found in premises in Sydney Valley, those suspicions are confirmed.

In the aftermath of the fire, San Franciscans are frustrated by their authorities' inability or unwillingness to deal with the Australian desperadoes, and their anger is fuelled by a series of earthquakes that rattle their scorched town and make the clean-up even more difficult and dangerous.

Then, on Saturday 22 June, a further reminder of rampant villainy and official impotence – another fire. Suspected of being started by arsonists using timed fuses, it begins at about 11 am on Powell Street and spreads in every direction to consume ten city blocks, destroying all in its path including the newly renovated City Hall and, for the second time this year, the Jenny Lind Theatre. The opulent theatre – named after the famed Swedish opera singer now touring America, but who will never set foot in California – was the pride of the city.

All this misery upon misery galvanises the public resolve that something has to be done about the Sydney Coves. Enough is enough!

In the travel journal of German businessman and pioneer archaeologist Heinrich Schliemann is a detailed eyewitness account of the fire, and a surprising conclusion as to the likely culprits.

'San Francisco, June 4th 1851. A most horrible disaster has befallen this city,' Schliemann writes. 'A conflagration greater than any of the preceding fires has reduced nearly the whole city to ashes.

'I arrived here last night at half past 10 o'clock and put up at the Union Hotel on the Plaza. I may have slept a quarter of an hour when I was awakened by loud cries in the street – "Fire! Fire!" – and by the awful sounds of the alarm bell. I sprang up in all haste, and looking out of the window I saw that a frame building only 20 or 30 paces from the Union Hotel was on fire.

'I dressed in all haste and ran out of the house, but scarcely had I reached the end of Clay Street when I saw already the hotel on fire from which I had just run out.

'Pushed on by a complete gale, the fire spread with an appalling rapidity, sweeping away in a few minutes whole streets of frame buildings. Neither the iron houses nor the brick houses hitherto (which were considered as quite fireproof) could resist the fury of the element. The latter crumbled together with incredible rapidity, while the former got red hot, then white hot, and fell together like card houses.

'Particularly in the iron houses, people considered themselves perfectly safe, and they remained in them to the last extremity. As soon as the walls of the iron houses were getting red hot, the goods inside began to smoke. The inhabitants wanted to get out, but usually it was already too late, for the locks and hinges of the doors having extended or partly melted by the heat, the doors were no more to be opened.

'Sometimes, by burning their hands and arms, people succeeded in opening the doors to get out, but finding themselves then surrounded by an ocean of flames, they made but a few paces, staggered and fell, rose again and fell again in order not to rise any more. It was tried in vain to arrest the progress of the fire by blowing up the houses with gunpowder.

'Wishing to avoid dangers I went up Montgomery Street and ascended Telegraph Hill, which is a mountain about 300 feet high, close to the city. It was a frightful but sublime view – in fact, the grandest spectacle I ever enjoyed. The fire continued to spread in all directions, sweeping away the whole of Washington Street, Kearney Street, Montgomery Street, California Street, Sansome Street and many others, and except for a few houses on Battery Street, Bush Street and on the hillside, the whole beautiful city was burned down.

'The roaring of the storm, the crackling of the gunpowder, the cracking of the falling stone walls and the cries of the people, and the wonderful spectacle of an immense city burning in a dark night all joined to make this catastrophe awful in the extreme.'[2]

Schliemann concludes with the following bombshell:

'A report having spread out among the people that the fire had been caused by French incendiaries, the scorn of the enraged populace fell upon the French, and many a poor French chap was thrown headlong into the flames and consumed.'[3]

But no such thing happened, and neither was Schliemann an eyewitness to the disaster. He was in Sacramento at the time and based his account on what he read in the papers, with a generous helping of fiction thrown in. He even gets the date wrong – the fire he describes is not the fire of June 1851 but the fire of May 1851.

In his business dealings, Schliemann will earn a reputation for being careless with the truth. As an archaeologist, he will win fame for his discovery of the treasures of Troy, but suspicion will persist among experts that some of the artefacts he unearthed – including the famous Mask of Agamemnon – are fakes.

Chapter 16

'Something must be done'

Sunday 8 June 1851 finds two San Francisco businessmen, James Neall Jnr and George Oaks, deep in conversation, ruminating on what Neall calls 'the perilous condition of society'.[1]

'We ought to take some steps to see if we could not change these things,' says Oaks, and suggests they go and have a word with Sam Brannan. The pair stroll up to Brannan's office on the corner of Samsome and Bush, where they find Brannan and his clerk busy at work.

'We sat down and talked the matter over,' Neall tells the *California Courier*. 'We discussed the subject and concluded that something must be done, and it was suggested that each one of us should give Mr Brannan's clerk, Mr Wardell, the names of such men as we could mention, whom we knew to be reliable, to invite them to meet us at noon the next day, at the California Engine House, to devise some means of protecting ourselves from the depredations of this hoard of ruffians, who seemed to have possession of the city. There was no such thing as doing anything with them before the courts – that had been tried in vain. Notices were sent out to parties to the effect that they were nominated, each as chairman of a committee for his neighbourhood, to invite their fellow citizens, good reliable men, to meet.'

So many men answer the call that at noon next day the meeting at the fire station is crowded.

'There they entered into a discussion upon the evils by which we were surrounded, and what the remedy should be,' Neall recalls, 'and the meeting then adjourned, to assemble again that evening at the old Brannan building for the purpose of organisation and settlement of a course of action. The adjourned meeting was held that evening, and a partial organisation was effected, and they adjourned to meet on Tuesday evening at the same place. There they perfected the organisation, and determined upon a method by which the society should be called together, in case of any disturbance, which was three taps of the bell on the California Engine House at the junction of Bush and Market Sts.'[2]

At that meeting, a constitution is drafted, declaring:

'Whereas it has become apparent to the citizens of San Francisco that there is no security for life and property, either under the regulations of society as it presently exists or under the laws as now administered, therefore the citizens whose names are hereunto attached do unite themselves into an association for the maintenance of the peace and good order of society and the preservation of the lives and property of the citizens of San Francisco and do bind themselves each unto the other to do and perform every lawful act for the maintenance of law and order and to sustain the laws when faithfully and properly administered, but we are determined no thief, burglar, incendiary assassin, professed gambler and other disturbers of the peace shall escape punishment either by the quibbles of the law, the insecurity of prison, the carelessness or corruption of police, or a laxity of those who pretend to administer justice.'[3]

The document is two pages long, proclaiming five aims.

First, the organisation's purpose, that being a 'committee of vigilance for the protection of the lives and property of the citizens and residents of the city of San Francisco.'[4]

Second, that the committee should have a station, to be manned at all hours, where citizens can report crimes of violence or damage to property. If the men on duty at the station judge that an incident reported 'justifies the interference of this committee in aiding in the execution of the laws or the prompt and summary punishment of the offender, the committee shall be at once assembled for the purpose of taking such action as a majority of the committee when assembled shall determine upon'.[5]

Third, that the alarm calling all committee members to assemble will be two peals of the fire bells of the California Engine House and the Monumental Engine House.

Fourth, that the decisions of the committee are binding on all members.

And lastly, that to qualify as a member, a person must be a 'respectable citizen'.[6]

Affixed to the constitution are the signatures of 705 men. Aside from president, secretary, treasurer, sergeant-at-arms and other executive positions, members assume roles on a Committee of Finance, responsible for collecting fees and fines; a Committee of Qualification to process applications for membership; a police force under the control of a chief of police and five deputies, responsible for patrolling the city; and a separate water police force, tasked with patrolling the bay.

The press is firmly onside. The *California Courier* thunders:

'It is clear to every man that San Francisco is partially in the hands of criminals, and that crime has reached a crisis where the fate of life and property are in imminent jeopardy. There is no alternative now left us but to lay aside business and direct our whole energies as a people to seek out the abodes of these villains and execute summary vengeance upon them.

'What now shall be done? Are we to continue to threaten, and nothing more? Why stop, under the present unsafe and uncertain state of affairs, to have a thief, or one who attempts to fire the city, placed in the hands of law officers, from whose clutches they can, with ease, be relieved by false swearing, and the ingenuity of lawyers? Or what is equally as certain, their escape from prison? Where the guilt of the criminal is clear and unquestionable, the first law of nature demands that they be instantly shot, hung, or burned alive. We must strike terror into their hearts.

'Those who object to this summary and terrible mode of punishment ought to recollect the men who were burned to death in the last fire. In thus punishing these criminals we may save the lives of hundreds of innocent beings. We can bear these things no longer. No man, since we became a city, has been hung in San Francisco. Some 50 murders have been committed, but no murderer has suffered death for his crimes.

'We ask again, what shall be done? We are in the midst of a revolution, and we should meet the emergencies of our condition with firm hearts and well-braced nerves. We have no time to talk about the defects of the laws on the dangers which beset us, but we must act, and act at once – act as men do in revolutionary times.

'We hope a meeting of the people will be called tomorrow afternoon at 4 o'clock, in the Plaza, to organise a powerful force and to establish some system of measures to rid this community of the criminals who infest it.

'Men of San Francisco, act, and act at once.'[7]

San Franciscans who rally to the cause will soon discover that the vigilantes have no respect for established rights and liberties. On 5 July the public is summarily informed:

'It having become necessary to the peace and quiet of this community that all criminals and abettors in crime should be driven from among us, no good citizen, having the welfare of San Francisco at heart, will deny the Committee of Vigilance such information as will enable them to carry out the above object. Nor will they interfere with said committee when they may deem it best to search any premises for suspicious characters or stolen property.

'Therefore resolved that we, the Vigilance Committee, do claim to ourselves the right to enter any person or persons' premises where we have good reason to believe that we shall find evidence to substantiate and carry out the object of this body; and further, deeming ourselves engaged in a good and just cause – we intend to maintain it.'[8]

It seems the newly formed San Francisco Committee of Vigilance will be a formidable force indeed, but whether or not it will be a force for good or evil remains to be seen.

Accusatory fingers invariably point to Sydney Valley, but there is at least one example of a solid citizen being tempted to indulge in a little larceny amid the chaos of a conflagration.

It's reported to the Vigilance Committee that after the June fire a Pacific Street watchmaker, an Englishman named Lee, left town suddenly and under suspicious circumstances, taking with him to Marysville his wife and four children, a large quantity of jewellery, and watches given to him to repair. It's also suspected that his wife, who sells cigars on the same premises, could have vital information regarding the fire.

The San Francisco committee writes to the recently formed Marysville Vigilance Committee (they are springing up everywhere lately), stating that Lee 'pretended to have lost everything by the fire, but there is every reason for believing that all his jewellery was saved and has been carried by him to some place. As several parties here have lost their watches by him we desire that you will investigate the matter and try and obtain from him some information his wife or family are possessed of, concerning threats made by some customers of her cigar shop here, relative to the firing of this city'.[9]

The suspicion is that not only has Mr Lee run off with goods belonging to his customers, but Mrs Lee, because she refused or was unable to pay protection money to the Sydney Valley gangsters, knows who struck the match.

One of the watchmaker's customers, Francis Dickerson, tells the vigilantes, 'My watch was with Mr Lee 10 or 12 days before the fire. I had paid him for cleaning it but it did not go well so I took it back.

'I went there on Friday before the fire. He said it was not done but would be finished Sunday morning. I did not go, being a fine day, until the alarm of fire. I rushed up to his house – the front doors were fastened. I pounded and pounded, saw nobody.

'By and by a big man came to the door from the inside. I told him I wanted my watch. He told me the watches were all gone. I looked around the place, could not see the watches as usual, nor cigars that were there – they were all gone. The man said they were all gone long ago.'

Shortly afterwards, Dickerson was in the alley behind Lee's place, helping another man shift sacks of grain away from the blaze, when Mr Lee appeared carrying a box of glass watch-face covers.

'He says, "For God's sake hold onto this until I can get my children!" I held it a little while until Mr Lee came along with two children. I did not see him any more for half an hour. He saw me again and said, "Help me out with my things." I ran up to get in his back gate but I got suffocated and came down the alley.

'I met his boy the night before last on the wharf. He said his father had lost all. He said he was on North Beach but when I asked him to show me where he would not do it.'[10]

Still determined to retrieve his watch, Dickerson made inquiries, found an address, and went to a house the Lees had rented on North Beach, only to find them gone. A woman who lived nearby told him they had stayed there only one day and 'went off in a hurry, with trunks and all, to Marysville'.

'The woman said she had no doubt from his manner that he had carried all the jewellery off,' Dickerson said. 'Lee's wife said to the woman that they had only lost some blankets.'[11]

History does not record whether or not Francis Dickerson's chronometric quest took him to Marysville, or if that town's vigilance committee investigated the matter. Most likely, neither of those things happened, or if they happened, nothing came of it.

Most likely, Francis Dickerson was fated to spend the rest of his days staring at the glint in other men's fob pockets with a mix of suspicion and envy.

Most likely, Lee the wicked watchmaker safely stashed his stolen goods then sold them on the quiet; and if his wife really did know who started the June fire she was sensible enough to keep it to herself.

The larcenous Lees were perhaps the only San Franciscans to escape the clutches of vigilantes, gangsters and irate citizens alike. And, most likely, they lived happily ever after.

Chapter 17

Comings and goings

Everyone who is anyone is here tonight. Mayor Geary, Senator Broderick, Sam Brannan – all those who stood on the dock cheering and waving as the guest of honour's ship pulled in. All those and more besides have come dressed in their best to the grand banquet.

Usually, escaped convicts from Australia are decidedly unwelcome in San Francisco – to put it mildly – but tonight's guest of honour, Terence Bellew MacManus, is an escaped political prisoner – an Irish rebel convicted of treason and transported to Van Diemen's Land. And that's an entirely different matter.

Anti-British sentiment is endemic in California, a relative newcomer to the American republic and at odds with all things imperial. Accordingly, Ireland's struggle against the Crown, as personified by Terry MacManus, is dear to many a Californian's heart, especially to politicians courting the Irish-American vote.

Early in 1847, at the height of the Potato Famine that would take more than a million lives and cause another million to flee the country, a secret revolutionary organisation, the Young Irelanders, was formed with the aim of forcing Britain to repeal the Act of Union. Outraged by Britain's reluctance to provide adequate famine relief, the rebels believed the only way to save the country from destruction was for Ireland to have its own parliament, enacting laws for the benefit of the Irish, not their English overlords.

Terry MacManus, from County Monaghan, had migrated to Liverpool where at just 25 years old he was a successful shipping agent. Though wealthy and respectable he was also a committed nationalist, and when he learned that the British Government intended to introduce arrest without trial in Ireland, he abandoned his business in Liverpool and returned to Ireland to join the rebel cause.

As a rebel leader, MacManus fought bravely in several battles between the insurgents and British forces, but the rebellion was doomed to failure. Outgunned and outnumbered, he and his comrades attempted to slip away; to live to fight another day. After he boarded a ship about to set sail for America, police came on board to search for another man, a suspect on the run. One of the constables, who happened to have spent time in Liverpool, recognised MacManus, who was arrested and charged with high treason.

In October 1848, MacManus and two other captured rebels, Thomas Meagher and Patrick O'Donaghue, stood in the dock at Clonmel courthouse. They had been found guilty of treason and were sentenced to be hanged and quartered.

Prior to a modification of the penalty in 1814, men convicted of treason were hanged, drawn and quartered, whereby they would be hanged almost to the point of death, emasculated, disembowelled, beheaded and their body chopped into four pieces and displayed in prominent places. In the modified version, men convicted of treason were hanged, then posthumously quartered.

Women, on the pretext of protecting their modesty, were burnt at the stake, an even more painful end.

In response to this gruesome sentence, Terry MacManus gave a speech that would make him immortal. After acknowledging the dedication and zeal of his defenders, he told the court:

'I am therefore content, and with regard to that I have nothing to say. But I have a word to say which no advocate, however anxious and devoted he may be, can utter for me. I say, whatever part I may have taken in the struggle for my country's independence, whatever part I may have acted in my short career, I stand before you, my lords, with a free heart and a light conscience, to abide the issue of your sentence.

'And now, my lords, this is perhaps the fittest time to put a sentence upon record, which is this – that standing in this dock, and called to ascend the scaffold – it may be tomorrow – it may be now – it may be never – whatever the result may be, I wish to put this on record – that in the part I have taken I was not actuated by enmity towards Englishmen, for among them I have passed some of the happiest days of my life, and the most prosperous; and in no part which I have taken was I actuated by enmity towards Englishmen individually, whatever I may have felt of the injustice of English rule in this island.

'I therefore say, that it is not because I loved England less, but because I loved Ireland more, that I now stand before you.'[1]

Fortunately, MacManus was not 'called to ascend the scaffold'. His sentence, along with those of Meagher, O'Donaghue and William Smith O'Brien, was commuted to transportation to Van Diemen's Land for life.

From the beginning, they were granted special treatment. The four rebels set sail for Australia not on a squalid convict ship but on the *Swift*, a trim naval vessel. Although under constant guard by marines, they were given a cabin – as befitted their station as gentlemen – rather than being crammed into airless, fetid spaces between decks like common criminals. They were provided with books, good food and wine, and were allowed on deck to take the air whenever they liked.

And if they assumed they were bound for the chain gang in some hellhole they were mistaken. On arrival in Hobart, the captain of the *Swift* delivered an official dispatch to Governor William Denison, ordering that the prisoners were to be immediately offered tickets of leave. That meant they could live anywhere in the colony they pleased, but there was a catch. They would have to agree in writing not to attempt to escape or to meet with one another.

All accepted the offer except William Smith O'Brien, a former Member of Parliament and rebel leader, who declared that to do so would be to recognise the British Crown, which was against his principles. O'Brien would later attempt to escape by ship, but would fail when betrayed by the ship's captain.

MacManus, on the other hand, saw the liberal treatment of political prisoners as a weakness to be exploited; a possible path to freedom. And unlike O'Brien, he made good his escape.

The timing was perfect. With the colony now abuzz with tall tales and true of the California gold rush, ships bound for the Golden Gate were leaving almost daily from Hobart and Launceston.

It was at Launceston, where MacManus was working as a farmhand, that, as gangplanks creaked with hordes of bustling gold-seekers, and with many a sympathetic Irish constable willing to look the other way, he had no difficulty smuggling himself aboard the *President*, an American brig bound for Monterey.

From Monterey, Terry MacManus took ship for San Francisco, and so here he is tonight at a dinner in his honour, in the company of starched-collared civic officials and leading citizens, glad-handing politicians, stiff-necked army officers, and their fine ladies – eyes and fans fluttering in seductive syncopation.

MacManus might be amused to know that over on the tacky side of town, in Sydney Valley, an ex-convict from Launceston named Tom Burns has marked the occasion by renaming his sleazy lodging house the MacManus Welcome.

The celebrity rebel would probably not be amused if he knew that soon, because Tom Burns' establishment is a noted haunt of the Sydney Coves, Burns will be deported to Launceston.

To the San Francisco press, the Irish rebel's escape to freedom is a cue to entreat Australians to do as Americans have done – to cast off the shackles of her abusive parent, Mother England.

'It is a pity that the British government did not learn to practise the lesson which the American Revolution was well calculated to teach,' the *Daily Alta California* opines.

'It is possible, indeed almost certain, that no line of policy could have been pursued by the British ministry and people which would have kept the colonies as integral portions of the empire for an indefinite period.

'But everyone knows, and England knows, that in a system founded in justice and equity one recognises the right of representation, the rights of Englishmen, whether natives or citizens of the colonies or the home country, might and would have retained the American colonies as a portion of her Empire, perhaps for centuries.

'Every man knows the consequence, has heard of the Boston Tea Party, of Concord, of Cowpens, of Yorktown, of the Old Thirteen, of the New Eighteen, of the Stars and Stripes, the Constitution, the peace and prosperity and power which have resulted. The world has learned that crossing an ocean and rescuing a continent from nature and the savage is not a school that teaches men to forget their origin, or to breed those incapable of appreciating and asserting the rights of free men. The only chance of retaining colonies capable of asserting their rights is to allow the exercise of them freely and fully as a bona fide portion of the nation. This lesson, European diplomats have yet to learn.

'Canada has been balancing in the scale for some years, and each year the hold of Great Britain is growing weaker. Yet she grows little wiser. She has planted colonies in the South Seas. A large portion of their inhabitants are of an excellent character. Many of them have voluntarily emigrated from the teeming shores of the Mother Country to a far-off land where they could stand a better chance of elbow room. Others are political convicts and their descendants.

'This class is usually the most intelligent and patriotic of a nation's citizens. A political crime does not necessarily imply a moral one. Yet the policy of Great Britain has been too generally for her own good, to lump them together or make such exceptions as to scarcely amount to a difference, as in the case of the Irish state prisoners on Van Diemen's Land.

'She has persisted in overflowing those colonies with her own refuse population until the system is looked upon and denounced by the better portion of the inhabitants as unwarrantable oppression; a tyranny and abuse.

'They cannot and will not endure it much longer. They say so openly and positively. They have been drawing closer and closer, and more firmly about themselves the strong cordon of a Southern Pacific Alliance, and are fast approaching that point when they will say to the Mother Country what was said to her from the old hall in Philadelphia 75 years ago.

'We do not rejoice over this condition of things. We sincerely wish the continued prosperity of Great Britain, but there is something of more consequence than even the glory and empire of Britain. It is the rights of man; the inalienable rights of "life, liberty and the pursuit of happiness", which taxation without representation utterly denies and abrogates.

'The people of Australia are at last ripening for revolt and independence. We see it in the tone of their papers just as distinctly as the Revolution may be traced in the language of Mr Jefferson.'[2]

Stirring words indeed – high-minded notions that are sure to bounce between sage heads nodding in agreement later tonight, as the famous Irish rebel and assorted Californian grandees, wallowing in overstuffed leather armchairs, chat over port and cigars before joining the ladies.

In a few days' time, however, after these self-proclaimed lovers of liberty have lynched an Australian in the town square, Terry MacManus, who fought against the denial of natural justice and was exiled for it, might be left wondering if he had washed up on a horribly familiar shore.

Lost in the crowd of chattering passengers and sullen Australian deportees on the dock of the bay, waiting to board ships that will carry them away, is a rather sweaty, portly man with a broad face, sad eyes and a distracted air. He has come to San Francisco by way of Valparaiso but he hasn't been here long – because he never stays anywhere for very long – and now he's leaving. He's waiting to board a ship bound for England, and from there, when the spirit moves him, another bound for Australia.

The sad-eyed man's name is Arthur Orton, and in a couple of years all the world will know of him.

In March 1853, Roger Tichborne, heir to a baronetcy, vast Hampshire estates and a family fortune, sails for South America. A month later, his ship, bound for Jamaica from Argentina, never reaches port and is presumed to have sunk with the loss of all hands. There are rumours, however, that survivors have been picked up and taken to Australia, and when Roger's mother, Lady Tichborne, is told by a clairvoyant that her son is alive, she places advertisements in Australian newspapers seeking information.

The unexpected response is a letter from a butcher in Wagga Wagga, New South Wales, claiming to be Sir Roger. The claimant, known in Australia as Tom Castro but also as Arthur Orton, sails to England where, despite the fact that he bears no resemblance to the missing heir – except perhaps for the sad eyes – and has none of the refined manners of an aristocrat, Lady Tichborne and many others swear he is Sir Roger.

Yet some family members are unconvinced, and seek to expose him as an imposter. What follows is one of the most sensational cases in British legal history, during which time the claimant becomes both a celebrity and a curiosity. And even though a court finds him guilty of impersonating the missing peer and sentences him to 14 years in prison, many continue to believe him, and a popular movement is formed to champion his cause. Released after ten years, the pretender takes to the stage, touring in music halls and circuses as the rightful Sir Roger. Eventually, though, his star fades and he dies in poverty.

Doubts will persist. Many will still wonder if Arthur Orton was really Sir Roger Tichborne. Or, some will ask, did the truth die with another claimant, William Cresswell, an inmate of a Sydney lunatic asylum, who was never released and never got to tell his story?

Chapter 18

'Speedy and terrible vengeance'

On Tuesday 10 June, two days after its formation, the Vigilance Committee gets its first victim. At about 9 pm, a group of watermen on Central Wharf notice a large man carrying a bag obviously containing something heavy jump into a boat and pull out from the wharf. A moment later, a shipping agent named Virgin comes puffing and panting down to the wharf. Virgin tells the watermen he is chasing a man who brazenly strolled into his office and walked out with a small safe containing a large amount of money. The watermen take to their boats and soon overhaul the thief who, on realising he can't escape, throws the safe overboard, and, after a desperate struggle, surrenders. It's John Jenkins of the Sydney Coves.

The watermen take Jenkins to Sam Brannan's office, where they find a select group of some 20 vigilantes busily engaged in forming an executive committee, comprised, fortuitously, of themselves. As the heart of the organisation, its role would be to consider important issues, delegate work to members of the

700-strong general committee, prepare reports and interrogate prisoners. In the running of what might well be the most corporatised vigilante group in history, Sam Brannan is to be president of both the executive and general committees.

Jenkins is handed over to the vigilantes, and the fire bells toll to summon all committee members. About 80 show up, the doors are closed, and a kangaroo court is quickly convened, with a jury and prosecutor selected from among the members. No defence counsel is appointed.

The watermen testify as witnesses for the prosecution, and, after a short deliberation, the prisoner is found guilty. And even though the safe, which has been fished out of the bay, contains only a small amount of money – making a lie of Virgin's claim – the crime is deemed grand larceny, for which the penalty is death. Jenkins, who curses and derides his captors throughout the farcical trial, is sentenced to hang.

When some members baulk at sanctioning an illegal execution, and suggest that Jenkins be handed over to the police, one prominent member, William Howard, reminds them, 'Gentlemen, as I understand it, we came here to hang somebody.'[1]

Word of Jenkins' capture has spread quickly, and, despite the late hour, a sizeable crowd has gathered outside. To test the level of public support for San Francisco's first lynching, Sam Brannan is appointed to address the crowd. At 1 am, he steps outside and recounts the case against Jenkins and asks whether or not he should be executed at once. When the response is an ardent chorus in favour of the noose, any hesitant members of the Vigilance Committee can now rest assured they have the people's blessing to enforce lynch law.

As John Jenkins is led through the streets towards Portsmouth

Square, flanked by a howling mob, word gets through to the Coves. They rush to the rescue but find themselves outnumbered and outgunned. Some manage to grab their comrade by the legs but cannot release him from the noose and have to let go and retreat.

Captain Ned Wakeman, the vigilante marshal and hangman, has hold of the rope. As he calls for assistance to haul the prisoner aloft, Sam Brannan shouts out, 'Every lover of liberty and good order lay hold of the rope!' and a dozen men oblige.

A police officer named North, who was on patrol when the lynch mob entered the plaza, surrounding John Jenkins, pushes through the crowd and manages to grasp hold of the prisoner for a second or two in an attempt to drag him away from the crowd. But he is forced to let go when one of the vigilantes draws a pistol on him.

Suddenly, Dutch Charley muscles his way into the mob. He tries to wrest the rope away from Wakeman and the others but is repelled at gunpoint, and hapless John Jenkins is hoisted to his death.

Sparing no lurid detail, the *Alta California* reports: 'Our city on the night of the 10th instant was the scene of one of the most appalling tragedies that has been enacted within its limits, an execution having taken place in the public Plaza known as Portsmouth Square, a body of citizens acting as judges and executioners, and a multitude aiding and supporting them by countenancing the deed by their presence and non-interference.

'About two o'clock the doors of the committee room were opened, and the condemned was for the first time presented to the populace. He was a tall man of very great muscular development, and with rather a forbidding countenance. He was smoking a cigar, and appeared rather pale, but composed. His arms were pinioned, and his hands tied behind him, while he was surrounded by a rope thickly manned by armed men, many others closing on them determined to prevent his escape.

'In this manner, followed by a large crowd, he was conducted to the public square. His arrival was announced by a shout and every description of vociferation – the wildest scene of confusion and excitement prevailing we have witnessed for a long time. The moon, obscured by clouds, shed no light, and the picture was wild and awful in the extreme. Some person climbed the liberty pole [flagpole] to rig a block for the execution, but a loud shout of "Don't hang him on the liberty pole!" arose.

'Voices screamed out, "To the Old Adobe!", and a rush was made for that edifice, formerly occupied as the custom house, on the end of which a block was rigged, and a long rope run through it.

'In the meantime, a number of the police, who were on the ground, made several attempts to obtain possession of the prisoner, but they were roughly handled and prevented. Had they persisted they would have been riddled with balls. Several citizens denounced the execution, and sought to aid the police.

'The prisoner by this time was nearly dead with fear and rough handling, when a rush was made towards him, a noose thrown over his head, the rope manned by 20 ready hands, and the heavy form of the convicted felon swept through the air and dangled from the block. A few fearful struggles, a quiver of the hempen cord, a few nervous twitches, and the crowd gazed upon the lifeless corpse of him upon whom such speedy and terrible vengeance had been executed by an outraged people.

'As he swung to and fro, and turned round and round, a feeling of awe appeared to spread through the crowd, who could not be otherwise than impressed by the terrible occurrence. Slowly they dispersed, but when day broke there were still many gazing upon the swollen, purple features of the doomed man.

'At six o'clock, the Marshal, Mr Crozier, repaired to the spot, cut down the body, and consigned it to the dead-house.

'Thus ended the first execution that ever took place in San Francisco, where more crime has been committed within the past year than in any other city of the same population in the Union, without one single instance of adequate punishment.

'Of the guilt of Jenkins there was no doubt. He has been known to the police for months as a desperate character from the penal colonies, where he had passed many years as a transported convict.'[2]

At the coroner's inquest into the death of John Jenkins, men known to have taken an active part in the lynching invoke their constitutional right to refuse to answer any question that might incriminate them.

A police officer tells of arriving at the scene to see Jenkins, in handcuffs, being marched down the street to the old adobe custom house by armed vigilantes, and a following crowd of a thousand or more. The officer saw that one of the men escorting Jenkins was carrying a rope, and he heard Jenkins cry out, 'Untie my hands!'[3]

Captain Wakeman slipped the rope around Jenkins' neck, drew his pistol and threatened to shoot anyone who attempted to cut Jenkins down, as some 25 men lent willing hands to hoist the prisoner aloft.

Another police officer, Constable Noyce, refuses to answer any questions unless the court is cleared. He swears, 'I have every reason to believe that there is a secret committee or inquisition in this city and if I should tell what I have seen and know as to what occurred that I should be in danger of my life.'[4]

The coroner agrees to his request, and behind closed doors Noyce tells the court that while walking his beat past the Brannan building he heard through an open window a voice he recognised as that of Sam Brannan call for a new trial, at which many voices protested, 'No, no!', and a man, presumably John Jenkins, cried out, 'Shoot me like a man! Don't hang me like a dog!'[5] At that, someone shut the window.

An hour later, in Portsmouth Square, as the mob gathered, Noyce asked other police on the scene if they had been ordered by the marshal or the mayor to rescue the prisoner from the vigilantes. When told there had been no such orders, he decided to try to rescue Jenkins as a civilian.

As the mob approached with Jenkins, handcuffed, in their midst, Constable North appeared beside Noyce and told him, 'I'm with you!'[6] and they seized hold of Jenkins.

Suddenly, Noyce felt the point of a gun in his ribs as a vigilante barked, 'Let go of the man or I'll blow your heart out!' As two more vigilantes levelled their pistols at him, a friend intervened. 'Why risk your life?' Noyce's friend asked, and pulled him out of harm's way.[7]

Noyce was not about to give up, however, and when the rope was raised aloft, he borrowed a knife and tried to cut it until his friends, again fearing for his life at the hands of the angry mob, dragged him away.

In evidence at the inquest, and at a mass meeting in the square following the lynching, Senator David Broderick decries the actions of the Vigilance Committee, describing its members as 'very bad men'. One member, William Jones, he describes as a particularly violent man who is 'in favour of hanging everybody not belonging to the Committee'. According to Broderick, Jones declared, 'To hell with all the courts! Let's take care of ourselves!'[8]

The jury at the inquest charges Sam Brannan and eight other vigilantes with murder. Unperturbed, the committee responds with the following statement:

'We, members of the Vigilance Committee, remark with surprise the invidious verdict rendered by the Coroner's Jury after their inquest upon the body of Jenkins, after we have all notified the said jury and public that we were all participators in the trial and execution of said Jenkins. We desire that the public will understand that Capt. Edgar Wakeman, W. M. H. Jones, T. K. Battelle, Benjamin Reynolds, J. S. Eagan, J. C. Derby, and Samuel Brannan, have been unnecessarily picked from our members, as the Coroner's Jury have had full evidence of the fact that all the undersigned have been equally implicated and are equally responsible with their above named associates.'[9]

A further 183 citizens have claimed shared responsibility for Jenkins' death, and the press is clearly on the side of the lynch mob. The *California Courier* opines, 'All laws are based upon the law of nature and when they are incapable either from positive imperfection or from an inefficient administration of them to protect our lives and property from the assassin and robber, the people, from whom all power is derived, have the indefeasible right to fall back upon the first principles of government, and do all that may be necessary and proper to protect their lives and property. This right was asserted by our ancestors, and it is a doctrine peculiar to republicans. The people have done the deed complained of and are ready to shoulder the consequences.'[10]

There will be no consequences. None of the vigilantes are prosecuted, an outcome celebrated by most of the citizenry, and blessed from the pulpit as at least two parsons preach sermons approving of the lynching. A sermon by Congregationalist pastor

Timothy Dwight Hunt, declaring that 'actual incapacity, or gross corruption, on the part of rulers may sometimes justify or even require a people to take power into their own hands'[11] is so popular it is circulated as a pamphlet.

Chapter 19

The grocer's apologia

Spicing up current events with a conspiracy theory, the *California Courier* snorts: 'We have been furnished by the Vigilance Committee with the following, which will go far to show what kind of people we have had to deal with in this city. We never doubted the correctness and propriety of the course of action adopted by them in re-shipping the escaped convicts to the colonies. This shows a state of facts, too, in regard to the officers in the British penal colonies that we have long suspected was the case. The idea of sending men among us whom they would not permit to live in their own country is an insult, and should be promptly resisted by our government.'[1]

The example provided of the 'kind of people' referred to is John Goff, landlord of the Panama House in Sydney Valley, who has been ordered by the vigilantes to take ship for Australia at once or suffer the consequences.

As proof of Goff's larcenous nature, the *Courier* prints a statement by Charles Marsh, now a citizen of California but formerly steward to New South Wales Governor Sir Richard Bourke. Marsh states that Goff 'was transported to New South Wales and assigned to Judge [Sir Francis] Forbes. He had conducted himself so well that the judge allowed him to keep a little grocery shop for his own account, he working also for the judge. While he kept the shop there was a person named Foss, a druggist and wholesale grocer. Goff and the porter at Foss's were connected together. Goff began to sell goods cheap, and did a large trade. He sold goods cheaper than Foss could.

'It was discovered that this man Goff obtained his goods through the porter. Goff was arrested, tried, and transported to Norfolk Island. He worked his seven years out and then went to Windsor. From there he came here. He is a bad character.'[2]

Goff tells a different story. He insists he was not assigned to Judge Forbes but to a Hunter Valley settler named Smith, and that he was not transported to Norfolk Island. However, he admits, 'I think I know a man by the name of Foss. I kept a grocery store in a town called Windsor. I have never bought any goods off Mr Foss but have taken goods from Mr Foss's store to people in the country.'[3]

He states that he was born in Huntingdon, in Cambridgeshire, England. At about 23 years of age he was convicted of housebreaking and sentenced to transportation for life, but was granted a ticket of leave, and left Australia for California.

Judge Forbes would beg to differ. In 1837, in evidence to a British parliamentary inquiry into the convict transportation system, Sir Francis Forbes stated that Goff 'kept a shop [in Pitt Street, Sydney] while he was nominally assigned to me, but under these conditions: that he had been in my service and had conducted himself very respectably for a number of years.

'While his ticket of leave was being processed, some stolen property – I believe a small amount – was found in his house, or his wife's house, or his wife's shop, and he was convicted of receiving stolen goods and was transferred to Norfolk Island.'[4]

A likely scenario is that Goff's ticket of leave application was revoked when stolen goods were found in his possession; that after serving his time at Norfolk Island penal settlement he settled in Windsor; and that in 1849 he was granted a conditional pardon. Convicts sentenced to life were eligible for conditional pardons after serving eight years – the condition being that they were now free but could not return to England or Ireland.

Goff has shown the Vigilance Committee a copy of his pardon, signed by Governor Sir Charles Fitzroy, and dated 1 May 1849, and the case has won him rare public sympathy. Yet the vigilantes are determined to deport him, perhaps because he has embarrassed them by pointing out that they are complicit in a terrible miscarriage of justice.

Goff says he arrived in San Francisco on the barque *Victoria* [on 18 February 1850], and that there were other ex-convicts among the passengers, including 'Berdue, the man now being tried at Marysville for murder. I never heard any harm of him at home, and he was quiet on board the ship. He had a wife at Sydney. I have seen him several times since he has been here. He brought four or five pounds of gold dust, which he left at my house.'[5]

Goff is certain Thomas Berdue and Jim Stuart are not the same man. There is 'some slight likeness', he says, but Berdue is shorter.

He states also that he had known William Windred back in New South Wales. 'I lived near him at Windsor,' he says.

'I was on intimate terms with Berdue and Windred in this country.'[6]

Regardless of public support in his favour, John Goff, who despite his past dishonest dealings has tried to save a man's life, is deported to Australia.

Chapter 20

The wrong man

In his youth, the prisoner in the dock at Marysville District Court was a thief. He was born Arthur Acteson, in 1818, son of a dockyard worker in the East End of London, and the eldest of 12 children.

At the age of 16, caught red-handed after snatching a woman's scarf on the street, Arthur gave a false name, Thomas Berdue, and under that name was convicted of theft and sentenced to transportation to New South Wales for seven years.

One of 230 male convicts taken aboard the *England* in June of 1835, Berdue arrived in Sydney in late September after a relatively fortunate passage.

'Most of the convicts were young and appeared healthy, and except for a few cases all were landed in good health at Sydney,' ship's surgeon Obediah Pineo reported. 'There were no epidemic diseases and with attention to food and clothing, most retained their health during the 16-week voyage. There were three mild cases of scurvy amongst the young. It took the form of discoloured legs with some hardness and spongy, bleeding gums. They were given port wine every day and lime juice with sugar and water.'[1]

After four years as an assigned servant at Windsor, west of Sydney on the Hawkesbury River, Berdue was granted a ticket of leave and, under the name Thomas Arthur Acteson, married Emma Arnold. The couple settled at Windsor, but in 1849 Berdue, touched by gold fever, and reverting once again to his alias, took ship for the American Eldorado, leaving his wife behind. Emma's fate is unknown.

It was in California where misfortune, in the shape of a squad of vigilantes, would find him.

The defence is not contesting the prosecution's contention that the outlaw James Stuart is guilty of the murder of Charles Moore. The case for the defence is that the prisoner in the dock is not James Stuart but an innocent man named Thomas Berdue.

For days, since the opening of this trial on 28 June 1851, the prosecution has produced witness after witness who has sworn that they know Stuart well and that the accused man is definitely him. Some say they have often shared his table; played cards with him; even shared a bed with him. They testify that, like the prisoner, Stuart has dark curly hair; that their eyes are the same colour; and – after the judge orders the prisoner to stand so that the witnesses and jury can see him better – that they are the same height and move in the same manner.

Witnesses testify that, like the prisoner, Stuart has a stiff middle finger on his right hand, and tattoos around one of his fingers and between the thumb and forefinger of each hand. The jury, on examining the prisoner's hands, confirm that his hands are tattooed in the manner described. They find, however, that his right middle finger is not stiff, but that his left middle finger is slightly misshapen.

Prosecution witnesses also claim that Stuart has a long scar on the right side of his face. Unable to examine the prisoner's face because he is lightly bearded, the judge orders that he be shaved before returning to court the next morning. And when, next morning, the prisoner appears with a scar running from jaw to neck down the right side of his face, the case for the defence looks shaky.

The defence's star witness, Judge Oliver Stidger, swears that Stuart had often been brought before his court at Foster's Bar, and that he is certain the prisoner is not the same man. There is a strong resemblance, Stidger admits, but Stuart is taller by at least two inches, their eyes are different colours and have different expressions, and their ways of moving are quite different. Stuart moves uncommonly fast, like a wildcat, says the judge.

Other defence witnesses support Judge Stidger's testimony, but it seems all eyes in the jury box are fixed on the scar on the prisoner's face. On Friday 4 July, after two days' deliberation, the jury returns a verdict of guilty. The man in the dock, still protesting his innocence, is sentenced to be hanged on Monday.

Chapter 21

The Night Watch

The appropriately named George Hopeful spends his nights skulking around the mean streets of Sydney Valley, sniffing out clues and reporting on comings and goings, no matter how seemingly trivial. Hopeful is a vigilante policeman, specifically a man of the Night Watch, a special unit created by the Vigilance Committee to gather intelligence on the Australian gangsters and their ilk. His report for the night of Saturday 14 June 1851 states:

'From information I have received this day, there is every reason to believe there is a most dangerous character living at the corner of Cat Alley and Jackson Street. He is a man about five feet and ten inches, well-built, very quick in his movement, decently dressed. Goes about armed with a revolver and slung shot. Shuns being seen in daylight.'[1]

Night Watch reports like Hopeful's provide a rare picture of Sydney Valley after dark:

'Detained squads of men in twos and threes to watch various suspicious places, some supposed and others known to be cribs for Sydney men. Reports from these confirm previous suspicions but detected nothing in particular. Up to one o'clock this morning neither Bums nor Arlington had closed their houses as ordered.

'Mrs Fawcett, who lives six or seven doors from Pacific Street, says she knows personally all the Sydney men in town and in Cat or Murderers' Alley, a quarter to which some rude folks have applied the name St Giles. She says two vessels are now hourly expected, having on board some 500 men who are completely organised in their various branches of crime; that they have been sent for from here and are all picked men; that if they are prevented from landing by the authorities they have made arrangements to lay off near the ship with boats and let the men jump overboard and swim until they pick them up; that they have their boats all ready and are in hourly expectation of the arrival of the ship. She also states that they are desperate men, thoroughly regardless of human life – their own as well as others – and have arranged to burn and plunder the town the moment they get ashore, and that they have told her that in less than six months they have numbers enough sufficient to take the town, and that in that time they will have full possession.'[2]

It is not known how much credence is given to Mrs Fawcett's warning of an impending invasion, it being quite obvious that she is either risibly gullible or barking mad.

From Captain of the Watch and vigilante Police Chief Jacob Van Bokkelen on 16 June: 'John Sullivan volunteered in my watch – was elected Boatman of the Committee – knows too many men of bad character – would recommend that he not be trusted too much.'[3]

Ironically, this is the same John Sullivan who a few weeks later will deliver to the vigilantes their greatest prize.

'This morning at 1 am a man named Yates, alias Wood, was arrested by Messrs Elleard, Spence and Ilossefros in a small house on Virginia Street, north side of Jackson, for an assault on his wife, as he called her, who was heard to say to Yates, as they were entering, "You did kill him. You know you did. You are a murderer!"

'At the time Yates was arrested there was another man in the house, not known to the parties arresting, but it has been proved since, almost beyond a doubt, that the man was Adams, the burglar [possibly George Adams, a member of the Sydney Coves]. He escaped after being knocked down by Mr Spence.

'Before Yates was taken out of the house he attempted to pass a watch to his woman, but which was taken from him, and is now in the possession of the Recorder, who has continued the case until tomorrow.'[4]

Next day: 'This morning at 9 o'clock a woman went to the house that Yates occupied and enquired for the parties living there. She was asked by Mr Matheson, the owner of the house, which she wanted, Yates or Adams. She replied that either of these gentlemen would answer.'[5]

Meanwhile: 'Belcher Kay was seen late last night on Powell Street, under suspicious circumstances, with a drunken man. After walking up to the farther end of Powell Street, and finding that he was watched, he walked back with him to the square.'[6]

Captain of the Watch John Ryder reports: 'Thomas Scott's premises were examined and well watched until past one o'clock. Saw very suspicious-looking characters congregated there. Obtained no positive information. Recommend this house be strictly watched.'[7]

Thomas Scott, a tailor, is arrested a few days later and deported to Sydney, along with Morris Russell alias Moe the Jew, Ben Sellers, and John Burgess alias Spring-heeled Jack.

Ryder's report continues: 'Visited John Smith's house, found everything quiet, no person to be seen about the premises.

'White house on Broadway watched until one o'clock. This house was visited during the night by some 60 characters at different times. Have no doubt that this house is a crib of the worst kind. The house of Lamb and Brady opposite is just as bad. The Australian Arms closed about half past nine. Parties passed into this house from the rear during the night.

'The Heart in Hand – house above James Howie's – all require further watching.

'The house next to the corner of Pacific is a very bad one. Mr Thomas Byrne was one of the visitors during the night. He remained in the house about an hour and a half.'[8]

Jacob Van Bokkelen reports: 'Last night the characters known as Sydney men were congregated at their haunts in large numbers with closed doors and very quiet. Your committee may rely upon it that a concert of action is on hand amongst the thieves. Action will be required, and each member of the committee is requested to carry his arms well prepared, and have them on their person every day and at all hours.

'The day police have been joined by the night police, making in all 40. It is expedient that 20 should serve each night. I would suggest the propriety of increasing the force to 60 by an addition of 20 more, who should be men of active disposition and willing to do their duty without fail. As many persons have put their names on the police roll who fail to report for duty, this subject should be placed before the general committee at a meeting this night.'[9]

Van Bokkelen finds there is little enthusiasm among members to volunteer for the Night Watch. It is, after all, the middle of winter.

Thanks to arrests based on observations of these night owls, Vigilance Committee reports are peppered with warts-and-all descriptions of Sydney Valley characters:

Morris Russell, alias Moe the Jew: 'Aged 40 years, height 5 ft 7–8 inches, black hair, swarthy complexion, dark beard, dark brown eyes, mouth broad, upper lip straight, scar on the right side of the chin, nose straight, eyes sunken – not like a Jew – very smooth and plausible in his address. He gives his eyes a peculiar expression. Married with one boy, two years old; round shoulders but strongly built, chin round.'[10]

Charles Becket: 'Aged 40, 5 ft 5 inches, nose rather hooked, hair dark, some front teeth gone, mouth down at the corners, little or no whiskers, chin pointed with a marked dimple in the centre, stoops, thin, small face, sallow dark eyes.'

A later note adds, 'Shot in San Francisco for stealing.'[11]

John Burgess, alias Spring-heeled Jack: 'Aged 33, 5 ft 11 inches or 6 ft, narrow, strong build, very wide mouth with irregular black teeth, high cheekbones, long and large feet, small pig eyes, sunken snub nose with bridge depressed, long upper lip, sandy whiskers – fresh colour. Single man. One front upper tooth, right side, gone.'[12]

Ben Sellers: 'Aged 41, 5 ft 11 inches or 6 ft, high cheekbones, freckled, pitted by smallpox, sunken eyes, grey-brown hair, no whiskers, strong, square build, active man, mouth very wide. Married with no children.'[13]

V. Fitzpatrick: 'Irish, aged 44, 5 ft 6 inches, pale, well made, dark hair, high cheekbones, small grey eyes, determined look, stands with his hands on his hips and has a habit of twisting his mouth when he speaks; broad across the jaw.'[14]

A report relayed to the Sydney press states:

'The San Francisco newspapers noticed the arrival in that place of a vessel direct from Sydney, without any regular clearance, and on board were some of whom were easily recognised as the regularly convicted felons of the criminal law, by the marks and brands of punishment.

'A few were so recently from confinement that the hair had not time to grow out of their shaved heads.'[15]

So maybe Mrs Fawcett isn't so crazy after all. Either that, or it's catching.

Chapter 22

Ecce homo

In his pocket is a note that reads:

'Old Fellow,

'Look out, the Hawks are abroad and after you both here and down below. You had better keep in the upper country at present. I can say no more at present.

'S.W.'[1]

Then again, maybe the smoke is clearing. Maybe after the tumult of the lynching of John Jenkins things have settled down enough to risk returning to Sydney Valley where he can hide out with his old friend the boatman, William Kitchen. But then again, maybe not.

Long Jim Stuart is cautiously making his way back on foot from the Old Mission, where he has been staking out a potential robbery, when he spies riders on the road ahead – a vigilante posse. It's too late to avoid them. To turn on his heel and head back the other way would surely attract suspicion, so he opts to stroll by with a smile and a nod.

It almost works, until the leader of the posse, Jim Adair, notices that the smiling traveller is armed with pistols and a bowie knife. Adair calls to Stuart, who pauses, confident as ever that he can bluff his way through any sticky situation.

Questioned by Adair, he introduces himself as William Stevens and claims he is returning to the city after visiting a cousin who works in a bakery at the mission. Adair, unconvinced, detains Stuart while some of his party ride to the mission to check his story. When they return to report that no such cousin exists, Stuart is arrested and escorted to vigilante headquarters in San Francisco.

When interrogated, Stuart, still claiming to be William Stevens, impresses his captors with his cool and confident manner. He tells them he was born in Brighton, England, on 3 March 1819, and that at the age of 16 he left England for Montreal, Canada, where he worked as a tailor. He left Canada two years ago, bound for the Atlantic port of Chagres, in Panama, and arrived in California late in 1849.

After trying his luck on the goldfields at Sullivan's Creek and on the Mariposa for several months, he arrived in San Francisco just last night, on foot.

'I slept last night on North Beach,' he says. 'A man by the name of Kitchen showed me the house. I do not know the occupants – it is a private house. I went to the place with Kitchen a little after dark, about 9 o'clock.'[2]

He says there were two other people in the house where he spent the night – a woman whose name he declines to mention because he slept with her, and a man he did not know.

'I left the woman soon after daylight this morning and went to the Mission,' he says. 'I have a cousin there named John Stevens.

He is working at a bakery there and has been in the country about 16 months.

'I arrived at the Mission at about 6 o'clock, remained there at least till 10 o'clock, left the Mission and took the road over the hills, thinking it was the nearest road.'[3]

It was while on that road he happened upon the vigilante posse, and was arrested on suspicion of a robbery of which he claims to know nothing. And despite the posse's failure to find any cousin at the mission, he calmly insists that such a person does indeed exist, and that his arrest was a simple but understandable case of mistaken identity. No offence taken.

It's a plausible story, and some of the vigilantes find it so convincing, and expressed with such apparent candour, that they recommend he be released at once. Others, however, are not so sure, and it is decided to detain him overnight while his story is checked more thoroughly.

Early next morning, the prisoner who some say reminds them of Christ is about to have a Pontius Pilate moment – *Ecce homo*: 'Behold the man.' A new guard enters the room where Stuart is being held.

'Hello, Jim!' he says. 'How did you come here?'[4]

Stuart looks up to see the face of John Sullivan, his former mining partner. He pretends not to know him.

'I know who you are,' the guard says. 'I worked for you six months at Foster's Bar.'[5]

With that, Sullivan leaves the room and announces that the man within is without doubt the outlaw Jim Stuart.

Confronted by vigilante police, Stuart continues to insist they have the wrong man, but his captors are now convinced that the wrong man is elsewhere. Word is sent to Marysville that Thomas

Berdue, convicted of the murder of Charles Moore and awaiting sentence, is not Jim Stuart and is probably innocent; that the real Jim Stuart is in the hands of the Vigilance Committee in San Francisco.

Stuart's lawyer, Frank Pixley, is called in to vigilante headquarters to confirm the prisoner's identity. Under oath to tell the truth, he is taken to Stuart's room, but when asked if the man before him is James Stuart he replies, 'You have no authority to ask me any questions. You are an illegal body.'[6]

Pixley's stonewalling is cold comfort for Long Jim. As a string of witnesses are brought in and identify him, he can hear voices outside chanting, 'Hang him! Hang him!',[7] unaware that it is Frank Pixley the mob wants to lynch.

'We had ropes and tackle all ready,' committee secretary Isaac Bluxome writes, 'and Jake just pushed him down the stairs or he would have been hung. The people were angry with him because he defended all the thieves. Then we knew that the prisoner was the genuine Stuart.'[8]

Chapter 23

Deeper and deeper

Late on the night of Tuesday 8 July 1851, at vigilante headquarters, sits a man in chains surrounded by committee men poised to record his confession. Seeing no other way to cheat the hangman, Jim Stuart has offered them a deal: to be handed over to the proper authorities in exchange for betraying members of his gang and collaborators. The vigilantes make no promises but agree to consider his offer, and so for the next several hours are treated to a rambling account of the rise and fall of the Sydney Coves.

The prisoner writes a few lines in his own hand, then dictates the rest to Sam Brannan. He begins with a statement of fact: 'My true name is James Stuart.'[1]

All that follows is contentious, however.

Stuart tells his captors he was born in Brighton, England, and at 16 was convicted of forgery and sentenced to transportation to New South Wales for life. He says that through the 'intercession of friends' he was granted his freedom, but does not name the 'friends' or explain the circumstances.

He says that as a free man he made his way to Adelaide, South Australia, where he remained for about five years, but offers no details of what he did there. From Adelaide he took ship for the seaport of Callao, in Peru. Again, he provides no details other than that he spent 'about two years and a half knocking about the southern continent'.[2]

He is vague about how he got to Panama – it was either directly on the ship *J. W. Coffin* or by way of Paita – a seaport in north-western Peru – in the *Coffin*, and thence to Panama in a smaller vessel. From Panama, he booked passage on the *Tennessee* to San Francisco.

'The day I arrived, I left for Sacramento in the *Senator*,' he tells his inquisitors. 'Next day to Marysville, and from Marysville to Foster's Bar [a gold-bearing sandbar on the Yuba River, and one of the earliest Californian goldfields].'[3]

On the diggings, he took a job with the Rock Mining Company. After working for the company for a month, he hired John Sullivan to work in his place for a month more while he went about four miles down the Yuba River to work a mining claim for himself.

About two weeks later, Stuart returned to Foster's Bar and hired another man to replace Sullivan, who he took with him to help work the claim downriver. 'He [Sullivan] finished his month out down the river, and for two days extra work I paid him $20.'[4]

If the claim paid out he does not mention it. Presumably it did not because he and Sullivan soon abandoned it and returned to Foster's Bar, where Stuart says he bought another claim, for $300, and a boat, for $400. He leased the boat as a river trading vessel, for $6 a day, then went with Sullivan to Slate Range, about eight miles upriver. There, they bought a claim for $50 each, but after just half a day's work Stuart decided the claim would not pay well enough. He left Sullivan to work the claim and went back to Foster's Bar alone, promising to return in the winter. He didn't.

'I found the claim [at Foster's] would not pay more than $12, and abandoned it, then went down the river to the old place and worked three weeks or a month longer.'[5]

Stuart, seldom if ever seen swinging a pick or shovel, realised a miner's life was not for him. 'I did nothing for a week and became tired of the life,' he says. 'I concluded to stay all winter and commenced building a house – the largest one there – for boarders. I did not finish it.'[6]

He then decided to become a merchant. 'I let the claim I paid $300 for to others, and they gave me a share for the privilege of working it. I then took a partner, Bernard Feather [or Feller], a German, and commenced store-keeping in my house. But the company to whom I left the $300 never paid me – they left.

'I bought off Daniel Casey, one of the company, all the things the company had left. Searching the house, I found a trunk. The trunk was open and full of clothes. I took them. I wore part of the clothes during the remainder of my stay.'[7]

One night, Stuart joined a card game at the house of a certain Captain Dodge. Luck wasn't with him and he lost about $200. Convinced that Dodge had cheated him, and having observed that Dodge kept all his money in a chest, he waited until all in the house were asleep, then broke in and stole the chest.

'Opening the chest, I found $4,300. There was one piece [of gold] worth about $1,568, another $738, the rest in dust and about $600 in silver. I took all this and secreted most of it in my garden.'[8]

Ten days later, he was arrested – not for stealing Captain Dodge's gold and silver but for theft of the trunk of clothes, which, in his opinion, belonged to him. He was committed to appear at Marysville for trial and released on $500 bail, but, three days later, was arrested for robbing Dodge of $4300, and committed again to Marysville on a charge of grand larceny.

'The mob that night wanted to hang me,' he tells the vigilantes. 'The judge swore in about 60 men to protect me. The next morning, Captain Dodge, the largest loser, came to me and said if I would give him the money he would let me go and see that I was not hurt.

'Another party came to me and told me that his wife and family were suffering at home, so I concluded to give it up, and all but about $150 was found, allowed that I had lost this, remained with the sheriff this afternoon, and then asked the judge about selling my things, called an auction, sold my things and gave my boat away to a friend. My things brought about $170.

'The sheriff [Edward Barr] kept this money in his possession, went out at night to collect some of this money, and while gone his cook came to me and said if he was in my place he'd go. I told him I couldn't well go without money. He said I had better go without it.'[9]

So, when darkness fell, Stuart made a run for it. After travelling some distance on foot he stole a horse and rode for Sacramento, arriving late the following evening. There, while keeping his head down, he made the acquaintance of a trio of horse thieves – an American named James Peet, another known only as 'Dab', and an Australian named Johnny Griffiths. Stuart agreed to a partnership selling the stolen horses, adding receiver of stolen goods to his criminal résumé. More ambitious villainy would soon follow.

Firstly, piracy. Johnny Griffiths got word of a ship in the river with a good deal of money aboard – about $20,000. Stuart,

Griffiths and two other Australians, John Edwards and George Smith, boarded the vessel and got clean away with all the money aboard, which turned out to be about $1200, not the rumoured $20,000, but still not bad for an easy night's work.

Stuart, Edwards and Smith – the core of what would become the Sydney Coves gang – agreed to band together and move down to San Francisco, where Edwards knew of another ship ripe for the picking. They were joined by Stuart's old friend James Burns, alias Jimmy from Town, whom he had smuggled aboard the *Tennessee* on the voyage from Panama to San Francisco. All agreed that Jim Stuart was the undisputed leader of the gang.

During the one-day trip downriver on the *New World*, Jimmy from Town robbed a Spaniard of 30 ounces of gold, which he gave to Stuart to be divided among the four comrades.

Arriving in San Francisco that night, they lost no time in boarding the brig *James Caskie*, wearing masks and armed with guns, knives and coshes. This time, they would meet resistance.

'Had some hard fighting on board,' Stuart says. 'The captain was desperate and we left him almost dead. In the fight, his wife came out of the cabin with a sword in her hand. I took it away from her.'[10]

Exerting his authority, Stuart ordered the others to guard the captain while he searched the cabin.

'His [Captain Allen's] wife gave me up what money there was on board. I then asked her if there were any arms on board. She gave me one of Allen's six-shooters, large size. I gave the money and pistols to one of the party – I do not remember which.

'The woman begged me not to take her husband's life. I said I did not want to do it if he would be quiet. I then looked in the cabin and saw that she had a splendid gold chronometer watch. She hoped I would not take it, as her mother had given it to her.

'I said, "On those conditions I will not take the watch." The others kicked up a row for not taking it. I told them I was master, they had made me so, and I would act as I liked.

'We tied the captain's hands behind him and shut him in the cabin. I told his wife not to speak for two hours as I should not leave the ship. We also tied up some boys who were on board at that time, and then went ashore.

'We supposed we would get $15,000 or $16,000, and only got $170. He [Captain Allen] advertised a loss of $200. When his wife gave me the money she said she had sent it nearly all home in the previous packet, or we should have got it, no doubt.'[11]

Having graduated to armed robbery and robbery with violence, Stuart tried his hand at safe-cracking. Hiding in Grayson and Guild's store until it closed, he spent all night trying to open the safe but failed. He then tried to remove the safe but found it was too heavy and left empty-handed.

A few days later he travelled back up to Sacramento where he won a good deal of money gambling, and, using the alias Campbell, sold a few stolen horses and mules for his rustler mates Peet, Dab and Griffiths.

His lodging in Sacramento was Moore's boarding house, a well-known thieves' kitchen, with notorious tenants including John Griffiths and John Morris Morgan, known as Old Jack. While Stuart was there, Moore died, and Stuart bought the premises from Moore's widow for $150. Overnight, he had become a landlord and receiver of stolen goods.

'A few days afterwards, Griffiths was arrested for picking a man's pocket of $800, and was committed to the prison brig [the prison ship *La Grange*, anchored in the Sacramento River]. Bail was set at $1,500.'[12]

None of Griffiths' associates would agree to put up 'straw bail'. 'So I took a team, loaded it from my house with stolen goods and started for Mormon Island [mining camp], sold all at Mormon Island and Salmon Falls [mining town on the American River] and returned to Sacramento county. I went to the sheriff of Sacramento, procured an order to go on board [the prison brig] and see Griffiths. But when I got on board I found that the night before, in trying to escape, he was drowned.'[13]

While Stuart was away raising bail for the late unlamented Johnny Griffiths, someone robbed his boarding house, clearing it of all his possessions, ill-gotten and otherwise. 'I did not think it worthwhile to open another house and went to live in a small house near the burying ground,' Stuart says.

A few days later, arrested for housebreaking, he found himself in need of a lawyer – a crooked one, preferably – and Frank Pixley was just the man. Pixley's criminal law practice was so lucrative that in 1852, when San Quentin prison opened, replacing the prison brig *Waban*, anchored in San Francisco harbour, he opened a law office next door to the prison.

'He got me out of it by one of my men swearing false,' Stuart admits. 'Old Jack swore false. I gave him $20, and Mr Pixley agreed to get me out of the scrape if I would give him $50 more. I told Pixley I was guilty.

'About a week or 10 days later I was arrested again for breaking into a house in a lumber yard. I very nearly got shot there – through my hat at all events. I got taken and committed aboard the brig for trial.'[14]

He admits that a few nights before his arrest he and Matt

Hopwood, known as Big Brummy, had robbed a clothing store of some $900 worth of goods. And while on the prison brig he had paid Frank Pixley $50 to defend Big Brummy, charged with robbing a woman.

Jim Stuart has reached the point in his confession where naming names and apparently frank admissions of guilt are not enough to save his neck. What he needs now is an alibi for murder.

Chapter 24

Law and disorder

It is near midnight now, as, at vigilante headquarters, Jim Stuart, bargaining for his life, continues to make his confession.

'Two days after I had been on board the prison brig a constable came down from Auburn and identified me as shooting the sheriff of Auburn,' he says. 'Two or three hours afterwards, two more constables came on board – one from Foster's Bar and one from Marysville. The one from Foster's Bar identified me as the man having committed murder at Foster's Bar.'[1]

The sheriff of Marysville came armed with a warrant, issued by Judge Russell Sackett, to take Stuart to Marysville for trial. But when Frank Pixley, appearing for Stuart, claimed the warrant was not legal, the sheriff had to return to Marysville to fetch another warrant.

'I then gave Mr Pixley my bag of gold dust to weigh out $600 and an order for $130, which he told me he had got and would pay me the next day.'[2]

But Stuart did not wait for his lawyer to return the next day. That night, he escaped from the prison brig.

'I walked to Dry Creek, halfway to Stockton, and the next day got into Stockton, disguised myself and came to San Francisco on a steamer – somewhere in the middle of December, then stopped in Edwards' house in Sydney Valley.'[3]

He claims John Edwards was unaware he had escaped from the brig. 'I never went out of the house during the day. During the night, I went to Port Phillip House, kept by McCormick and Whitaker. Jansen at that time lived next door to Whitaker's.'[4]

For the Coves, it was straight back to business, with mixed results. 'Whitaker had got information of there being $800 or $900 in a butcher's shop in Broadway,' Stuart says. 'Myself, John Edwards, Whitaker and George Adams went, took the window out, got the safe into the street and could get it no further.

'The next thing was [shipping agent] Charles Minturn's safe. We got this information from Belcher Kay. Kay had gone several times during the three days previous to inquire about the money. He was acquainted there. Myself, Edwards, Teddy McCormick, Whitaker, George Adams, Belcher Kay and Bob McKenzie took a boat with us, made shears to take with us, put a feather bed in the boat, augurs and saws to cut away with, and went pretty well armed.

'We managed to get inside, three or four of us, and moved the safe somewhat, made a few augur holes in the floor, and intended cutting the floor away.

'Someone came to the door – a false alarm. We had to run! McKenzie spoilt it by not knowing his instructions. We should not have stirred for one man or two, with so big a haul. McKenzie gave the wrong signals, and we jumped into the water and swam away.

'The next thing was a jeweller's shop Belcher Kay had examined. He allowed that there was $2,000 or $3,000 in diamonds etc. We went to look at it at night, myself and Edwards. I gave my opinion that we could not do it; there was too much risk with some four or five people in the shop below, and gave it up as a bad job.

'The next thing Kay got for us was Macondray's store. He had been watching it for a month. He told us there were three safes and a vault with lots of money, as much as we could take away in a boat. Come up to the night to do it, and some backed out, considering there were 11 men in the building, and gave it up.

'The night after, Whitaker informed us of [Charles] Jansen's place. He said that when Jansen moved he had a bag which he supposed contained $10,000 to $15,000. We agreed to go and get it – myself, Jim Briggs, J. M. [Old Jack] Morgan, Sam Whitaker, Teddy McCormick, Billy Hughes, Belcher Kay and John Edwards. All of us had been together for 10 days, except Briggs and Morgan, who had just come up from Monterey.

'Morgan went into Jansen's store first. The rest of us stopped in the road. Whitaker and myself stood at the window at this time. I thought he was too long and would get no money, so I went in to help him.

'I got halfway up the shop behind the counter, heard Jansen ask Morgan what he wanted there. Morgan told him that he wanted to look at some blankets. He turns round, sees me behind the counter. I also told him I wanted blankets. He stepped about two yards to show me some blankets – we had cloaks on for a disguise – and I hit him on the head with a slungshot and knocked him down. I then left Morgan to take charge of him while I looked after the money. I only hit him once. I opened a desk and took out a shot bag containing money.

'We then carried the money to Sydney Valley. I carried the money. I counted the money. There was $1,568 in gold coin. We divided it in eight parts, making $96 each. We then came downtown again, went into Mrs Hogan's, stopped there two or three hours and then went home again. Mrs Hogan lived on Sansome Street.

'The next day there was quite a fuss about town. We did not commit more robberies while the men arrested for striking Jansen were under trial, as we did not wish them hung as they were innocent. We would have shot 50 men rather than they should be hung. We agreed that if the above men were hung, which we expected they would on Sunday night, to burn down the town.

'A few nights after, we agreed to rob a bank kept by Beeboe, Ludlow and Co on Montgomery Street. In this we were assisted by [corrupt police officers] Rob McIntyre and Andy McCarty. We opened the outside door by false keys, watched it for two days and concluded there was not money enough to attempt the robbery, as we observed the porter of the bank come each morning from Argenti's [bank] with bags of money deposited the evening previous.

'The next night we went to Mr Young's bank, next to the Eldorado [gambling house] in Washington Street. Morgan helped to build the vault, and gave us the information. Went down the Eldorado steps, opened the door with false keys, entered and found two beds, discovered there were too many people sleeping there, considered it too dangerous and gave it up.

'Belcher Kay was an accomplice with us. There were eight in the gang. Kay was generally an outsider, and did the watching.

'The next night we stole a small safe out of Emerson and Dunbar's auction store, and the next night stole a safe from Gladwin and Whitmore, took it up on the sandhills, where we were discovered before we had broken it open. Morgan and James Briggs were arrested by the police in this scrape. Here we lost all our tools, which were worth $500 to us.

'We went to Mrs Hogan's house. Not liking to see men go to the watch-house, I wanted the others to come and rescue them from the watch-house by force, but they refused. They thought that by employing Lawyer Parbut they would be cleared. The next day, Morgan was acquitted and Briggs was committed to gaol.'[5]

Deciding to get out of town until the heat died down, Stuart took ship for Trinidad Bay, California, 250 nautical miles north of San Francisco. There, he ran across his old rustler friends Dab and Peet, who were laying low after selling some 60 horses stolen from Sacramento City.

'I found Trinidad to be a bad place for me,' Stuart recalls. 'I played cards with Dab and won all his money, about $300. I then came back to San Francisco and paid the passage of Dab and Peet also. We arrived in San Francisco on a Sunday, and Dab threatened to inform on me if I didn't give him money. I gave him $50.

'The same day, Dab and a policeman stopped me in the street. The policeman wanted to arrest me. I drew my pistol to shoot him and he stood off. There were many people about, and I gave him $100 to quieten him.

'I went and saw Mrs Hogan. She told me that there was a warrant out for Whitaker and Long Charley for robbing a man in her house of $1,500. She advised me to leave town, said the police were searching her house, and said she had secreted Whitaker at the Mission.

'The next morning, I hired a horse at a stable and rode to Monterey. At this time I had just taken the name of Carlisle – I previously was called Campbell. The day I arrived at Monterey, [gang members] Jim Briggs and Dick Osman were about to be tried for robbing the Monterey Custom House. I went to Monterey purposely to attend the trial, went to the watch-house and saw the prisoners. The second night my horse was stolen from me.

'Dick Osman was first to be put on trial. Parbut went down from San Francisco to defend him, and I appeared [under the alias Carlisle] as a witness in his favour. We all knew the parties were guilty. Although they took $13,000 down from San Francisco, all that was robbed was $8,000.

'The fact is that Parbut, McDonald and Judge Merritt were counsel for the prisoners, and Colonel Weller, Boots and Wallace for the prosecution. There was a great deal of swearing falsely and bribery.

'The sheriff of Monterey [William Roach] received $700 and a gold watch for stacking the jury and other services, and Morrison, a juryman, received $100 from the prisoners, which was paid after the trial. Dennis McCarthy [a corrupt police officer] received $100 for false swearing. The judge knew nothing about it. Jim Carson, a juryman, held out for guilty – he was bribed by the prosecution.

'All the money was taken from the prisoners – the court charges, amounting to $1,000, were first taken out, and the balance of $13,000, say $12,000, was equally divided between the prisoners and prosecuting counsel. The prisoners then paid their own lawyers.

'Parbut told me to let the prisoners out of jail, and I broke the door down and let them out.'[6]

From Monterey, Stuart started on foot for the southern mines. In San Jose he stole a horse, saddle and bridle, but was captured near San Joaquin.

'I got in a row with 11 Mexicans who took my gun from me, stating I had stolen their horse. They took me back to Livermore's Pass. I gave them my watch and chain to release me, and went on foot to Sonora. From there, I went to Sullivan's [goldfield near Sonora] and worked about a week, did not like mining, then went to Mariposa. I worked there for about five weeks, and met two Americans who knew me, and did not think myself safe to stay where I was known, and left for San Francisco on foot.

'I arrived here Tuesday night, saw Kitchen at the Eldorado, and went to the house where he used to live. Wednesday morning arose and I went to the Mission to see an acquaintance who lives at a bakery at the Mission. I went to see about robbing an old Spaniard at the Mission. The acquaintance at the Mission is short and had on a black hat.'[7]

Here, Sam Brannan, recording Stuart's statement, notes: 'It is known to our committee who this friend is.'[8]

Stuart continues: 'I went into the Mission house and looked at the safe, and told him I would see him again about it. I took to the hills on the way back from the Mission to avoid being seen, and was arrested on the sandhills doing nothing. I was on the way to North Beach.'[9]

It's been a long night. Stuart has brought his story up to date, but then, as an afterthought, adds a couple more exploits to the record – the first proving that to the Sydney Coves nothing was sacred.

'In coming from San Jose to San Francisco last January or February, I came on the steamer *North Star* with one Smith, who was afterwards shot in Sacramento City, robbing a house. We went from San Francisco to San Jose and Santa Clara to rob the churches of silver and gold images. We were told there was a gold image weighing 10 pounds, but although I attended Mass regularly I could not find it.

'On the passage to San Francisco the boat got stuck on a mud flat. In the morning, all hands were called in and told that a passenger had been robbed of $100 in gold dust. They took my gold dust and that of another man, a passenger, but I did not rob it and knew nothing about it.

'On arrival here I advised robbing the steamer *Star*. I met Teddy McCormick and John Edwards and went down to the steamboat. I went on board, opened the window and robbed the desk of about $250.'[10]

It is near dawn now, and while Stuart has finished his statement his captors are not satisfied, particularly since his long and convoluted confession has conveniently avoided any mention of the Charles Moore murder and other violent crimes attributed to the Sydney Coves.

They fire a series of questions at Stuart. His answers are recorded but the questions, apparently, are not. He tells them:

'I knew Jenkins. I knew Windred – I think he is gone out of the country. I do not know where he is now.

'I know Nelson and Wilson, horse thieves in Sacramento City.

'When I landed from the *James Caskie*, I went to Edwards' house. John Edwards has red whiskers, is an Englishman.

'We broke into Smith's lumber yard at about 8 o'clock at night.

'Jimmy from Town stole a trunk from Mr A. J. Ellis' house.

'Jimmy from Town robbed Dow's safe and blew it up with powder.

'I gave Pixley an order for my money in the name of James Campbell.

'I arrived at Foster's Bar in the middle of April. I hired Sullivan, Hunt and Howes to work at Foster's Bar. I never committed more crimes at Foster's Bar than I have stated.

'Dodge and Co kept a gambling house at Foster's Bar.

'I think I knew of every robbery committed in Sacramento when I was there.

'I have worn a serape [a blanket worn as a cloak, similar to a poncho but with no neck hole] and rode on horseback in San Francisco.

'I generally board at Edwards' house. Some of my friends have boarded at the Port Phillip House.

'John [Old Jack] Morgan is known here as John Morris and lives with Briggs. He is 50 years old, a large, stout fellow and weighs 15 stone.

'I have heard hundreds remark here that the day would soon come when this country would be taken by the Sydney people.

'We have had an understanding with police officers McIntyre and McCarty for a long time. They were concerned with us in the robbery of Young's Bank, next to the Eldorado.

'I don't know who makes burglar's tools. Briggs makes some.

'I knew Otis, a horse thief, saw him arrested and saw him on trial.

'I know Pico. I did not know Fisher, nor Hill or Hull at Monterey. Ryan was the only one who robbed the Monterey Custom House that reaped any benefit.

'I gave Pixley an order for $113 on Lowe. He lives in Front Street, Sacramento City – very pretty house, has a bay window in it.

'Money stolen from Jansen was divided in Edwards' house, near Clarke's Point. A quarrel between Belcher Kay and Whitaker was caused because they did not equally divide the money.

'We should certainly have fired the town, in three or four places, had the men arrested for striking Jansen been hung.

'The men who committed the jewellery robbery here were George Adams and Teddy McCormick.

'I have been to Angel Island [in San Francisco Bay], and generally stop at Daniel Wilder's house. I think there are no robbers there.

'Mrs Hogan's house is a crib for stolen property. She wears my daguerreotype. She knows all about our motions. Mr Hogan is innocent.'[11]

And Long Jim Stuart is doomed.

Chapter 25

A 'quiet and orderly' occasion

In a last-ditch attempt to rescue Jim Stuart from the vigilantes, Frank Pixley appeals to the Californian Supreme Court and is granted a writ of habeas corpus on the grounds that Stuart is being held captive by an illegal organisation.

The writ orders that his client be handed over to the legal authorities at 11 the following morning, but when Sheriff Jack Hays – a poor choice for the job – inspects vigilante headquarters Stuart is no longer there. He has been taken into hiding elsewhere.

Committee secretary Isaac Bluxome writes, 'We knew the writ was coming and we did not want to refuse it, and so I borrowed a long cloak and slouch hat, and Oaks and I dressed Stuart up in them and took him to Endicott and Oaks' building on First Street, between Market and Mission. We showed him two pistols and said to him, "If you attempt to run we will shoot you."

'We put him down the cellar there. When Endicott went home, we placed a guard over him. Endicott came back and said, "This won't do! I am a city official [an alderman] and have taken the oath to support the government." This was in his own building.

'Rube Maloney, who was also a member of the committee, said, "I will put him in my house." So we walked him up there to his house to keep him clear of the habeas corpus.

'About 12 o'clock, down came Maloney and said he could not keep him any longer. We sent a guard and took him to some other place, and he was shifted round to keep him away from the sheriff.'[1]

Sheriff Hays enters court to report that Jim Stuart is nowhere to be found. He searched the city, he says, and even followed a carriage out as far as the mission in case it was the outlaw on the run. It wasn't.

With rescue attempts stymied, Senator David Broderick calls a public meeting in hopes of forming a community group to support the civil authorities and prevent the punishment of citizens without due process of law. In other words, an Anti-vigilante Vigilance Committee. When Broderick's proposal fails through lack of interest, Jim Stuart's would-be saviours have run out of time and ideas.

From the *San Francisco Herald*: 'The tapping of the alarm bell on the Monumental Engine House, about 9 o'clock this morning, startled the citizens, for it was the well-known signal for the assembling of the Committee of Vigilance, and is never heard except when a case of life and death is pending. The members of the committee repaired in great numbers to their room, where they remained in session until 2 o'clock, engaged in the trial of Jim Stuart, who confesses to six aliases – a native of England, and former convict. He was convicted and sentenced to death.'[2]

While Stuart made no such admission in his confession, the committee declares that the charge of murder against him was clearly proven at the trial.

For Jim Stuart, in the guardhouse awaiting the verdict, the result is surely obvious when a clergyman enters the room. He tells Reverend Flavel Scott Mines, rector of Trinity Church, that if there is a Hell he is bound to go there. When Rev. Mines suggests he might yet be saved, Stuart replies that it would be too great a work to be done in such a short time. And besides, he is no longer convinced that God exists.

At a later meeting with the minister, Stuart says he has accepted his fate and can trust only in divine mercy. Miles offers to accompany him to the gallows but he refuses.

At about 2 pm, some 300 vigilantes emerge from their headquarters in the Brannan Building, led by the hangman, Captain Ned Wakeman, and with the prisoner in tow – his arms tied behind his back. He appears calm and resolute.

'They marched two abreast, arm in arm, along Battery Street to Market Street wharf, down which they took their way to its extremity, where a derrick stood with everything ready for the execution.'[3]

The 'derrick' is a makeshift gallows of two posts and a crossbeam, used for hauling freight. As onlookers on the wharf scramble for the best views of the hanging, and people on ships in the bay crowd the decks and clamber up the rigging, Stuart's composure shatters. 'The prisoner was nearly overcome with fear,' the *Herald* reports, 'so that his guards had almost to support him.'[4]

As Stuart stands at the foot of the gallows, the correspondent for the *Daily Alta California* notes, 'He appeared to feel as though he was satisfied with his sentence and did not desire to live longer.'[5]

As a hush comes over the crowd, Stuart is heard to say, 'I die reconciled, my sentence is just.'[6]

The *Alta* continues: 'The rope was pulled, and in a moment he was dangling in the air. As he went up, he closed his eyes and clasped his hands together. He had previously requested that his face might not be covered. He scarcely gave a struggle, and although the knot was on the back of his neck, appeared to be in little pain.'[7]

The *Herald*: 'Twice only he drew up his body and shoulders, and then swung dangling in the breeze. After remaining suspended for about 25 minutes, life being entirely extinct, he was slowly let down, and the committee having satisfied themselves that he was in reality dead, his body was lowered from the wharf into a boat and carried off into the harbour.'[8]

The *Herald* notes also that an expected rescue attempt by Stuart's gang did not occur. 'Not the slightest resistance was offered by anyone to the proceedings of the Committee. All was quiet and orderly, and becoming gravity sat upon the faces of all.'[9]

Life was not 'entirely extinct', however. Those who had 'satisfied themselves' that the hanged man was dead were negligent or worse. Jim Stuart was still alive.

'An inquest was held yesterday morning, by Coroner Gallagher, upon the body of James Stuart,' the *Daily Alta California* reports, 'and after examining three witnesses, the jury returned a verdict that "the deceased came to his death by strangulation, by hanging, at the hands of a body of men styling themselves the Vigilance Committee of San Francisco".

'It is said that life was not extinct in Stuart for several hours after he was brought to the station house, and an intelligent physician has stated that had the proper means been employed he could have been resuscitated.

'Three hours after he was cut down, an incision was made in the arm, from which the blood flowed freely. The expression of his features was calm and composed, and there was none of that distortion which is usually observed upon the countenances of men who have met with a violent death. He had, on the whole, a fine appearance, with a broad, high and intellectual forehead. Pity for him was it that his talents had not received a better direction.

'The grave has closed over the cold form of the robber, of the probable murderer. It is to be hoped that another terrible example like his will never be required to be made among us.'[10]

Two questions would remain unanswered. As Jim Stuart lay unconscious on a mortuary slab, why was no attempt made to revive him? And if he had been resuscitated, would the vigilantes have nursed him back to health only to hang him again?

Appalled by Stuart's lynching, San Francisco's new mayor, Charles James Brenham, a tough former steamship captain, issues a proclamation:

'We have arrived at an important crisis in the civil and social condition and prospects of our city. A voluntary association of men has been formed, under peculiar bonds to each other, and assuming most extraordinary and irresponsible powers, and have undertaken to institute extra judicial proceedings in forms not known to the laws. This association claims and exercises the right to indict penalties upon those adjudged by them of crime, even to the penalty of death, and has publicly and boldly inflicted that penalty in two instances.

'They claim and exercise the right of domiciliary visits, without any accountability, of a character not known under any other than inquisitorial governments. The great and sacred writ of habeas corpus has been rendered by them ineffectual, and the authority of the highest tribunal of the State disregarded.

'The circumstances in which the authorities are placed, in consequence, seem to demand of me, as the constituted Chief Magistrate, some action by which the views and purposes of the city government, over which I have been called to preside, may be indicated to the citizens, to the country and to the world.'[11]

Brenham is a brave man, and on a past occasion stood alone in the face of a lynch mob. He calmly pulled out his pocket watch and gave the mob ten minutes to disperse or be arrested. By the time ten minutes had passed, the crowd had dissolved peacefully into the night.

Hoping to end the present crisis, Brenham strengthens the police presence guarding accused criminals to protect them from vigilante lynch mobs. He calls upon those who have joined the Committee of Vigilance to resign, and for all citizens to deny the vigilantes aid or support. His calls are ignored.

Chapter 26

The hangman's banner

Captain Ned Wakeman, of the steamer *New World*, is the very image of a crusty sea dog. His friend Mark Twain will, in later years, describe him as 'rough as a bear in voice and action, and yet as kind-hearted and tender as a woman. He is a burly, hairy, sunburnt, stormy-voiced old salt who mixes strange oaths with incomprehensible sailor phraseology and the gentlest and most touching pathos, and is tattooed from head to foot like a Fiji islander.

'He knows nothing of policy or the ways of the world, but he can keep cheered-up any company of passengers that ever travelled in a ship. He never drinks a drop, never gambles, and never swears where a lady or a child may chance to hear him.'[1]

Twain, who first meets Wakeman in 1866 on a voyage from San Francisco to New York, is mightily impressed with this 'handsome, weather-beaten, symmetrically built and powerful creature, with coal-black hair and whiskers and the kind of eye which men obey without talking back.

'He was full of human nature, and the best kind of human and loving a soul as I have found, and when his temper was up he performed all the functions of an earthquake, without the noise.'[2]

So impressed is Twain that he uses Wakeman as the model for his characters Captain Ned Blakely in *Roughing It*, Captain Hurricane Jones in *Some Rambling Notes of an Idle Excursion*, Captain Stormfield in *Captain Stormfield's Visit to Heaven*, Captain Saltmarsh in *American Claimant*, Captain Davis in *The Great Dark*, and Admiral Abner Stormfield in *Refuge of the Derelicts*.

Born in 1818, Edgar 'Ned' Wakeman, a Connecticut farmer's son, ran away to sea at age 12. By the age of 20, in an adventurous life at sea, he had braved the many perils of the ocean, survived shipwrecks, pestilence and being mauled by a tiger in Sumatra, fought countless brawls, and, in Havana, had killed a man in a knife fight.

Of course, some of these tales might not be true, or, if true, could be heavily embroidered, given Wakeman's legendary reputation as a spinner of rollicking yarns.

In a notable example, overheard by Mark Twain in the bar of the Grand Hotel, Panama, and included in his *Travels with Mr Brown*, Wakeman is holding forth about an encounter with seagoing monkeys.

'Monkeys!' he snorts. 'Don't tell me nothing about monkeys, sir! I know all about 'em. Didn't I take the *Mary Ann* through the Monkey Islands? Snakes as big as a ship's mainmast, sir, and monkeys!

'God bless my soul, sir, just at daylight she fetched up at a dead standstill, sir. And what do you suppose it was, sir? It was monkeys! Millions of 'em, sir – banked up as high as the cat-heads [wooden beams on the sides of the bow of a sailing ship], sir – trying to swim across the channel, sir, and crammed it full.

'I took my glass to see 13 miles of monkeys, two miles wide and 60 fathoms deep, sir. Counted 97 million of 'em, and the mate set 'em down, sir – kept tally til his pencils was all used up and his arm was paralysed, sir.

'Don't tell me nothing about monkeys, sir, because I've been there. I know all about 'em, sir.'[3]

While the above tale is preposterous, and probably intentionally so, Mark Twain's *Roughing It* includes a story he says is based on an actual incident related to him by Ned Wakeman, renamed Ned Blakely in the book. The story, Twain tells us, is 'a scrap of history familiar to all old Californians, and worthy to be known by other peoples of the earth that love simple, straight-forward justice unencumbered with nonsense'.[4] And the name Ned Blakely 'will answer as well as any other fictitious one (for he was still with the living at last accounts, and may not desire to be famous) – sailed ships out of the harbour of San Francisco for many years'.[5]

The fictionalised account is set in the Chincha Islands, a group of three small islands off Peru, with large deposits of guano – the accumulated droppings of birds, bats and seals, mined for use as fertiliser. Blakely, the skipper of a guano carrier visiting the islands, is challenged to a fight by a notorious waterfront thug, Bill Noakes, who has boarded Blakely's ship uninvited. Blakely beats Noakes almost to a pulp and throws him overboard to swim ashore.

A week later, Noakes, who has sworn revenge but knows he is no match for the captain, turns his attention to the first mate, Blakely's close friend and trusted shipmate. Noakes tries to pick a fight with the mate, who turns and runs away, whereupon Noakes draws a pistol and shoots him dead.

Captain Blakely, on learning of the cowardly murder of his mate, arms himself with a double-barrel shotgun, goes ashore, arrests Noakes and drags him back to his ship in irons. He sends word to the captains of vessels then in port that he intends to hang Noakes from the yardarm next morning, and cordially invites them all to attend the lynching.

When other captains protest that the accused man should be given a fair trial, Blakely compromises. He will agree to a trial, he says, only if he can hang him afterwards. A kangaroo court is quickly convened ashore, Noakes is found guilty and led to a nearby canyon.

There, with his fellow captains as witnesses, Blakely sets a noose around Noakes' neck and throws the rope over the branch of a tree. He recites from the *Book of Genesis*, calls on Noakes to confess, and, when Noakes refuses, takes hold of the rope and hoists him up to strangle. After tying off the rope, Blakely calmly takes out his watch, waits half an hour then lets the body down.

Concluding this tale, Mark Twain writes, 'When the history of this affair reached California (it was in the "early days") it made a deal of talk, but did not diminish the captain's popularity in any degree. It increased it, indeed. California had a population then that "inflicted" justice after a fashion that was simplicity and primitiveness itself, and could therefore admire appreciatively when the same fashion was followed elsewhere.'[6]

Ned Wakeman arrived in San Francisco in July of 1850 as master of the *New World*, a brand-new steamer built in New York for the California run. The ship's owner, William Brown, threatened with bankruptcy, had taken as a silent partner the sheriff of New York City, Andrew Hodges. As the ship sat at its mooring in New York harbour, preparing for its maiden voyage to San Francisco, the sheriff and a number of deputies came aboard with the intention of impounding the vessel until debts were paid.

Captain Wakeman had other ideas. When Hodges noticed that the ship was casting off, Wakeman convinced him that it was merely for a short sea trial; to wear the rust off the bearings and make sure the steam engine was working well. But when the ship steamed out of harbour and out to sea, Hodges realised he had been duped. But it was all too late. The sheriff and his deputies, outnumbered by the crew, were put ashore in rowboats and the *New World* set course around the Horn for Panama, then on to San Francisco.

So when Ned Wakeman docked in San Francisco he was effectively a pirate, yet he was never prosecuted as such – rather, he was warmly welcomed. Perhaps, arriving as he did at a critical time in the stand-off between the Sydney Coves and the supporters of Sam Brannan, his reputation as a champion of lynch law had preceded him. He was among the first to join the Committee of Vigilance and was duly appointed executioner.

As the man who hanged John Jenkins and Jim Stuart, Captain Wakeman is a celebrity in San Francisco, feted and fawned upon by the many and demonised by the few. Promoting a dinner in his honour, the *Daily Alta California* gushes, 'Captain W. has been favourably known to the public of San Francisco and Sacramento for a length of time, and borne a very high reputation as a seaman and a citizen. His connection with the recent action of the very large body of our fellow citizens comprising the Vigilance

Committee has brought him somewhat into notice and caused him to be condemned by that small portion of the community opposed to their acts.'[7]

After two years plying between San Francisco and Sacramento, on the occasion of his departure on the *New Orleans*, bound for Australia, the good folk of San Francisco have a parting gift for the captain. Presented to him with due pomp and ceremony aboard his new ship, the *Independence*, it is a satin signal flag featuring a large lone star with the word 'Vigilance' above and the word 'Eureka' below.

On behalf of the grateful citizens of San Francisco he is told, 'This flag, designed by your friends as your private signal, bears for its leading motto a sentiment deemed peculiarly appropriate for one placed in your position, and a sentiment which should be a guiding motto through life for us all.'[8]

Responding to these and many other flowery phrases, a visibly moved Ned Wakeman vows 'to exhibit ere long your gift, my signal, at the fore-topmast head of the *Independence* as she enters the Golden Gate of the Bay of San Francisco'.[9]

And all he had to do for it was to strangle two helpless wild colonials at the end of a rope.

The captain's signal flag, impressive though it may be, is not half as grand as the banner presented to the Vigilance Committee by the ladies of Trinity Parish, lovingly made with their own sweet hands.

The presentation takes place at the vigilantes' new headquarters over Middleton and Smiley's store, on the corner of Sacramento and Battery streets. The meeting room is elegantly furnished and carpeted, with maps and pictures on the wall and neatly curtained windows. At one end of the room is a rostrum with a suitably impressive desk and chair for the president, in front of a large mirror. In the centre of the room is a table with books, stationery and an ornamental inkstand, and at the far end of the room, opposite the rostrum, is a cabinet on which the daily papers are filed.

Speaking on behalf of the ladies, a Mr Brooks tells the assembled vigilantes:

'The ornaments of the banner are intended to assist in expressing the confidence of the donors in this association, their reliance upon its strength and protection, and their confidence in the blessings which will flow from its existence and its action. On that side of the banner which bears the name of this association, the date of its organisation and the purposes of its creation, the inscription is enclosed in a wreath of live oak, an emblem of their strength that defies the storms and tempests that howl and threaten around it.

'Entwined with this emblem on one side is the fig – the emblem of home, with all its pictures of quiet delight, of prosperity, of happy faces and loving hearts. On the other side, the oak entwines with the olive – because from your strength comes peace. Under the protection of your vigilance and strength, our rights, our lives, our persons and our property is safe from rapine and violence. But what is of far more importance, and what I feel from the bottom of my heart is, that in your banded strength, our dearest treasures, our wives and children, find a safe and sure protection.

'On the reverse side of the banner, which bears upon its more delicately tinted front the names of those who gave the banner and the reason why it was given, a simple wreath of varied flowers encircles this inscription.

'This gift comes with peculiar appropriateness from the ladies,' Brooks tells the assembled vigilantes. 'At the time that this society was organised our situation was very different from what it is at present. It is true that the strong man with loaded revolvers in his pocket and bowie knife concealed in his breast might defy the attacks of the Sydney convict and the refuse of all the world which infested our city. But it was different for the weak and defenceless woman – she who sits patiently at home waiting for her husband's return from his business. In every noise about the house she fears the burglar and the robber. If her husband is delayed beyond his usual time, a thousand fears, a thousand horrid visions of murder and outrage and violence come upon her heart, and fill her with anguish and dismay.

'Such was San Francisco – but now we live in peace. We sit beneath our vine and fig tree happy and secure, and a woman's heart feels, and this her gift expresses, her gratitude.

'Gentlemen, accept this gift, and in all your actions, in all the assaults which may be made upon you by those who hate or those who fear or those who doubt, remember the motto which it bears, "Do right and fear not", for in the end blessings will ever reward you for your laborious vigilance for the protection of our lives and property.'[10]

With appropriate expressions of appreciation, and with all due humility, the vigilantes accept the banner and do with it what they do best – they hang it – at least until the ladies have gone. Then it is taken down, rolled up and left to gather dust in a small side room where they keep their handcuffs, chains and other tools of the trade.

On 20 May 1853, a letter to the editor signed simply 'a British citizen' appears in the *Sydney Morning Herald*.

'It is asserted, on the evidence of several credible witnesses,' says the unnamed writer, 'that the individual who acted as hangman on the occasion of Jenkins and another miserable fellow-creature being murdered under the authority of the self-constituted Vigilance Committee of San Francisco, in 1851, has recently arrived in Sydney. The witnesses are fully prepared to prove his identity.

'Will you allow me to inquire, through your columns, whether the offender is not answerable to our laws, as for murder; and whether a criminal information exhibited against him, and substantiated by witnesses of unimpeachable credit, would not be sufficient to warrant his committal to take his trial before the Supreme Criminal Court of this colony.'[11]

The editor comments:

'We are afraid that the individual alluded to by our correspondent, even if guilty, is beyond the pale of British colonial law, having escaped that of the United States.

'We think, however, that it would be well to give the individual referred to a gentle hint to return to the more congenial atmosphere of California, or it may become necessary to send to that distant land and request the presence of Judge Lynch in Sydney, for this occasion only.'[12]

Chapter 27

Close but no cigar

It's old news – two months old – by the time it reaches Australia, but 'as many of your readers have friends and relations in California,' a returning Sydneysider writes to the *Empire*, 'the following latest intelligence may not be uninteresting to them.'[1]

Prefaced by a headline screaming, 'California – the almost certain prospect of civil war,' the letter from an unnamed 'respectable and well-known resident of Sydney' lately returned from San Francisco, reports: 'The Committee of Vigilance were as powerful and as vigorously engaged in punishing offenders as ever. Every vessel coming from Sydney has been boarded by them, and persons who had the misfortune to be emancipists, not permitted to land; and one, a respectable and well-conducted man, sent back.

'The committee have publicly stated that they will not suffer any man who has been sent out from the Mother Country as a convict, no matter what his subsequent character may be, to land in their country.

'They intend to send everyone of this class out of the country. They have already ordered one or two to quit or stand the consequence, i.e., to be forcibly expelled or shot down like dogs.

'A detachment of their body searched our vessel before leaving on the 21st July, and they informed us that they had arrested two persons implicated in Stuart's confession, whom they expected to lynch.

'One of them informed me that on the previous night a notorious gambler named Charles Duane [alias Dutch Charley] had shot a man who was dressed as a lady at a masquerade ball that took place that evening in the California Exchange. The cause of the quarrel was unknown, Duane had been arrested by the committee, and, as there had been "a down" on him, my informant told me he would be lynched, and also that they were about to try one of their judges. All the efforts of the authorities to put down the Committee of Vigilance were utterly abortive. An Act by which the Executive was authorised to enforce martial law had been published, and the attention of the citizens directed to it, but without effect. The public mind had completely run out – all were for lynch law, and a law-and-order man was looked upon with the most sovereign contempt.

'Just as I left, it was publicly rumoured that the Governor would announce San Francisco in a state of insurrection, and proclaim martial law in a few days. What the upshot of this will be, no-one could conjecture.

'According to the best opinions I heard, a civil war or "rush with the authorities" as they termed it, was inevitable, and in the event, the condition of the Sydney people there would be anything but pleasant, the prejudice against them being bitter and dangerous.'[2]

Gold prospectors, California, c. 1850.

Capital of the Wild West. San Francisco Bay in 1851. (US Library of Congress Prints and Photographs Division)

Where lynch law ruled. Portsmouth Square, c. 1850, looking north. (US Library of Congress Prints and Photographs Division)

PORTSMOUTH SQUARE, SAN FRANCISCO.

Portsmouth Square, 1850. (British Library)

*Rabble rouser.
Vigilante leader
Sam Brannan.*

A group portrait of Sharpshooters of the Committee of Vigilance. (Oakland Museum of California)

Father of the Australian gold rush. The mercurial Edward Hargraves. (Painting by Thomas Tyrwhitt Balcombe, National Museum of Australia)

Blame it on the Sydney Coves. The Great Fire of San Francisco, 22 June 1851.

Leaderless now. The lynching of Long Jim Stuart on Market Street Wharf.
(Bancroft Library, University of California, Berkeley)

A willing hand on the rope. Vigilante hangman Captain Ned Wakeman. (Painting by William Smith Jewett, c. 1851, Oakland Museum of California)

Mouthpiece for the mob. Sydney Coves' attorney Frank Pixley. (California State Library)

Respectability at last. Joseph alias William Windred, lone survivor of the Sydney Coves.

HANGING OF WHITTAKER AND McKENZIE,
By the San Francisco Vigilance Committee.

The awful price of vigilance. The hanging of Whittaker and McKenzie.

Californian diggers join an Australian rebellion. The Battle of the Eureka Stockade, 1854. (Watercolour by J. B. Henderson, c. 1854, State Library of NSW)

A cross of stars on a field of blue. Designer of the Eureka Flag, Canadian rebel leader Henry Ross. (Photo by S. J. Dixon, c. 1849, Bendigo Art Gallery)

The wrong man to cross. Gunfighter Jonathan Davis.

No signs of a dark past. Portsmouth Square today.
(All photos by author)

Where the mob once howled, tourists now stroll. Market Street Wharf today.

The great survivor. The Mission of San Francisco.

The same issue includes a letter from Captain Isaac Harris of the English barque *Timandra*, concerning 'the outrage perpetrated upon [him] in the city of San Francisco' by the Committee of Vigilance, which he denounces as 'a banded body of armed barbarians' and a 'moral pestilence'.[3]

The *Empire* predicts that the name of Captain Harris, 'in connection with the infamies inflicted on innocent persons by the Vigilance Committee, will yet be made familiar to every Christian people in the civilised world'.[4]

The *Empire* reprints an unpublished letter Harris sent to the *Daily Alta California* newspaper on 24 June, describing how he arrived in San Francisco to find the city alight, and joined others in fighting the fire, moving from place to place, wherever he could lend a hand.

While crossing Portsmouth Square, opposite the *Alta California* office, he saw a burning barrel of tar.

'Its close proximity to sundry packages of merchandise gave uneasiness to some, speculation to others, and who knows but pleasure to not a few,' he wrote. 'Still, of all the medley groups, not one seemed to adopt means to extinguish it. I stepped forward, and with a drag of my feet along the ground, threw sand and ashes upon it, so as to smother it.'

With the fire soon under control, Harris, to his surprise and horror, was accused by a 'large, idle-looking fellow' of having set the barrel alight.

'In a moment, I was surrounded, and cries of "Thief, thief, Sydney thief!" And "Take him to the committee!" became astounding and universal. A man of powerful frame came forward and seized me violently by the throat, in the name of this committee, followed by many others of like character and brutality.

'By this time, a mob of many hundreds has assembled from all quarters. The regular police force demanded me; the Vigilance refused; the most horrible imprecations were bandied; revolvers pointed; bowie knives glittered and clashed. My position became fearfully critical.

'Every declaration of my innocence, name and capacity was unheeded, nay, it exasperated them even more, so when I cried, "Try me by the Vigilance Committee", I yielded to necessity. Had I appealed to the legal force, sought their aid and protection, I have no hesitation in saying that I should have met with almost instant death, for my captors looked upon me as so entirely theirs that to part with me living, give me up to the officers of the law, to be placed by them for a week or two in the county jail, and then allowed to escape, was too monstrous to be thought of.

'No, the city had been burnt; the citizens cried aloud for vengeance; I was the victim; my blood was to quench the flame, extinguish the embers.'

Harris is dragged along through a mob screaming abuse, demanding that he be hanged at once from a lamppost. By the time he reaches vigilante headquarters he is bloodied from savage blows and kicks, and is naked, his clothes having been ripped from his body while running the gauntlet.

'It was now ascertained who I was, every manifestation of regret and apology was made, I was clothed and conducted to apartments – poor amends for the past.'[5]

Harris's experience with vigilante justice was not over yet. He immediately reported the incident to the British consul who, to the captain's disgust, contacted not the proper authorities but the Vigilance Committee. The following day, a group of vigilantes boarded his vessel and asked him to come to the committee rooms where a gold watch and chain lost during his arrest would be returned to him.

In the committee rooms were some 200 men, many of them draining tumblers of whisky with marked enthusiasm. Harris was shown a book he had signed in a confused and terrified state after his arrest, listing him as a new member of the Vigilance Committee. He recalls: 'I was told that if I signed it they would protect me with their lives, for that the people outdoors were still howling for my life.'[6] He asked that his name be erased, and was promised that would be done, but later learned it was not done.

Sam Brannan mounted a platform and called the meeting to order. 'Gentlemen,' he said, 'you all know for what purpose we organised ourselves. It was, gentlemen, to exterminate the thieves who are in our midst – the scoundrels poured in from the shores of New South Wales.'[7]

Fortunately for Harris – knowing that many Americans saw no distinction between Englishmen and their colonial cousins – Brannan added, 'Now, gentlemen, what we have to deal with tonight differs somewhat from this.'[8]

The matter for discussion was the latest outrage by Dutch Charley Duane. 'His crime, gentlemen, you all know,' Brannan continued, 'and for which he has been tried by the judges, but, owing to some dissentient jurors, he was acquitted. Now, gentlemen, you who are in favour of trying him by this body will say aye, on the contrary, no.'[9]

Brannan announced that the ayes had it, but someone disputed his call, and another attempt showed both sides equally divided. A show of hands failed to resolve the issue, as did a call for those in favour to stand and those against to remain seated. Brannan then called, 'You who are in favour of the motion, pass to the right; on the contrary, to the left,' but it seemed many among the liberally libated membership could no longer tell right from left, and mistakenly voted against trying Dutch Charley. This was immediately and vigorously disputed, and as a man standing near Harris cried, 'Did you ever know such a goddamn shame? That fellow ought to be strung up and no mistake, that's a fact!'[10]

Taking advantage of the chaos, and an open door, Harris fled the meeting – without his watch. He remained determined to retrieve his property, however, and wrote to the committee requesting its return. The day before he was due to set sail for Sydney, having received no reply to his letter, he went to the committee rooms, where he was told he had to state his case to an executive committee.

Brought before Sam Brannan and 14 others, seated at a long table, he was asked by 'a Herculean, Yankee-looking fellow':

'Captain Harris, I find you have sent in to this committee a claim for a watch you lost the day of the last fire. Do you, sir, call that gentlemanly? You see before you the most respectable gentlemen in San Francisco – gentlemen who watch night and day over the property of their fellow citizens.'[11]

Fixing Harris with a menacing stare, he continued, 'We spend a deal of money, we do, and determined we are to exterminate all the scoundrels that the penal settlements of New South Wales pour in upon us.

'Now, sir, do you think we stole your watch? You have been speaking disparagingly of us.'

'I think, Captain,' said another man, 'that you are making a goddamn fool of yourself, and the sooner you clear out of this the better.'[12]

Then another, armed with a pistol and a bowie knife, as were they all, told him that if he suspected them of having stolen his watch they would have to detain him in order to prove it. To avoid this fate, he could sign a document presented to him. It affirmed that the Vigilance Committee had rescued him from a lynch mob, brought him to their quarters and 'honourably acquitted' him. Convinced by the men's threatening manner that to refuse would surely mean a bullet or a noose, Harris signed the document, dashed out the door and left San Francisco the following day vowing never to return, and to hell with his gold watch and chain.

'What, I ask, can compensate for such a flagrant and monstrous outrage?' he demanded in his letter to the *Alta California*. 'Publish these facts, and let the world comment. Such at present is all I ask.'

The *Alta California* did not publish Captain Harris's letter. In September, when the letter is printed in Australian newspapers, Harris adds a blistering opinion of the San Francisco vigilantes and those who support them.

Convinced that the vigilantes are intent upon 'exterminating the Australian', he warns those with notions of 'golden San Francisco' what they can expect to find 'should they determine to visit it, for against them is the vengeance of this Committee of Vigilance more particularly directed'.

'This banded body of armed barbarians is too mighty to be put down by the physical force of those who are opposed to them, and those who should wield the moral power of the state, the press, are clamorous in their support of this most villainous assembly.

'However, it must be remembered that even editors are not revolver-proof, nor their offices citadels.'

Harris disputes the vigilantes' claim that Australian ex-convicts are the instigators of the city's crime wave. 'This I deny,' he says, 'although we all know that the convicts of Britain are bad, yes, for the most part a wicked and degraded people, and many of whom are there. Nevertheless, there are of their own, unconvicted hundreds who are infinitely worse – moving, to all seeming, respectable citizens; even the ruffian of the western wilderness, the crafty gambler, swindler and repudiator of her cities, let loose over a land where their misdeeds can go unchecked; nay, farther, and which is to the point, where they may at any moment resolve themselves into the arbiters of an Englishman's fate, with bowie knife, revolver and halter – the judge, jury and executioners of their ferocious will.'[13]

The actual source of the vigilantes' 'deep-seated aversion to the people of New South Wales', says Harris, is not a righteous determination to stamp out lawlessness and corruption but an attempt to repress all foreign competition in commerce. 'And the first *suspected* infringement of the monopoly, as in the case of Jenkins, was punished with death, to prove that the suns of Australia have but little chance to culminate over the American stars.'

As for the fires which so frequently rage through the city: 'Every fire is declared to be the work of an incendiary, and all incendiaries Australians.' Yet, says Harris, it's clear to even the most casual observer that San Francisco is a tinderbox. 'A vast collection of parched pine boards, hastily knocked together, is what they call a city. Every crevice is filled with shavings.'

So a more likely cause of fire, he suggests, rather implausibly, is not the colonial arsonist but the corona cigar. 'The judge on the bench, the merchant in his counting house, the loafer on the

street and the drunkard in his lair, bear eternally a firebrand –
Manilla or Havana.

'Now, danger may indeed be apprehended from a power, the
creation of these misdeeds and cruelties. A mighty avenger might
be germinated in the blood they have wantonly spilt, and be
nurtured in the bosom of the injuries and injustices daily practised. The best and bravest might be rendered ferocious by such
deeds as those of the Vigilance Committee – much less people who
perhaps are already tainted by crime. Hence may it be wondered
at, if assassins and incendiaries should *now* arise to exercise the
terrible functions of retributive justice?

'Such is the state of that land, and such is the state to which
Australians residing in California are reduced; save, indeed, it be a
few who cringe and fawn, spaniel like, to their barbarian oppres-
sors, forswear the great land of their nativity or adoption, and,
to give the crowing point to their depravity, go to the length of
pointing out to the Committee of Vigilance some of their suffering brethren as fit subjects for the fangs of these bloodhounds.'[14]

Harris's letter sparks indignant responses from apologists for
the vigilantes. On 23 September, Captain White, master of the
Cameo, writes to the *Empire*:

'Respecting the late letter which appeared in the *Empire* of the
22nd, respecting a Mr Harris, formerly of the *Timandra*, I can
justly state that his statement, as respecting an American judge
smoking a cigar on the bench, is quite untrue. Also, the low slang
language is perfectly false. The Committee of Vigilance are above
using bad language.

'As a gentleman, I can safely say they are above inflicting
bad treatment, and if Mr Harris justly considered the exciting
language he used on the Plaza to the American citizens he should

feel thankful to the Committee of Vigilance for protecting him from violence. As to loyalty for the British flag, he should have shown his courage in San Francisco and not in Sydney. I merely state this in justice due to the American citizens.'[15]

Captain White seems to have taken greater offence at Harris's comment on cigar-smoking judges and cussing vigilantes than on his claims regarding the violence done to him. And, unsurprisingly, White does not mention that he (White) made a deal with the Vigilance Committee to take with him to Sydney on the *Cameo* any Australians they cared to deport, at $100 a head. On the *Cameo*'s passenger list, none of the names are those of known members or associates of the Sydney Coves, so there is no way of knowing how much the captain earned from the forced repatriation of Australians, guilty or otherwise.

The next day's edition of the *Empire* includes a scathing reply to Captain White's letter by Captain Harris, headlined 'The Vigilance Committee and their apologists.'

To White's assertion that he should be grateful to the Vigilance Committee for saving him from the mob, he asks, 'What are mobs? People unlawfully assembled; people who are set at defiance of the laws determined by the elected senators of their country. What then are the Vigilance Committee? The Vigilance Committee does good and is supported by all, say some. Then why should they arm themselves with bowie knives and revolvers, and try their victims in secrecy?'

And on a more controversial matter: 'With regard to the judge smoking on the bench, is that strange? Who that has seen the Congress of the United States at Washington can disbelieve it? Surely, if the rulers of that mighty republic can indulge in it, when in solemn enclave, it cannot be a great stretch of authority in the judges of San Francisco, whom carters and boatmen can displace.'[16]

The last shot in this war of words, waged with ink and column inches, is fired on 8 November by Australian journalist Thomas Hinigan, in a letter to the *Sydney Morning Herald*. A former California correspondent for the *Herald*, now shipping reporter for the *Alta California*, Hinigan agrees that Harris 'got a rough handling from a crowd of people', but insists he had only himself to blame.

An unabashed Americophile, Thomas Hinigan is one of a small number of upper-crust Australian expatriates who are members or supporters of the vigilantes, some of whom meet incoming ships to prevent Australians deemed low on the social scale from landing. Australian merchants in San Francisco are making a fortune importing flour, dried fruit, vegetables, tents, wagons and other goods, all at greatly inflated prices. A barrel of flour worth £11 in Hobart, for example, will fetch £40 a barrel in San Francisco. The city's Australian merchants, with ambitions of becoming the permanent providores to Eldorado, are determined to thwart the arrival of possible competitors for the American dollar, even if that means daubing their innocent or reformed countrymen with the convict stain.

Thomas Hinigan writes that he had been in company with Isaac Harris and other sea captains on the day of the fire. According to Hinigan, Harris had been boasting of his success in fighting the fire, and 'speaking very much against Americans in general'. He advised Harris to curb his tongue. 'You are only a sojourner here for a short time,' he told him, 'and if you cannot speak in favour of Americans, speak not to their disparagement.'[17]

Hinigan says he also advised Harris not to go uptown, concerned that his indiscretion would get him into trouble.

'Two hours afterwards, however, he proceeded to the Plaza, and there quarrelled with a man in liquor, respecting the putting out of a blazing tar barrel. A crowd collected, and a report rapidly spread that Harris had been caught kindling a fire.'[18]

Hinigan says the crowd was leading Harris away to lynch him when men of the Vigilance Committee arrived to save the day. 'They rescued him from the mob and conducted him to their rooms. His clothes being torn very much, they gave him others to put on, and, when the mob had dispersed from outside, he was conducted in safety to his vessel. Indeed, I was told that while in the committee room he drank and smoked with them.'[19]

Hinigan goes on to claim that the *Alta California* failed to publish Harris's letter not due to fear of the vigilantes but simply because it did not have the space. He further claims Harris's original letter – as sent to the *Alta California* – thanked the committee for rescuing him, unlike the supposed copy of the letter published in Sydney.

The Committee of Vigilance, Hinigan says, is made up of the great and the good of the city – 'merchants, bankers and trades-people; men of wealth, honesty and integrity; men of family, men of heart and feeling, many of whom have their wives and daughters around them.

'These men, finding that their laws were insufficiently admin-istered by those whom they had placed in office; that murderers and thieves of every description, after having been secured, had been let loose again on society through means of legal quibbles, by false testimony, by bribery or connivance with the police, that robberies and slung-shot murders were of nightly occurrence, and that there was no possibility of putting these corrupt administrators of the law out of office until the period for which they had been elected had expired, felt it necessary for the well-being of the community to put their shoulders to the wheel in order to bring about a change, and with a firmness of purpose and tenacious adherence to justice, they have pursued the course indicated by the laws of nature. They have arrested, tried and executed four of the most daring villains that ever infested society – all of whom confessed to their guilt, and their accomplices – the latter they have sent out of the country, but I have yet to learn that any man of honour and respectability, whether from England, the Australian colonies, or any other part of the world, has been injured by their proceedings.'[20]

Hinigan has no doubt that Captain Harris, being himself a respectable man, asked to join the Vigilance Committee, and did not sign up under duress, as he claimed.

As to the causes of fire in the city, Hinigan, like Captain White, is scandalised by the suggestion that cigar-toting judges might be at fault. 'I believe that at least three out of the six fires I have witnessed in San Francisco have been the work of some villains who wished to destroy the city for plunder,' he writes.[21]

And Captain Harris's missing gold watch? Hinigan is sure the vigilantes – upright and honest almost to a fault – made every effort to find it, but, regrettably, without success.

Following the unfolding San Francisco saga from a distance, many Australians, like Captain Harris, are sceptical about claims that the fires were deliberately lit by the Sydney Coves. Speculation varies as to other possible causes, but according to one newspaper, the *Maitland Mercury*, arson is simply un-Australian:

'The recent fires in California – at San Francisco and Stockton – have led to a repetition, and in a more direct and offensive form, of the uncivil things which the Californians have been in the habit of saying of the people from this side of the Pacific. The Californians assume that the five fires which have devastated San Francisco, and the recent fire at Stockton, have been caused by incendiaries from these colonies, and without deeming it necessary to obtain proof of the correctness of this assumption, they forthwith assemble a public meeting, and pass a string of resolutions which reflect infinitely more discredit on them than on those whom they abuse and vilify.

'A comparison of the histories of the United States and of these colonies for the last 20 years will show, not only that fires are proportionately more frequent there than here, but that the crime of incendiarism is more common in the "glorious republic" than in the penal colonies of Great Britain. However crime-stained our annals may have been, arson has been comparatively a rare offence amongst us. It is not therefore likely that our fellow colonists who have emigrated to California, of whatever class, would suddenly be converted into "systematic incendiaries", and occupy themselves in firing the cities in which they had taken up their residences, and in which probably all they were worth was at stake.

'It seems to us an unreasonable conclusion to assume that the extensive fires which have occurred in the cities of California have been caused by incendiaries. Looking at the inflammable materials of which nearly all the houses there are built, and at the gambling, dissolute, stop-up-all-night habits of many of the population, it seems much more reasonable to ascribe the origin of all these fires to drunken carelessness than to deliberate villainy. And the fact that these extensive conflagrations have originated from the firing of single buildings strengthens this conclusion.

'Admitting, however, for the sake of argument, that the fires have been caused by incendiarism, there is at least as much ground for charging the crime on American citizens as on emigrants from these colonies.

'While, however, we condemn the unreasoning injustice with which the Californians have acted in their wholesale vilification of the emigrants from Australia, we cannot deny that they would be justified in protecting themselves, in a regular, legitimate way, from the evils which may arise from the introduction into their country of the criminals of another. The great majority of us in this colony maintain that the Mother Country has no right to inflict on us the evils of transportation – either direct or indirect. We cannot, therefore, with any consistency or fairness, dispute the right of the Californians to maintain a kindred principle in regard to a foreign state.

'Luckily, our complimentary friends on the other side of the Pacific are not likely to be called upon to put their expulsion doctrines into practice. The discovery of a goldfield of our own will render any such difficult and unpleasant proceeding on their part unnecessary. They will not be troubled with many more emigrants from these colonies, and some of the Australians already located there will probably now feel inclined to voluntarily transfer themselves back to their old homes.

'Should any of the citizens of the "American sovereign state" feel inclined to accompany them and take up their quarters amongst us, we think we may venture to guarantee to them here an immunity from any such wholesale abuse as has been heaped upon our countrymen in California.'[22]

Beneath the editorial, as if to drive home the point, is the latest news from the Australian goldfields.

'The report that 106 pounds of gold had been found in one spot proves to be correct. One of the sable sons of the soil made the discovery, near the Merroo Creek, about midway between Mudgee and the Macquarie River.

'Whether the Californian goldfields exceed ours in general richness or not, no such quantity of gold as this has yet been found there in one mass. This finding of a hundred weight of gold, as it has been aptly termed, has produced considerable excitement in the colony, but it will tell with still greater effect at a distance. Increased immigration from neighbouring countries may be looked for as an immediate consequence, and the news will reach home just in time to swell the stream of immigration hither which the first intelligence of our gold discovery will have induced.

'With the reports of success are however mingled the opposite accounts of those who have been unsuccessful; and some of the returners give most doleful accounts of the condition of many of the miners.

'We are glad to see that the government have made provision for a weekly escort of the mail from the mines, and for undertaking the transmission of gold from Ophir to Sydney by the conveyance so guarded. This arrangement will have a wholesome effect in repressing any inclination which may be felt for finding gold without the trouble of washing and digging for it, and may so prevent some loss of life, considerable waste of property, and save to the community the cost of convicting and punishing bushrangers and mail robbers.

'The government have also made provision for holding petty

sessions at Ophir. This will materially aid their efforts to preserve order in the mining districts. We hope to hear that they are also maintaining an uncompromising crusade against gambling and sly grog selling.'[23]

Chapter 28

Pillars of propriety

There are more than 700 members of the San Francisco Committee of Vigilance, most of them foot soldiers or minor functionaries. Of prominent members, Sam Brannan, fiery tempered, filthy rich and eminently respectable – these days – is the undisputed standard-bearer of the organisation. By his side, but not necessarily in his shadow, stand the self-appointed great and good of San Francisco. Some are colourful and larger than life, such as Captain Ned Wakeman (see Chapter 26) and Selim Woodworth (see Chapter 33). Others, while drab on the outside, conceal more than meets the eye.

Isaac Bluxome, the committee secretary, is a merchant whose business has been burnt out in three successive arson attacks. He won the city's respect back in 1849 when he formed and led Bluxome's Battery, a militia unit that expelled the Hounds, a band of ex-soldiers terrorising San Francisco. He keeps an Australian mistress in Sydney Valley, however, and when that secret is revealed his role in the committee will be compromised and his reputation ruined.

Colonel Jonathan Stevenson, former commander of the New York Volunteers, Masonic Grand Master, and a successful land speculator until his recent bankruptcy, joined the vigilantes after one of his properties was robbed and another set alight – crimes attributed to the Sydney Coves. Yet back when the Hounds were running riot he defended them on the grounds that some were former members of his regiment.

'Little George' Ward, the committee treasurer, is something of a dandy, fancies himself with the ladies and is short not only of stature but of temper. Reputedly, during a heated argument with a man named Michael Reese, he drew his pistol, thrust it point-blank at Reese and yelled, 'Be careful, sir, or by God, I'll blow your brains out!' but could only reach up to the bottom of Reese's waistcoat.

In a classic case of gallows humour, at the lynching of John Jenkins, the excitable Ward waved his gun about so recklessly that someone was heard to cry, 'Take that pistol away from that boy or he will hurt somebody!'[1]

There is more to James King of William than his unusual name. In the District of Columbia, where he grew up, there were quite a number of men named James King, so he decided to distinguish himself from the rest by adding to his surname the first name of his father, William. In 1849, in San Francisco, he established the James King of William Bank, which holds the account of the Vigilance Committee.

King of William is known for his business acumen, not as a man of action. Yet on one occasion he was so convinced of the innocence of a man arrested by the Vigilance Committee that he drew a gun and threatened to shoot any of his fellow vigilantes who dared to harm the prisoner. His comrades, knowing the banker with the quaint moniker had the courage of his convictions, backed off and the prisoner was released.

Nobody trusts James 'Rube' Maloney. The vigilantes are suspicious of him because he has close ties with Sydney Valley gangsters and other undesirables, and the gangsters and other undesirables mistrust him because he's a member of the Vigilance Committee. Curiously, when Jim Stuart was spirited away from vigilante headquarters at gunpoint to prevent his being rescued by the sheriff, Rube volunteered to hide him at his house, then inexplicably changed his mind.

So is Rube a vigilante informer or an underworld plant? Neither side is sure. To be safe, the vigilantes only tell Rube what they want him to know, and exclude him from attending vital meetings by changing the password. The Sydney Coves tell him nothing.

Shipping magnate William Tell Coleman – a staunch advocate of vigilantism – is a motivating force on the Vigilance Committee.

Yet there was an incident when a lynch mob intent on dragging Thomas Berdue and William Windred from the gaol and hanging them on the spot was subdued by the commanding voice of an unidentified man smoking a fat cigar (see Chapter 14). The unidentified man, who convinced the mob to wait until the prisoners had been tried by the committee, thereby saving their lives, was William Tell Coleman.

In later life, in an 1891 magazine article, Coleman reveals his role in the incident. 'I had always a horror of a mob, and its wild and hasty excesses,' he writes, 'and it occurred to me that a middle course might be adopted, and a fair and speedy trial be secured by a court of the people.'[2]

Pushing his way to the front of the mob, he climbed to a balcony overlooking the crowd and somehow soothed the beast.

'Never in my life had I heard a more instantaneous and tumultuous shout of applause,' Coleman recalls. 'It was light breaking through the dark overhanging cloud. It solved the problem and satisfied the longings of the people.'[3]

Felix Argenti, head of the banking company that bears his name, and one of the wealthiest men in San Francisco, bears also the unwelcome title of the only vigilante to be sued by an Australian immigrant. Peter Metcalf, formerly a Sydney carpenter, now a San Francisco publican, is suing Argenti for $20,000 in damages.

Metcalf's complaint is that Argenti, leading a force of some 30 vigilante police, and accompanied by a woman believed to be a prostitute, invaded his home in the middle of the night, upsetting his wife and children, and ransacked the house searching for stolen goods.

Argenti's defence is that during the last fire he employed Metcalf to move some furniture and goods out of harm's way, but when Metcalf returned the goods, items belonging to the woman who accompanied him on the search of Metcalf's house were missing. The woman – who was not named in court – is Argenti's mistress. He testifies that many fine items were found during the search, but admits that none of them belonged to his mistress.

The case is a test of the Vigilance Committee's presumed right to illegally search private residences, and the closing argument by Melcalf's attorney, Rufus Lockwood, is a scathing attack upon the committee and the San Francisco press – a speech destined to become famous in Australia.

'It is said that our Committee is composed of "nice men" – men of wealth and respectability – "our best and most influential citizens",' Lockwood begins, 'and that no honest man can suffer wrong or injury from their clean and immaculate hands.'

He goes on to compare committee members to 'the "nice men" of Jerusalem' – the Pharisees who 'sought for false proof against Jesus, that they might put him to death'.

'When those worthy prototypes – and, to great extent, progenitors of our worthy committee – haled to death the Son of Man, doubtless a feeling of awe fell upon the spectators, as deep and solemn as that so graphically portrayed by our venal and corrupt press, when, with base, pandering servility, with fulsome, sickening adulation, they lauded the tragic murders of the wretched Jenkins and Stuart.

'And shall those blood-stained men be allowed to assert and maintain, on behalf of their association, an exemption from legal liability for gross and wanton outrages upon the most sacred rights of our citizens? Shall the members of that band of felons and traitors against the laws of God and their country be permitted to claim a licence and indulgence to wrong individuals with impunity, upon the sham and insolent plea that they are organised and acting for the public good?

'The public good! Great God, gentlemen, how long will our corrupt editors abuse and insult us with their shameless and absurd falsehoods as to the great good accomplished by the stern and inflexible, the noble-minded and never-enough-to-be-rewarded Vigilance Committee? What have those mushroom noblemen – those sweet-scented, starch-collared, counter-jumping aristocracy who, in one short night, by the foul purchase of a goodly quantity of dirty ink and printing materials, became suddenly metamorphosed from cheating haberdashers and close-fisted and soulless money dealers into an august body of patriotic noblemen – in the name of sense, what have they accomplished for the community?

'I almost feel like cowering before the rage of popular clamour and the insolence of combined wealth. But when I consider that I am not merely pleading the cause of Peter Metcalf – an inoffensive and wronged man – but that I am also advocating the cause of you and me, and those who shall come after us in this world-known land – that I am standing up in defence of human rights and lawful freedom against the insolent assaults of usurping wealth and its hired minions. I cannot rest, I will not believe that you will suffer these proud lordlings to trample with impunity upon my injured client.'

Lockwood concludes by pleading with the jury to 'bleed these purse-proud lordlings to the last cent of the $20,000 claimed by this complaint, and you will perform an act not only of limited justice between these parties, but one of which yourselves, and the community and the whole civilised world will long and justly be proud.'[4]

In the end, Rufus Lockwood's stirring speech wins Peter Metcalf a moral victory but not a financial one. The jury finds in his favour but awards him just $201.

Chapter 29

Chasing the wily Cove

In his confession, the outlaw James Stuart named some 25 people – members of his gang and collaborators – making outlaws of them all. The Vigilance Committee has provided Stuart's statement to be published in the newspapers, and suddenly for all those named there is an urgent need to run fast and far.

The vigilantes scour the city and dispatch posses north and south, and first to fall into their hands is Jimmy from Town, captured at Marysville on 16 July. His arrest is followed two days later by that of George 'Jack Dandy' Adams at his hiding place on the American River.

At his trial, James Burns alias Jimmy from Town is charged 'with having, on the 2nd day of July, feloniously taken away a trunk containing a large quantity of goods from the house of Edward A. Breed'.[1]

Since the quantity of goods stolen was valued at from $300 to $400, defined as grand larceny, the penalty is death, at the discretion of the jury.

'Mr Breed testified that his trunk was standing on the veranda in front of his house on the night of the robbery, protected from the street only by a railing. Officers Card and O'Donnell testified that they met Burns and Robinson, who was tried and acquitted on the same charge a few days since, at an early hour in the morning, with their pockets and persons stuffed with the clothing which the trunk contained. Burns stated that they had found the trunk in the bushes on the hillside, where it was afterwards found by the officers.

'A man named Hayes, who had been in the county jail with Burns, testified that he had made a confession of his guilt in this transaction to him.'[2]

The defence argues that the death penalty is not appropriate in this case, the jury retires to consider its verdict, and returns half an hour later with a verdict of guilty and a sentence of ten years' imprisonment.

The horse thief known as Dab is captured at Marysville on 17 July but, on being delivered to vigilante headquarters in San Francisco, is inexplicably released by Sam Brannan. When the vigilantes' chief of police, Jacob Van Bokkelen, and others protest and attempt to prevent Brannan releasing the prisoner, Brannan draws his pistol and threatens to shoot anyone who gets in his way. Amid the hubbub, Brannan opens the door and Dab dissolves into the night, never to be seen again. Why Sam Brannan let Dab escape is never explained, and the incident results in Brannan no longer playing an active role on the committee, but it is possible that he and the rustler had a past connection.

In the hunt for fugitive Australians, notably Sam Whitaker – who is considered by the vigilantes to have been Stuart's lieutenant – a posse combs the country around Sacramento and

Stockton but returns empty-handed. Undeterred, a second, then a third posse extend the dragnet to the Chinese diggings, George-town, Jamestown, Shaw's Flat and Sonora. On 29 July, Robert McKenzie is apprehended in Sacramento but Sam Whitaker is still at large and his trail has gone cold.

Mary Ann Hogan – reputedly the lover of both Jim Stuart and Sam Whitaker, and, it is rumoured, the cause of bad blood between those rivals for her affection – is detained aboard a ship about to set sail for Sydney. Mary Ann, along with her husband Michael, is bundled into a handsome carriage hired by the committee and taken to vigilante headquarters for questioning.

The *San Francisco Daily Herald* reports, 'The famous Mrs Hogan was seized on board a ship in the harbour and removed to the Committee Rooms. She is about 35 years of age, quite genteel in appearance, and one who might safely keep a crib without ever being suspected.

'Her carriage, the most elegant in the city, was waiting on Saturday morning at the door of the Committee Rooms. For what, cannot be said, certainly not for the interesting female within.'[3]

Mary Ann claims she has no idea where Sam Whitaker might be hiding, and denies having had an affair with him, even though they had been seen together many times in bars, at the races and around town, and appeared to be on intimate terms. A search of the Hogans' premises fails to find the photograph of Whitaker she is said to keep, nor do they find the photo of Jim Stuart that both Whitaker and Stuart himself claimed she had.

Michael Hogan is in no doubt that his wife was unfaithful to him with Sam Whitaker. He voices his anger at having been deceived, and his loathing of Whitaker, but, like Mary Ann, offers no clue as to Whitaker's likely whereabouts.

The Hogans are released, but when Mary Ann leaves San Francisco for Stockton she is followed in case she plans to meet Whitaker there. She doesn't, and the surveillance is called off. She does plan to rendezvous with Whitaker in San Diego, however, and slips away from Stockton unnoticed. Meanwhile, a vigilante posse is searching inlets and swamps along the Sacramento River.

By the time Mary Ann makes it to San Diego her lover has been captured. Whitaker, while on his way to meet her there, is recognised in Santa Barbara on 8 August and arrested by the county sheriff, Valentine Hearne.

When Sheriff Hearne arrives in San Francisco on the steamer *Ohio*, intending to deliver his prisoner to Sheriff Jack Hays, he happens to mention to a certain Cyrus Palmer, who has rooms in the same building as the sheriff's office, that he has the notorious Sam Whitaker in custody, and that Whitaker is on the *Ohio* at long Wharf, under guard by the ship's captain. Palmer passes on the information to his friend James Wadsworth, who also has a room in the building and happens to be an officer of the Vigilance Committee.

Wadsworth rushes down to Long Wharf where he has no difficulty persuading the captain of the *Ohio* to hand over his prisoner. Whitaker is taken from the ship to vigilante headquarters, and Sheriff Hearne, apparently untroubled by losing his prisoner to an illegal body, returns to Santa Barbara with money in his pocket – paid to him by the committee to cover his expenses.

Being reliant on outdated reports from pro-vigilante Californian newspapers, Australia gets a skewed version of events in San Francisco, as is obvious from these items in Hobart's *Colonial Times* of 24 October 1851.

'The re-building of San Francisco was actively progressing, and the Vigilance Committee were doing their utmost to suppress crime, but in spite of all their efforts, burglary, murder, and other offences of a serious character prevailed to a fearful extent.

'We extract the following from the *Daily Pacific Star* and the *San Francisco Herald* of the latest dates:

'Nearly all the parties implicated in Stuart's crime, the man who was so recently executed by the Vigilance Committee, have been taken. Among them is a Mrs Hogan, to all appearances a highly respectable lady, and kept her carriage.

'The Vigilance Committee had disposed of more criminal cases in two weeks than any judicial court of the government had ever done before in the same period, and their proceedings seemed to give universal satisfaction.

'The number of arrests for various offences committed in San Francisco for the month of July was 250.

'A man of the name of John Goff, or Gough, from Van Diemen's Land, had received notice from the Vigilance Committee to quit California.'[4]

Chapter 30

Never a kind word

San Francisco's newspapers have sold out today. Everyone is keen to know the latest from the Vigilance Committee:

'The following confessions and testimony, taken in the cases of McKenzie, Whitaker and Mary Ann Hogan, are respectfully submitted to the public, in order that any other evidence that may exist may be presented to the committee, and that the people of California may be placed on guard as to those named in the confession, and if possible, that the offenders not in custody may be apprehended and brought to a just punishment.'[1]

The confession of Robert McKenzie is judged to be 'a tissue of prevarications, showing great obstinacy, refusing to answer, and declaring himself guiltless of any crime.'[2]

McKenzie states, 'My right name is Robert McKinney. I am 26 years of age. I was born in Cumberland, England. I left Liverpool, England, with my parents on the ship *Verandah*, for New Orleans. I lived in New Orleans until about March 1849, when I left for California, via Panama, and arrived on the steamer *California*.'[3]

After a long and convoluted story of his experiences as a waterman in San Francisco, trader in Trinidad, miner, wagoner and Indian fighter in northern California, he claims to know no more about the dirty deeds of the Sydney Coves than he has read about in the papers.

Later, however, he admits to having made the acquaintance of Long Jim Stuart, Belcher Kay and other members of the gang, and, as his tongue loosens up, confesses to having acted as lookout at a robbery, of having been a drunken but innocent bystander at the highway robbery of a Chinese digger by one of the Coves, and having witnessed meetings between Stuart and corrupt police.

He testifies that the first time he met Stuart, 'Jim had on a cloak and a hat drawn down over his eyes. They said he was the man who broke out of the prison brig at Sacramento.'[4]

He next encountered Stuart at Trinidad Bay, California. 'He was gambling in a house at night with a policeman named Joseph Wall, who I knew in New Orleans. I asked [Wall] what sent him down there. He said, "You don't know me, sir."' McKenzie says he was told that the police took bribes.

Apropos of nothing, McKenzie concludes with an item of salacious gossip. 'Mrs Hogan was the woman whom Whitaker was said to sleep with. The husband was jealous of him. Husband and wife parted, and the woman was sent back to Sydney.'[5]

It has been made clear to Sam Whitaker, firmly but gently, that neither continued stubborn silence nor a heartfelt admission of guilt can save him from his fate. A woman is brought into the interview room – a prostitute named Harriet Langmeade – who swears that during an argument involving herself, one of her clients, Whitaker and Belcher Kay, her pimp, during which the client attacked Kay with a knife, Whitaker shot at her and missed. With attempted murder now on his slate, Sam Whitaker accepts the inevitable and unburdens his soul. And in doing so, he not only confesses his crimes – holding nothing back – but voices a damning opinion of many of his comrades and collaborators, and utter contempt for official functionaries of law and order.

Sam Whitaker, 32, an English-born former convict, transported to New South Wales for life in 1836 for housebreaking, admits his name is an alias but refuses to disclose his true identity. His interrogator records, 'It [Whitaker] was the name under which he was transported, and he desires to suppress his real name for family considerations, and as an act of humanity.'[6]

Whitaker says he was granted a conditional pardon in 1849 and arrived in San Francisco that same year. He found work as a steward in a pub on Broadway, ran a delivery business, then a butchery before going into partnership with Coves member Teddy McCormick in the Port Phillip House hotel, in Jackson Street.

He admits, with perverse pride, having served on a jury that sentenced a man to prison for stealing a pistol while violent criminals of his acquaintance, clearly guilty, were invariably found not guilty and walked free.

He derides the politicians and officials he found so easily and eagerly corruptible, and instances how he secured the election of Malachi Fallon as town marshal by buying the votes of ex-convicts from Australia.

His views on his fellow gangsters are scathing for the most part, and he doesn't hesitate to incriminate them – naming erstwhile comrades as thieves, arsonists and worse.

He tells the vigilantes, 'I began my career of crime in San Francisco at the time I formed my connection with McCormick.'[7]

When a horse he had bought from a man named Curry turned out to be stolen, Whitaker tracked him down and turned him in to the police. But when Curry walked free without trial and the police, who had taken charge of the money paid for the horse refused to return it Whitaker decided that the justice system in San Francisco was corrupt; that it was a place where 'a thief had a better chance than an honest man'.[8]

He admits that the first crime he committed in San Francisco was the robbery of $900 from a bear hunter named Vyse, and that Teddy McCormick, Bob McKenzie, Morris Morgan and other Coves were also involved.

The gang divided the loot, but then things got complicated. It turned out that the money stolen from the bear hunter was not his own but belonged to a bare-knuckle boxer named Kelly.

'Shortly after, McKenzie went to Sacramento City and told Kelly it was McCormick that robbed him. On this information Kelly came down from Sacramento. I was then at Monterey. Kelly had McCormick arrested and put in jail. They threatened to lynch McCormick, and got from him some instrument by which they sold out the Port Phillip House to reimburse the loss.'[9]

He goes on to confess to a string of robberies and vicious assaults, and to implicate more of his fellow gangsters, including Jim Stuart, Jim Briggs, John Edwards, Billy Hughes, Jimmy from Town, and Belcher Kay, whom he describes as an alcoholic and 'an ignorant man' who 'can hardly read or write'.[10]

Of the robbery and assault at Jansen's store, he says, 'Jansen lived next door to me. Many persons from the colonies frequented my house, and on learning that the country generally wanted sovereigns, Jansen told me that he usually had them and would gladly sell them, and would be obliged to me to take them.' So the Coves decided to do just that.

Stuart, Briggs, McCormick, Edwards, Kay and Whitaker were strolling past Jansen's store one evening after closing time when they noticed a dim light within. Morgan went in, intending to quietly steal the money but after waiting a while for Morgan to return, Jim Stuart, growing impatient, said, 'If I don't go in there no money will be got.'

Stuart, who was wearing a cloak and carrying 'a stick, on the head of which there was a lump of lead as large as a man's fist', went into the store and knocked Jansen to the floor.

'Jansen screamed, but it was only for an instant,' says Whitaker. The gang relieved the victim of his money and his watch, and left him there bleeding and unconscious.

On another occasion, at the notorious Port Phillip House, Whitaker demanded a share of a thief's takings. The thief refused, and he and another man attacked Whitaker. 'I knocked them down,' he recalls. 'I broke the jaw of one in three places. He prosecuted me for assault and battery. I was arrested.'[11]

At trial, he was fined $100, ordered to pay the victim's medical bills, and sentenced to ten days' jail. However, by slipping certain officials a quiet $230 he walked free. 'I state this case also to show the manner in which the laws are administered, and the corruption,' Whitaker says, 'and if it had not been for the manner in which I have been treated and saw others treated, I should not now be here.'[12]

Whitaker declares that William Windred and Thomas Berdue, who were convicted of the Jansen robbery, are innocent. He says he heard Jim Stuart and others swear that if Windred and Berdue were hanged for the crime they would set fire to the city. 'It was to be fired at night in four or five different places,' he adds. 'It was the only time that I heard the colonial people say anything about burning the city.'

A few robberies later: 'McCormick, Stuart and I went together to shoot a man named O'Flaherty, who had testified in court that McCormick had robbed him in the colonies. He was going to shoot him for it.

'It was a moonlit night. I said to McCormick that it was too light and it would be better to wait until some other time, so he gave up. I did this to save the man.'

While portraying himself as a decent man at heart, laid low by bad company, Whitaker has no qualms about dropping his confederates and supporters right in it.

Of Mary Ann Hogan he states, 'I lived with Mrs Hogan for four months during Mr Hogan's absence. During that time I lived with Mrs Hogan as man and wife – we slept together. Indeed she never intended to live with Hogan any more. I knew her in the colony. I have heard she was transported.'

He claims that Mary Ann kept a portrait of Jim Stuart in her bedroom drawer, and another of himself.

'Mrs Hogan knew all the men I have mentioned,' he says. 'They used to frequent her house.'

Of John Edwards, he states that after he and Edwards won $600 gambling, a man named Gallagher 'went to my bedroom at Mrs Hogan's on tiptoe, with a drawn dagger, to look for me. Mrs Hogan told him I was not there. There was considerable talk about his going around trying to kill me.

A day or two after, Gallagher was found dead on the street by Edwards' house. 'I think that Gallagher knew too much about Edwards' business, and for that reason Edwards poisoned him.'

Of corrupt police: 'I gave McCarty three ounces [of gold], one each for Edwards, Kay and myself. I told McCarty that McCormick had got some $500, and that he should get some out of him, too. Brown, in the police, is the man who did the dirty work for policemen McCarty and McIntyre.

'Purcell, a police officer, used to take money. He took money off Hughes; he would take money from anyone.'

When asked to name fellow Coves and associates of the gang, Whitaker doesn't hold back.

'[Jim] Stuart and [George] Smith told me they shot a man on the Stockton road. It was foggy when they shot him. The man had considerable money. He ran towards the house after he was shot, and died nearly as soon as he had entered.

'Billy Hughes, John Edwards and Morris Morgan are runaway convicts. They come from Van Diemen's Land. There is no comparison between the convicts from Sydney and Van Diemen's Land. The latter are so bad they would not allow them to come into Sydney.

'William Clay is from the colonies. I believe him to be a convict. I know him to be a thief.

'William Gregory is from Van Diemen's Land. He is a low-sized and low-set man, very much pock-marked.

'Edward Edwards and Charles Edwards are brothers of John Edwards. They came from the colonies. I believe they are convicts and they are thieves. These Edwardses had a boat and used to steal and trade up and down the river.

'Dick Smith is from the colonies. He is connected with the police. He is a "putter-up" – a sort of go-between for the thief and the police. He told me that if any of my friends got into trouble he would get them out. He would go or get straw bail.

'Thomas Holt is a native of Sydney, with dark complexion and hair, and black teeth. He is a thief. His parents are reputedly rich.

'A dirty-looking little pock-marked Jew, whose name I do not know, keeps a store on the levee at Sacramento City. Long Jim [Stuart] wanted to sell him his goods, and because Long Jim would not take the price offered by the Jew, the Jew went and informed against him, and Jim threatened to kill him if he got a chance. The Jew is a receiver of stolen goods.

'John Darke is from Sydney. He is five feet five inches high with dark complexion and dark curly hair. I don't know who his associates are – rather I think he stole on his own account.'

Of Joseph Turner and his wife, exponents of the extortion racket known as the 'badger game': 'Turner is a tall, good-looking man, dark complexion. He is from the colonies. His wife will meet a man in the street, gets into a conversation, leads the man into a bye place, then Turner comes up suddenly and says, "What are you doing with my wife?", by which he gets money from the man who his wife thus decoys.

'Thomas Williams is from the colonies. This is the man who decoyed a man into the upstairs of Crockstein's house, without Crockstein's knowledge, and there robbed him of $2,000.

'P. J. Barnes is a tinman from the colonies; a convict. He is a stout man, rather surly looking. He will buy stolen goods, or steal them.

'Palmer the Birdstuffer is supposed to be a receiver of stolen goods.

'Robert Ogden is from the colonies. I think he is a convict. He kept a house called "Live and Let Live" on Broadway. I believe him to be a thief.'

As for Mary Ann Hogan, he not only refutes her claim that he and she were just good friends, but suggests he bought her affections with lavish gifts – presumably of stolen goods.

'To do her justice,' he adds, 'I must say that she done all in her power to break up my associations and to lead a different life.'[13]

Whitaker tells his inquisitors it was he who smuggled William Windred out of the country after Windred broke out of jail.

'I took Windred to a stable, got a horse, and took him to Dr Lambert's, where he stayed for two weeks. I paid his board. Dr Lambert is a man from the colonies.

'At the end of that time I engaged passage for Windred, and appointed a night to put him on board. I told [William] Kitchen to stand by with his boat, that I had a man to put on board.'[14]

Whitaker describes William Kitchen, a stout, heavily whisk-ered man in his thirties, as 'a rough, boatman-looking fellow, dirty, very dirty' who confirms his low opinion of convicts from Van Diemen's Land. Yet Kitchen, unlike others of Whitaker's acquaintance, has virtue to his credit. A boatman from Chester, England, he was sentenced in 1843 to ten years' transportation for stealing ten pounds of sugar. Kitchen proved a model prisoner, and in 1846, having served just three years of his sentence, was granted a ticket of leave after risking his life to save two men from drowning. Two years later, he was granted a conditional pardon, and took ship for San Francisco, where he keeps a boarding house on Battery Street, near Clarke's Point, and plies the river as a boatman.

'I put [Windred] down a passageway at Clarke's Point,' Whitaker says. 'Mrs Hogan and Mrs Windred were in waiting – Mrs Windred in men's clothing. In that disguise I had taken her frequently to see her husband. Both women bade Windred goodbye, and I put him on board Kitchen's boat, who took him to the ship.

'The vessel in which Windred was placed remained in port a fortnight, and I feared he would be apprehended again. Windred sent for his wife to go with him, and she went on board, and sailed with him the morning after the May fire.'

Saving the most damning statement until last, Whitaker claims that William Kitchen, for his part in Windred's escape, was paid in blood money. He states, 'Kitchen has a [gold] specimen, of the value of $140, which Long Jim Stuart took from the body of the man Moore, who he murdered.'[15]

Recalled for a second interview, Mary Ann Hogan, after having been read Whitaker's confession, admits they were lovers, but says she finds his insinuation that her affection could be bought with gifts to be insulting. She insists she was like a dutiful wife to him.

Mary Ann states that at two or three years of age she left England for New South Wales, presumably with one or both parents. 'I married in the colonies, and kept a public house in Sydney,' she says. 'I left Sydney about two years since. During my residence in the colonies I was never charged with the commission of crime.

'On our arrival in San Francisco, my husband commenced a general business. We changed this business into that of keeping a public house.

'I became acquainted with Whitaker at my own house in Sansome Street at the time my husband went to Oregon [on business]. I became acquainted with Whitaker through Jim Briggs. I also knew [Belcher] Kay, [John] Edwards and Jim Stuart. These men were in the habit of frequenting my house in Sansome Street.

'I recall a man coming to my house with a dagger drawn, and said he was looking for Whitaker, to kill him. I told him Whitaker was not there. I did hear of a man being found dead near Edwards' house. I never saw the man; do not know if it was the man who came looking for Whitaker with a dagger.'

She admits she knew of Whitaker's involvement with the Sydney Coves, but that she had hoped to persuade him to change his ways and seek honest work.

'I have heard all the confession of Whitaker, read to me carefully, and I have heard Whitaker make the statements. All that he has said is, so far as my knowledge extends, true. I have heard some of the men state the same. I have reason to believe the statements, so far as they go, to be true.'[16]

At some point during the interview Whitaker is brought in to confront her, but what passed between them is not recorded. Mary Ann Hogan's only crime, people will say, was in loving a bad man.

Chapter 31

Flash and counter-flash

It's a foregone conclusion. Although neither Whitaker nor McKenzie have confessed to murder, and there is no hard evidence supporting a charge of homicide, the Executive Committee nonetheless recommends the death penalty on the grounds that the Australians have admitted to robbery and are therefore a menace to society. The executive also cautions that it would be unsafe to hand them over to the authorities.

No one in the general committee, it seems, has any difficulty accepting that verdict. There is some debate, though, about what might be the most suitable venue for the hanging. Some suggest Portsmouth Square, as usual, but a majority opt to hang him from the yardarm of a ship in the harbour close to shore – the advantage being that the execution could attract a bigger audience on shore.

Governor John McDougall, on learning of the intended lynchings from certain vigilantes with twinges of conscience, hurries to San Francisco from Monterey, arriving at midnight, and, with much frantic doorknocking in the wee small hours, enlists the support of Mayor Brenham, and searches the city for a judge willing to issue a warrant to seize the prisoners from the vigilantes. Judge Myron Norton complies, and Sheriff Jack Hays is ordered to serve the warrant.

The trouble is, Sheriff Hays has been corrupted. The Vigilance Committee had offered to finance the upgrade of his gaol, with a little sweetener thrown in for himself, for expenses and certain considerations.

Still, it is his sworn duty to serve the warrant and he cannot refuse without arousing suspicion that he has been compromised. So it is that, early the next morning, Hays and his deputy John Caperton, along with the governor and the mayor, make their way to vigilante headquarters, passing by the guard who, drowsy from having been on duty all night, forgets to ask the password.

Rushing upstairs to where Whitaker and McKenzie are being held, Deputy Caperton easily shoves the guards aside and tells the prisoners, 'I am an officer. I've come to save you!'[1]

As the guards flail about in confusion, the prisoners lock arms with Caperton and dash out the door and onto the street. It's all over in a flash, and no one on either side has fired a shot or even drawn a weapon.

The vigilantes have been made fools of; seriously embarrassed. Yet the committee's response, surprisingly, is to cordially invite the governor, mayor, sheriff and deputy sheriff to vigilante headquarters to discuss the situation. Ever more surprisingly, all four agree.

The vigilantes are keen to know if any of their number tipped off the governor about the impending executions. The answer is yes, but McDougall refuses to name them. The outcome is a censure of those members who 'were so derelict in duty as to inform the Governor of the intended action of the Committee, which rendered it imperative upon him to adopt the course he did',[2] and a resolution that in future any loose-lipped members would be expelled. When their guests have gone, however, the vigilantes vote to attempt to recapture and execute the prisoners as soon as possible.

Sheriff Hays obligingly allows the committee's chief interrogator, Gerrit Ryckman, to visit the prisoners at the county gaol.

'Mr Ryckman,' says Sam Whitaker, 'I hope you are not sorry that we made our escape.'

'You have not made your escape,' Ryckman replies. 'You have been convicted and you will be executed beyond a shadow of a doubt. There is no power on earth that can save you.'[3]

Despite dire threats of expulsion, the Vigilance Committee still leaks like a sieve, and Governor McDougall soon learns there are moves afoot to recapture and hang Whitaker and McKenzie. On 20 August 1851 he issues a thunderous proclamation:

'Whereas an armed and organised body of the citizens of San Francisco County has, in defiance of the Constitution and laws of this state, assumed to exercise the powers of the Courts of Criminal Jurisdiction, and to pass and carry into effect extra-judicial sentences of death – and whereas a spirit of opposition to the officers of the law, while engaged in the execution of their duty, has been openly and publicly manifested; and there is reason to believe that further attempts may be made to interfere with the regular administration of justice in said county; and especially to take from the custody of the Sheriff certain prisoners now confined in the gaol of said County.

'Now, therefore, I John McDougall, Governor of the State of California, do hereby call upon all good citizens of said County to unite for the purpose of sustaining public law and tranquillity, to aid the public officers in the discharge of their duty, and by all lawful means to discountenance any and every attempt which may be made to substitute the despotic control of a self-constituted association, unknown and acting in defiance of the laws, in the place of the regularly organised government of the County. And I hereby call upon all public officers to be active, vigilant and faithful in the performance of their trusts, and to resist to the utmost of their power all efforts which may be made to subvert the law and trample upon the Constitution.

'And I hereby warn those who are disposed to resist the legal authorities, that they cannot do so without involving the community of which they are members in all the horrors of Civil War, subjecting life, liberty and property to the most fearful sacrifices.

'The Government is determined, at all hazards, to sustain the Constitution and laws. Public peace can only be secured, and public liberty can only be maintained by a strict adherence to that feeling of subordination to the law, and respect for its ministers, which have heretofore characterised the American people.'[4]

That same day, leaving the public confused as to who to believe, the vigilantes counter with:

'We, the undersigned, do hereby aver that the present Governor, McDougall, asked to be introduced to the Executive Committee of the Committee of Vigilance, which was allowed, and an hour fixed.

'The Governor, upon being introduced, stated that he approved the acts of the Committee, and that much good had taken place. He hoped that they would go on, and endeavour to act in concert with the authorities, and in case any judge should be guilty of maladministration, to hang him, and he would appoint others.'[5]

It's signed by executive committee members George Schenck, George Oaks, Isaac Bluxome Jnr and Samuel Payran.

Two days later, Captain Cartwright of the vigilante police is issued an order:

'You are hereby authorised to detail a guard such as you think proper and arrest two prisoners, to wit – Sam Whitaker and R. McKenzie, and bring them into custody of the Committee of Vigilance.'[6]

And a further two days later, Captain Cartwright can report:

'Agreeably to your orders above I detailed 30 men who proceeded in three divisions, under the respective orders of Colonel W. G. White, Captain Calhoun and Mr Oscar Smith, and in the short space of five minutes from the first charge the prisoners above named were on their way to your headquarters.'[7]

Yes, indeed, the raid on the county gaol to recapture Whitaker and McKenzie took a mere five minutes, and here's why: on the day of the raid, Sheriff Jack Hays is conveniently absent. His Vigilance Committee friend George Schenck has invited him to a bullfight at the Old Mission.

On the day before the raid, Isaac Bluxome visits the gaol, supposedly to see Thomas Berdue – who is still lodged there awaiting release – but actually to check whether or not the guns in the gaol's armoury are loaded. They are not.

On the day of the raid, Cartwright deploys his men near the front and rear entrances of the gaol. In the exercise yard, a religious service is underway. Sam Whitaker and Robert McKenzie are among the flock of felons praising the Lord, and some of the vigilantes persuade the unsuspecting guards to let them inside to join the congregation.

At 2.30 pm, as the prayer meeting concludes, a lookout on

Telegraph Hill, with a clear view of the exercise yard, gives the signal to attack. The vigilantes inside restrain the guards while those outside break down the doors, seize Whitaker and McKenzie, and, with pistols at their heads, force them outside and into a waiting carriage. The carriage races through the city to vigilante headquarters on Battery Street, and Whitaker and McKenzie, who just five minutes earlier were singing about being safe in the arms of Jesus, are flung back into the jaws of doom.

Chapter 32

Osiris rising

The fire bell clangs and, around vigilante headquarters, the streets are soon packed with people, at first shouting and chattering, pushing and shoving, then standing in silence. There are as many as 15,000 people, some say, all with eyes fixed on two doorways on the second storey of Middleton & Smiley's store, with projecting beams for hoisting freight by block and tackle.

As they watch, the second-storey doors are opened, ropes are pulled through the blocks and the ends of the ropes taken inside.

Sam Whitaker and Robert McKenzie appear in the doorways, each with a noose around his neck. They are dressed in white cotton shirts and their arms have been tied behind their backs.

McKenzie's face is contorted with terror, Whitaker's a study in resolute composure. Without ceremony, they are pushed out of the doorways to drop to their deaths. The crowd has barely time to gasp.

The dangling bodies have scarcely stopped twitching when Sam Brannan appears at one of the doorways above and assures the crowd that both men had confessed their guilt. For what, he does not say. Implausibly, he announces that both agreed that they deserved to die, and each blamed his descent into criminality on weak and corrupt authorities.

After about three-quarters of an hour the bodies are lowered to the ground, the coroner goes about his gruesome business, and the crowd disperses. The carnival is over.

An eyewitness to the lynching is appalled by the silence of the crowd. 'They did not seem like men but like judges sent like Osiris from the nether world,' he writes, 'so stern and implacable was their expression.'[1]

At a coroner's inquest, held on the day of the executions, all the witnesses called are members of the Vigilance Committee. The jury finds that 'Samuel Whitaker and Robert McKenzie came to their death by being hanged by the neck, thereby producing strangulation, by the act of a body of citizens styling themselves the Vigilance Committee of San Francisco, on the afternoon of Sunday, August 24th, instant, at about three o'clock, in front of the Vigilance Committee Rooms, on Battery Street, near California Street, from the second story thereof.'[2]

When news of the lynchings reaches Australia, outrage and anger abounds.

'More blood', cries the *Sydney Morning Herald*.

'Setting aside the laws of God and man, "the people" have committed three more murders. It is no longer to be denied that law and order are at an end in California, and that a "Reign of Terror" exists.'

After a detailed report on the dramatic events leading up to the lynching, and of the executions, the *Herald* adds, 'Some documents professing to be the confessions of these unfortunate wretches are published in the papers, from which it appears that they had committed, in connection with several others, a great number of robberies, most of which were said to be planned at the house of a Mrs Hogan, a woman who with her husband formerly kept a public-house in Sydney.

'We look with some suspicion on these confessions, as they were evidently extorted; there is no doubt, however, that both these men had committed crimes for which they by the law of California subjected themselves to the punishment of lengthened imprisonment. Mrs Hogan was in custody of the Committee, and it was supposed would be sent on to Sydney.

'These cruel murders were approved of and justified by the press. The *Alta California*, the leading paper in the state, writing on this subject says, "But the Croakers [complainers, doomsayers], where are they? Where are the men who affectedly anticipate from such proceedings the worst consequences? Where are the men who hear the words lynch law with blanched cheeks and trembling limbs? It matters but little. They are behind the times, the age, and the wants of this country."

'But if anything were wanting to show how much the mass of the population must be corrupted,' the *Herald* concludes, 'it is found in the fact that when these fearful murders were completed a flag was unfurled which had been presented to the murderers by the ladies of Trinity Church.'[3]

Counterbalancing these grim tidings are signs of a turning tide: 'The news of our goldfields had reached San Francisco, and caused great excitement, particularly among those connected with these colonies. Several vessels were immediately laid on for Sydney, and we may expect a large number of arrivals before the end of the year.'[4]

*

Thomas Berdue is free at last, and the due credit, he believes, belongs to his new best friends – the vigilantes. Committee members have given evidence that Jim Stuart assumed the guilt for the Jansen assault and robbery, exonerating Berdue and William Windred.

The judge, advised that Berdue is penniless, suggests that gentlemen present dig deep into their pockets for his benefit. Jansen offers to return the money taken from Berdue when he was arrested, and Vigilance Committee members take up a collection for him. It amounts to $302.

In gratitude, Berdue places the following notice in a newspaper:

'I have kindly to thank those gentlemen for what they have done for me; for certainly, through their vigilance and the kind providence of Almighty God, they succeeded in capturing the criminal for whom I have suffered so much.'[5]

Thomas Berdue will soon be penniless again. He will lose all the money donated to him in a mining venture that goes bust, and will petition the California State Legislature for $4000 compensation for injuries sustained during his wrongful imprisonment. His petition will fail, and, while some say he was last sighted working as a monte dealer in a waterfront saloon, others claim he was seen soon after his release boarding a ship for parts unknown.

The truth is that Thomas Berdue will make his way back to Australia, return to Windsor where he will make a modest but comfortable living as a storekeeper, marry for a second time, and die peacefully in his sleep on 7 February 1898 at the age of 79.

Chapter 33

Better angels

While the vigilantes' campaign to eradicate the Sydney Coves continues, their treatment of non-Australian miscreants shows that the quality of their mercy is strained.

Lately, rather than calling in the police, San Franciscans who believe they have been victims of crime prefer to make a citizen's arrest and drag the accused person to vigilante headquarters for judgement. And the suspects, unless they hail from Sydney Valley, tend to get a fair hearing.

The committee's verdict on Samuel Church is a case in point. Church, an army deserter and known horse thief, is accused by Lieutenant George Derby – an army engineer and author of popular fiction – of stealing his favourite saddle horse. Derby provides a string of witnesses testifying as to Church's guilt, and – fine wordsmith that he is – delivers an eloquent argument for the death penalty in this case.

Derby, who declares that Sam Church is a dangerous criminal who deserves nothing less than the noose, is apoplectic when the vigilantes find Church guilty but deliver him not to the hangman but to the military authorities, where the most severe punishment he can expect is a flogging.

Another army deserter, a Private Howard, is sent back to his post, where his commanding officer can decide his fate. Similarly, a sailor who jumped ship in San Francisco is returned to his vessel for the judgement of his captain, even though the sailor is a convicted murderer who escaped from prison in Panama. He is returned to Panama to serve out his sentence on the chain gang.

The committee reasoned that 'it would be contrary to equity that he should be punished by us in the absence of all proof, and for crimes beyond our jurisdiction'.[1]

It seems the men who so eagerly strung up four Australians have forgotten that in the eyes of the law they have no jurisdiction.

When foul play is suspected in the death of a former Mexican magistrate and prosperous landowner, Don Francisco Guerrero, apparently thrown from his horse on the Mission Road, the vigilantes track down and arrest his alleged killer, a Frenchman named François le Bras. The word is that le Bras, who is reputedly not the sharpest *outil* in the *cabanon*, has been used as a dupe by land speculators with greedy eyes on Guerrero's property.

Although a coroner's inquest finds that le Bras killed Guerrero by striking him on the head, the committee, having been convinced by the French consul that le Bras is innocent, refuse to hand him over to the proper authorities, defying even a writ of habeas corpus. A week later, however, after gathering evidence in defence of the Frenchman, the vigilantes deliver him to Sheriff Jack Hays, confident that at trial he will be acquitted. He is.

When the battered body of Thomas Wheeler is found on the Mission Road, William Jones, an influential citizen and brother-in-law of the victim's former employer, Colonel Fremont, appeals to the vigilantes for help.

Jones is surprised to learn that the committee already has two suspects in custody. As luck would have it, Sam Brannan happened to be in the vicinity of the crime a short time after the discovery of the body, and noticed two riders acting suspiciously. On being approached by Brannan, they bolted into the scrub. Brannan spurred his horse, gave chase, caught up with the fleeing duo and arrested them at gunpoint.

Yet even though Sam Brannan's Wild-West-style capture of the suspects promises to be a public relations coup for the vigilantes, the men are tried by the committee, found not guilty and set free.

Young Daniel Jenks, who stole $1000 from a man at Jacksonville, is dragged before a mass meeting in that town, where the good citizens vote in favour of flogging.

Jenks does not suffer the lash, however. Instead, he is sent to San Francisco where the Vigilance Committee, informed that the young man had previously been of good character, and assuming that the theft was a first offence, dismisses the charge with no punishment.

John Williams is languishing in the county gaol, convicted of assault with intent to kill. But then, at the instigation of Sheriff Hays, the Vigilance Committee petitions Governor McDougall, claiming that Williams acted in self-defence. The governor concurs and the prisoner is set free.

On the advice of Norman Ah Sing, a prominent member of San Francisco's Chinese community, the vigilantes arrest four Chinese men and one Chinese woman, Ah Toy, charged with keeping a bawdy house. Ah Toy, renowned for her beauty, is the madam of the establishment and the most famous Chinese prostitute in San Francisco. She is also the richest, thanks to her string of brothels and her famous peep shows, which offer punters a quick glimpse of her naked body for an ounce of gold.

The committee has all but decided to deport the prisoners to China when something rather curious happens. Selim Woodworth, a wealthy merchant and president of the general committee, intercedes on behalf of the accused, announcing himself as a 'Mandarin of the Celestial Empire and Chinese Counsel' – grand titles he has bestowed upon himself in recognition of his involvement in the importation of cheap Chinese labour.

Woodworth argues that the charge against the four accused is nothing more than a conspiracy to deprive them of their liberty. His fellow vigilantes are convinced, and the four are released.

The truth of the matter is that Woodworth, entranced by the beautiful Ah Toy – like half the men in San Francisco – is desperate to stymie attempts by Norman Ah Sing to have her repatriated to China. Ah Sing, leading a moral mission to end the shame of prostitution in his community, had tried to gain guardianship of Ah Toy through the city courts but was told it was impossible to exclude Ah Toy from 'the tolerance granted by the police of San Francisco to a thousand women at least – American, French, German and Spanish'.[2]

An appeal to the Vigilance Committee was Ah Sing's last resort, and history will hear no more of him. Selim Woodworth will win the praise of President Lincoln for his bravery as a naval commander during the Civil War, father 11 children and die peacefully in San Francisco in 1871. Ah Toy, the pay-per-view odalisque of so many men's fancy, will go back to China – voluntarily this time – as a wealthy woman, but will eventually return to California to live quietly and in comfort until her death in San Jose in 1928 – just short of her hundredth birthday.

Chapter 34

A scattering of Coves

There is a dark cloud over Sydney Valley. Long Jim is dead. Sam Whitaker and Bobby McKenzie are dead, all hanged like poor Johnny Jenkins before them. Jimmy from Town is breaking rocks, and even Dutch Charley has flown the coop. Of the rest, those who haven't been shipped back to the colonies, whether they like it or not, have scattered to the four winds. It's over.

The hunt continues for gangsters on the run. Acting on information in Jim Stuart's confession, former port warden Belcher Kay is arrested in Sacramento but somehow convinces his captors to grant him one night's parole. Declaring his faith in merciful vigilante justice, he writes to the Vigilance Committee:

'Being informed that certain grave charges have been preferred against me by the man Stuart, and that you wish to try me on said charges, I now state that I am ready and willing to meet the same, and will voluntarily deliver myself up the moment you may send for me, trusting to your honour for a fair and impartial trial, and beg of you the favour to secure for me as counsel Alcalde [Mayor] Geary, Esq.'[1]

Having given his solemn word that he will surrender the next morning, Kay wastes no time doing the opposite. He slips quietly out of town disguised as an old woman, and returns to San Francisco.

There, while hiding out in Sydney Valley, Kay asks a friend, Captain William Thompson Jnr, to help save him from the vigilantes' noose. Asserting that in Sacramento Kay had been unlawfully imprisoned by the vigilantes, Thompson obtains a writ demanding that Sheriff Jack Hays produce Kay in court, and in the meantime take him into custody to protect him from the lynch mob.

When Kay gets his day in court, the case is dismissed on the grounds that the county cannot afford to lose a case of unlawful detention. The vigilantes stake out the gaol and the docks, but Kay manages to slip past them and take ship for Panama. He is last heard of as a member of a street gang in Valparaiso, Chile, in 1855.

Luck was with Belcher Kay in escaping San Francisco. Just a few days later, Sam Whitaker and Robert McKenzie were singing like birds, and Kay's name was prominent in a litany of crimes.

Like Belcher Kay, Edwards, Osman, Briggs, Morgan and Hughes manage to escape arrest and flee the city. When word reaches the committee that the fugitives have boarded a ship in San Diego, bound for Panama, an attempt is made to arrest them when the ship calls into Mazatlan, in Mexico, but the vigilantes arrive too late. Come October, rumour has it that the five ex-Coves have returned to San Francisco, but either the rumour is false or once again they have avoided capture.

Of 86 people incriminated in the statements of Stuart, Whitaker and McKenzie, 21 are ex-convicts. Most of the gang are free men from Sydney and Hobart. Three have been hanged and 15 imprisoned by the Committee of Vigilance, and the remainder, apart from those who have escaped, consent to being sent back to Australia on the condition that they make a full and frank confession. The only alternative, their interrogators impress upon them, is the noose.

Within a few weeks, the crime rate has plummeted, the police and courts are pursuing wrongdoers with renewed vigour, making sure justice is seen to be done, Sydney Valley is all but deserted and the Committee of Vigilance, having served its purpose, is considering disbanding.

Jimmy from Town, serving ten years' imprisonment, and George 'Jack Dandy' Adams, given 20 years, are kept busy by Sheriff Hays renovating his gaol – Jimmy mixing mortar and Adams wielding a shovel.

In January 1852 Jimmy from Town escapes but is soon recaptured. In May, he tries again, along with Adams. Both are recaptured and flogged, and Jimmy is transferred to the new state prison at San Quentin. In 1854, he and five other inmates break out of San Quentin and are never seen again.

Under Senator David Broderick's patronage, Dutch Charley enjoyed a licence to do as he pleased. Brutal assaults on citizens went unpunished or earned him a fine of a few dollars; likewise his brawling and riotous behaviour in the gambling dens of Sydney Valley.

When a police officer tried to arrest him for shooting a dog that bit him, narrowly missing an innocent bystander, Dutch Charley beat the officer almost to death, but was fined just $100.

And when, in a saloon, Amedee Fayolle, the actor-manager of a touring French troupe, pointed him out as the man who had earlier entered the Adelphi Theatre without a ticket and assaulted two of the staff, Dutch Charley knocked him to the floor and kicked him in the head. As Fayolle struggled to his feet, Dutch Charley drew his revolver and shot the Frenchman in the back, shouting, 'The son of a bitch has got a pistol!'[2]

Fayolle, who was unarmed, was badly wounded but survived, and although Dutch Charley was charged with attempted murder, his trial was aborted when Fayolle failed to appear. The word was that David Broderick had paid the actor handsomely to leave town in a hurry.

Dutch Charley's luck ran out after he assaulted Frank Ball, a member of the Vigilance Committee. Although he was arrested and sentenced to a year in prison, Broderick persuaded Governor John McDougall to overturn the conviction. McDougall, an avowed and vocal opponent of the vigilantes, granted Dutch Charley a full pardon. The committee, not to be outdone, offered Charley an ultimatum: leave San Francisco and live, or stay and be hanged.

Well aware that not even Broderick could save him from the lynch mob, Dutch Charley took ship for Central America.

William Windred, who escaped to Australia, and whose actual name was Joseph Windred, died a wealthy and well-respected man on 13 January 1901.

His obituary reads: 'On Sunday last, at the residence of his nephew (Mr G. Windred), West End, the above old and popular gentleman breathed his last. Mr Windred had almost attained the age of 79 years, and had remained in these parts for a lengthy period. He was a man whose word was his bond, and his generosity was always an embargo to his amassing wealth.

'He was a native of Windsor, and a fine stamp of the natives of that historic settlement.'[3]

Not so much an obituary as a hagiography, an article on Windred's life and times in the *Windsor and Richmond Gazette*, on 26 January, includes what is presumably Windred's own version of events in California:

'Mr Joseph Windred was, in his youth, as fine a specimen of manhood as one could wish to see. He was a magnificently built man, of towering height and splendid proportions, with the one unfortunate drawback of having a maimed foot, which, though a disfigurement, seemed to be of no serious impediment to his movements until later years. He belonged to the older type of white native who flourished some 40 or 50 years ago in the Hawkesbury district, where physical prowess was esteemed more highly than mental gifts or intellectual accomplishments.

'He belonged to that old school of Australians who believe that the proper reply to an insult was a blow, and the right punishment of the wrongdoer was physical chastisement, and those who dared to insult or injure him had reason to repent their conduct. Like most fearless men, he was the last man to provoke a conflict but there was a limit to his forbearance. When the discovery of gold took place in California in 1848, like thousands of others, Mr Windred went to try his luck on the rich "placer" goldfields, where gold was got almost as easily as it was in later years at Bendigo and Forest Creek and other Victorian goldfields in the fifties. He arrived at San Francisco when the gold fever was at its height and when in lieu of any regularly constituted authority or legal rule the diggers established a Vigilance Committee, before which alleged offenders were tried in the most summary fashion and severely punished either by imprisonment, flogging, or by death for offences of an aggravated nature.

'While the Vigilance Committee acted as an effective check to crime and was a real terror to evil doers, unfortunately its hasty and reckless methods often led to the conviction of men innocent of the crimes they were accused for. Among the sufferers from the precipitate action of the Vigilance Committee Mr Windred was one of the innocent victims.'[4]

The article goes on to review at length the Jansen robbery, Windred's arrest and the mistaken identification of Thomas Berdue as Jim Stuart, and justifies the execution of Australians by a lynch mob as democracy in action. 'This was not a mob, but the people, in the highest sense of the term,' the *Gazette* declares. 'They wanted only a leader to advise and guide them to any undertaking that promised relief from the awful state of social danger and terror to which they were reduced.'[5]

A romantic version of Windred's escape from prison portrays a daring jailbreak 'due to the ingenuity, resourcefulness and daring of his wife'. Mary Windred, with her hair cut short and disguised as a man, aided by Samuel Whitaker, who the newspaper wrongly describes as the Chief of Police, gained entry into the prison with smuggled tools. Windred tunnelled under the prison wall and escaped, managed to elude capture, and was at last proved innocent of the crime.

The article's claim that, on news of the discovery of gold in New South Wales, Windred returned home to try his luck on the Australian diggings is at odds with Sam Whitaker's account of smuggling Windred aboard a ship leaving San Francisco for Sydney soon after the jailbreak.

The *Gazette* mentions that in the 1860s Windred was the proprietor of 'an orderly, well conducted hotel' at Lambing Flat (now Young, in south-western New South Wales). It does not mention that Windred's partner in the hotel was Jim Torpy, a leader of the miners, whose inflammatory speeches sparked anti-Chinese riots on the Lambing Flat diggings. In the summer of 1861, thousands of white miners who objected to the presence of Chinese miners on the goldfields attacked the Chinese camp, seriously injuring hundreds of Chinese diggers. Soldiers and police eventually quelled the violence, but the unrest continued for several months. The New South Wales government, reacting to public opinion, responded not by protecting Chinese miners from harassment and assault but by restricting Chinese immigration.

Around 1866, Windred moved to Orange, in the central west, where he became a pillar of the community – hotelier, auctioneer, stock and station agent, racehorse owner, town alderman and twice mayor, and a Justice of the Peace.

The article concludes, 'Mr Windred held strong opinions on everything, whether in politics, municipal matters, or on religion, and had no moral doubt as to the absolute soundness of his own peculiar views. He never even suspected that he might have formed wrong conclusions or that the other side might be right and his side wrong. He gave no quarter and asked for none.

'He acted according to his lights in everything, many of his undoubted weaknesses or deficiencies being due to unfavourable environments and lack of liberal education rather than to defective natural endowments. He was a kind-hearted and affectionate brother and a good son. He was married to one of the sweetest, gentlest, and most devoted of wives, and one of the handsomest women in Australia in her prime. They had no children.'[6]

Erased from Joseph Windred's life story was the four years he served in Van Diemen's Land, convicted of having robbed his own aunt, his known association with the Sydney Coves, and his boast, on returning to Australia, that after his escape from prison he started the Great San Francisco Fire.

Chapter 35

What goes around . . .

For more than a year Sam Brannan's body remained unclaimed in the San Diego Receiving Yard, yet there was a time when he was Mister California – 'King of the Gold Rush'.

In 1852, after the Vigilance Committee he had founded voted to quietly adjourn, its mission to eradicate the Sydney Coves accomplished, Sam Brannan chanced his hand at politics. As usual, he was successful. Elected a California State Senator in 1853, he became a notable mover and shaker in the corridors of power, always keeping an eye out for the main chance where his business interests were concerned. He was influential in developing trade deals with China and Mexico, founded banks, railroads and telegraph companies, and by the 1860s the man dubbed the richest man in California was even richer.

At about the same time it was noticed that Brannan was hitting the bottle rather heavily, not only affecting his health but making his famously short temper even shorter.

After a visit to the Napa Valley's hot springs, Brannan was inspired to build a resort there, reflecting the current fad for 'taking the waters' at spa resorts such as Bath in England and Saratoga Springs in New York. He bought land in the upper Napa Valley, in a canyon at the base of Mount St Helena, named it Calistoga – a combination of the words California and Saratoga – and set about building his spa resort and a railroad to bring tourists to it.

One Napa Valley resident, upset by the disturbance to his tranquility, protested by shooting Brannan in the hip. Left partially paralysed, he walked with a cane for the rest of his life, but that didn't stop him expanding his interests in the valley.

By 1870, with Calistoga a hit with the rich and fashionable, he had bought up more land to establish vineyards, a brandy distillery, a tea plantation and a thoroughbred horse stud. Meanwhile, he had convinced his estranged wife Ann Eliza, who preferred living in Paris, to return to America and live with him at Calistoga. It was a disastrous move, and in 1872 she divorced him, citing his increasingly violent drunken rages.

For Sam Brannan this was the beginning of the end. When the court ruled that Ann Eliza was entitled to half his holdings, payable in cash, totalling some half a million dollars, he was forced to liquidate his entire holdings. And most of his wealth was in property, sold off for cents in the dollar to pay the divorce settlement.

In the years to follow, whatever money Brannan had left slipped through his fingers, wasted on a series of bad investments, leaving him bankrupt. He died in Escondido, California, of inflammation of the bowel, on 5 May 1889, at the age of 70. Unable to pay for his own funeral, his body lay unclaimed for more than a year, until an anonymous benefactor paid for a gravestone. It reads,

'Sam Brannan, 1819–1889, California pioneer of '46. Dreamer, leader and empire builder.'[1]

Ann Eliza Brannan lived on until 1916, but, at the age of 93, she too died penniless, despite the fortune she acquired in the divorce settlement. Like her ex-husband, she lost it all on bad investments.

In the winter of 1872, as Captain Ned Wakeman, former marshal and hangman for the San Francisco vigilantes, lies on his deathbed in Brooklyn, flat broke and all but forgotten, his old friend Mark Twain makes a public appeal on his behalf.

In a letter to the *Daily Alta California*, Twain writes:

'Certain gentlemen here in the past have done me the honour to make me their mouthpiece in a matter which should command the interest and the sympathy of many Californians. They represent that the veteran Captain Ned Wakeman is lying paralysed and helpless at his home near your city, and they beg that his old friends on the Pacific Coast will do unto him as they would gladly do themselves if they were back now in San Francisco – that is, take the old mariner's case in hand and assist him and his family to the pecuniary aid they stand in such sore need of. His house is mortgaged for $5,000 and he will be sold out and turned shelterless upon the world in January unless this is done.

'I have made voyages with the old man when fortune was a friend to him, and am aware that he gave with a generous heart and willing hand to all the needy that came in his way; and now that twenty years of rough toil on the watery highways of the far West find him wrecked and in distress, I am sure that the splendid generosity which has made the name of California to be honoured in all lands, will come to him in such a shape that he shall confess that the seeds sowed in better days did not fall upon unfruitful soil.

'Will not some of the old friends of Captain Wakeman in your city take this matter in hand, and do by him as he would surely do by them were their cases reversed?

'Very truly yours,

'Mark Twain

'Hartford, December 3, 1872'[2]

Ned Wakeman dies at his home a week later, leaving a wife, Mary, and five children. His obituary praises him as 'generous to a fault, single-minded and pure-hearted', recalling his adventures at sea, and that 'during the stormy days of the Vigilantes, Captain Wakeman acted as Marshal of the organisation, and was presented with an immense satin banner, inscribed with their mottoes, on the occasion of his leaving upon the steamer *New Orleans* for Australia.'[3]

If any of the captain's 'old friends' answered Mark Twain's plea to rescue his family from penury, history does not record.

At his Cow Hollow ranch on 11 August 1895, two days after the suicide of his 'niece' Fanny Weller, who was actually his illegitimate daughter, Frank Pixley died of liver failure.

His obituary lauds an impressive list of achievements by a New York farm boy who in 1848 rode to California on a mule: City Attorney of San Francisco; Attorney-General of California; Civil War correspondent who posed as a US senator so that he could ride with General Ulysses S. Grant, who became a lifelong friend; crusading editor and founder of *The Argonaut* newspaper; appointee to seats on various boards and commissions; successful real estate speculator; patron of the arts; much admired bon vivant and lavish entertainer; quietly generous philanthropist; and founder of a town that bears his name – Pixley, California.

'Recently, Mr Pixley began to feel the advance of years,' his obituarist writes, 'and the strain upon his energies was so strong that he decided to retire from active work in journalism. So he sold his interest in *The Argonaut*, and since then the journal has ceased to be a reflex of the rugged opinions of its founder.'[4]

Frank Pixley's 'rugged opinions' showed that he shared many of the prejudices of his day. He was virulently anti-Chinese, opposing their further entry into California for fear that continued Asian immigration could overwhelm white majority rule in the state.

'They cannot intermarry [with whites],' he declared, 'but are thoroughly antagonistic in every particular, in race, colour, language, religion, civilisation and habits of life altogether different from our people.'[5]

Pixley held a similarly low opinion of African-Americans. He had no objection to slavery as long as blacks stayed down south and did not spread west into California.

These being mainstream views, it's hardly surprising that his obituary makes no mention of them. It would be quite a surprise indeed, though, if it had mentioned his most controversial achievement in San Francisco: the defence attorney who narrowly avoided being lynched after refusing to identify his client, the outlaw Jim Stuart.

Chapter 36

Showgirls and charlatans

Robert Collyer, the showman and quack known as the *Model Artistes* Man because of his popular nudie show at the Athenaeum Theatre, has whipped up a new act. Since the Athenaeum burnt down in the Great Fire of 1851 he has reinvented himself as an expert in the pseudoscience of phrenology. That is, he claims he can determine people's abilities and character traits by examining the bumps on their heads, and is more than willing to demonstrate this amazing technique to a paying audience.

Phrenology is not the self-styled 'Doctor' Collyer's first venture with scientific snake oil. Previously, he had toured the country lecturing on the phenomenon of 'mesmeric suspension' – the ability to keep a dying person alive indefinitely by putting them in a hypnotic trance.

Collyer's interest in mesmeric suspension was inspired by an article in the December 1845 edition of *American Review*, written by Edgar Allan Poe. In 'The Facts in the Case of M. Valdemar', Poe describes an experiment in which a scientist who hypnotises a dying friend discovers that his friend, rather than waking in a few moments, as is usual, remains suspended in a trance for seven months.

Collyer, then a travelling stage hypnotist, dashed off a letter to the *Broadway Journal*, supporting the findings in the experiment reported by Poe, and claiming to have taken the experiment a step – or rather, a giant leap – forward.

'Your account of M. Valdemar's Case has been universally copied in this city and has created a very great sensation,' he wrote. 'It requires from me no apology in stating that I have not the least doubt of the possibility of such a phenomenon, for I did actually restore to active animation a person who died from excessive drinking of ardent spirits.'[1]

Robert Collyer, while claiming the divine ability to raise the dead, was peculiarly unable to tell fact from fiction. Edgar Allan Poe's article was an evident work of fiction. While written in the dry style of a medical report and laced with mock-scientific jargon, its macabre subject matter was pure Poe. After his *Broadway Journal* letter appeared, Collyer, an overnight laughing stock, abandoned mesmerism, and, while making a relatively honest living delighting audiences with his troupe of nude models, studied phrenology in his spare time.

A quack he may be, but 'Doctor' Collyer is a consummate showman. At the close of one of his lectures in the South, he called on anyone among the audience who fancied having their skull examined to come to the stage. A big burly fellow volunteered, sat on a chair onstage, and Collyer, after measuring the bumps on his head, announced, 'Sir, your phrenological developments are those which belong only to an infamous villain – destructiveness and combativeness enormous, conscientiousness very small, and all the moral and reflective regions perfectly contemptible. You only lack opportunity to become a rascal.'

With that, the enraged man leapt to his feet and struck Collyer a mighty blow, knocking him to the floor.

'Ladies and gentlemen,' cried Collyer, bouncing to his feet. 'There is the strongest proof of the truth of phrenology I have ever seen in the entire course of my career. The villain has proved every word I told him to be the truth.'[2]

In September of 1851, a card is delivered to vigilante headquarters. Addressed to 'The President and Members of the Executive Committee of the Vigilance Committee of San Francisco', it is an invitation to a lecture titled 'The Anatomy of Crime' to be delivered the following evening by Robert Collyer, and demonstrated with the skulls of Jim Stuart, Sam Whitaker, Robert McKenzie and John Jenkins.

'Should you feel interested in the physiology and philosophy of the causes of mental action which prompted these men to pursue an evil course in life,' Collyer writes, 'I will be most happy for you to accept an invitation, which I now tender to you, to form part of my audience.'[3]

It's not known how many of the Executive Committee accepted the invitation, if any. While it is not uncommon or illegal in the 1850s for the bodies of executed criminals to be procured for scientific study, most Americans, even Californian lynch mobs, find the very idea of grave robbing repulsive.

Curiously, Collyer's lecture is not reported in the press. Perhaps no one showed up.

Chapter 37

Turnabout

Americans have been told, in no uncertain terms, that they are not welcome Down Under. When the world learns, in 1851, that Australia's goldfields at Ballarat, Bendigo and Castlemaine, in Victoria, are the richest ever found, the exodus from Australia to California slips into reverse. Unfortunately for the first Americans joining the Australian gold rush, their arrival coincides with news of the lynchings in San Francisco and the culture of violence spreading throughout the state. As a result, newcomers from California, however innocent, are tarred with the vigilante brush.

'Anarchy, murder, and every other crime continue to rage at California,' the *Sydney Morning Herald* wails, not for the first or the last time, 'and in addition to her internal foes, the State begins to tremble for the consequences of her outrages upon foreigners. That she will have a serious reckoning to answer with Great Britain there now remains no question. France is about to prefer a heavy claim for goods confiscated on pretence of the State's revenue laws not having been complied with by French merchants, and the

Government had received notice from Chihuahua that claims to the amount of $20 million for damages done to Mexican property, by the Indians from the side of the Rio Grande, have been filed with Mexican authorities for presentation to the central Government under the treaty which provides that the United States shall prevent Indian depredations. Thus it would seem that, for California, a fearful day of retribution was at hand.'[1]

The *Herald* follows up with what it calls 'a catalogue of the most frightful events':

A gunfight between the men of rival mining companies, at Colonia, leaves 11 killed and many more wounded.

The *Herald* notes that the *Alta California*, reporting the carnage, matter-of-factly observes that 'the long disputes between the two companies are said to have occasioned this murderous strife'.[2]

Miners' murderous contempt for Indians is revealed in an account by a recent visitor to northern California, who observes that 'the miners always kill the Indians whenever an opportunity presents, but they cannot spend the time necessary to follow them to their strongholds in the mountains, and thus hundreds of the rascals unfortunately escape'.[3]

And of Indians who do not escape, a typical report:

'This evening another party of 15 men, who started out some few days since, commanded by Captain B. F. Harvey, returned from an Indian hunt. Captain Harvey informs me that this morning, about 9 o'clock, he made an attack upon some 800 Pitt River Indian, on this side of the Sacramento, some 20 miles from this place.

'A warm fire immediately commenced, and was kept up for some considerable time, during which time some 60 or 70 were killed, and a large number mortally wounded. The party captured and brought in four squaws, and one young child about six years old.

'This morning, 150 men, well armed, left for Pitt River, and all other parts of the country where the Indians are to be found.'

And another:

'Captain Harvey and company returned from an Indian hunt yesterday evening. The Captain informs me that on the morning of the 1st instant, he made an attack on a Ranchería, killing some 50 Indians, and wounding many more. He captured and brought in some six or eight prisoners.

'Our town is nightly infested by these troublesome hombres, who, no doubt, are after their wives and children we hold as prisoners.'[4]

And yet another:

'Some short time since a man was brutally murdered by a digger, with an axe. He was in the employ of James Maclay Esq., cutting hay some 16 miles from this place.

'A party of 15 men was immediately headed by Mr Maclay, who pursued him to a rancho where a large body of Indians had collected for the purpose of making an attack on the whites, upon which a hot fire immediately commenced and kept up for some two hours, killing some 20 of their number and wounding as many more. The party brought in three captives.'[5]

Sydney's self-declared voice of the people, the *Empire* newspaper, rails against the 'degenerate, dechristianised, disglorified miscreants who have so fearfully shamed the noble nations of their birth by their fiendish deeds of blood in the city of San Francisco.

'Let it be seen that the white savages of California can find no resting place under an Englishman's roof, no shelter but the gaol or the madhouse.'[6]

Suggesting that American gold-seekers should be prevented from even stepping ashore, the *Empire* thunders: 'Let no door be opened to receive these blood-stained wretches if they dare to plant their unholy feet on our soil. Let them be driven back from our shores by a tempest of scorn and shame which shall flame and hiss, with insatiable fury, in their memory ever afterwards.'[7]

By November of 1851, tempests of scorn and shame notwithstanding, at least two have managed to plant their unholy feet on Australian soil, judging by this report in the *Herald*:

'Complaints have been received that two men, who claim to be fresh from the San Francisco goldfields, have sold respectable citizens in various parts of the colony bricks that they claim are pure gold.

'After the men receive their price they invariably make themselves scarce, and are out of the district by the time their dupes discover that the "gold" is a mere coating on base metal.'[8]

By 1854 some 1000 Americans have made their way to Ballarat, Australia's richest goldfields, where they will make their mark on Australian history. There, trouble is brewing over a move by Victoria's governor, Sir Charles Hotham, to enforce the collection of licensing fees from miners. Until now, the fees – £2 for three months – have been easily evaded, and the imposition of the system, and the heavy-handed approach of the police checking licences – now several times a day instead of once a month – is the cause of dark mutterings among the diggers.

The spark that will ignite the famous battle of the Eureka Stockade, fought on Sunday 3 December 1854, is not confrontation over the hated licences but the murder of James Scobie, one of two drunken Scotsmen who cause an altercation at the Eureka Hotel, in Ballarat, by trying to break in after hours. The publican, James Bentley, throws them out, but, incensed by an insult Scobie has hurled at his wife, grabs a shovel and pursues the pair, joined by his wife and two friends. While Scobie's mate, Peter Martin, manages to flee, Scobie is knocked to the ground and repeatedly kicked, and next morning is found dead in the street.

When a coroner's inquest into Scobie's death fails to indict James Bentley and the others for murder, and it is discovered that Bentley, the coroner, and the gold commissioner in charge of issuing mining licences are regular drinking companions, an Irish digger named Peter Lalor organises a protest meeting.

On 17 October, at the spot where James Scobie was killed, up to 5000 miners gather to condemn the coroner's verdict and call for democratic reforms such as universal suffrage and secret ballots. They form an association, the Ballarat Reform League, to advocate for their rights, and Peter Lalor – eloquent, well-educated and a commanding presence – is elected leader. No one calls for lynch law – not even the Californians present, who have yet to live down a reputation for taking the law into their own hands – and the meeting ends peacefully.

But the peace is shattered soon afterwards when fighting breaks out between a crowd of miners and mounted troopers sent to guard the Eureka Hotel. Insults and curses are exchanged, a rock is thrown, then a barrage of rocks, escalating into a full-scale riot as the crowd rampages through the hotel.

The troopers, with sabres drawn, manage to push the miners back, but are themselves forced outside when a fire breaks out in an adjoining bowling alley. The fire soon rages out of control and the Eureka Hotel burns to the ground.

Governor Hotham, determined to put these fractious miners firmly in their place, sends to Ballarat hundreds of extra police, soldiers, and even artillery. He is equally determined to prosecute the ringleaders of the riot, and while four are identified, only three – miners Henry Westerby, Thomas Fletcher and Andrew McIntyre – are indicted. The man not charged, John Kelly, is an American, freed by Governor Hotham at the request of James Tarleton, the United States consul.

Kelly is not the only American known to have taken part in the riot, yet in a letter dated 24 October, from Tarleton to Hotham, Tarleton assures Hotham that 'the Americans did not participate in the late riot at Ballarat, but, on the contrary, the bowling saloon that was burnt belonged in part to an American.

'The riot was got up, and the prime movers were Scotchmen, as the murdered man was one of their countrymen.

'I am happy in hearing, and believing, and thus informing your Excellency of this good account of my countrymen, and I hope and trust their future conduct may be such as to entitle them to the high position of law-loving and law-abiding citizens.'[9]

Hoping to defuse the situation, Governor Hotham grudgingly concedes to an inquiry into the Scobie killing, and, finding that the trial of Scobie's alleged murderers was a farce, as the miners claimed, has James Bentley and his accomplices re-arrested and tried for murder. All three are convicted and sentenced to three years' hard labour, but that does little to ease tensions because, at the same time, Westerby, Fletcher and McIntyre are given the same sentence for burning down the Eureka Hotel.

The diggers, outraged, threaten armed insurrection if the three men are not released, and when Hotham refuses, and, after meeting a delegation, also refuses to make concessions on licence fees, posters appear around the goldfields inviting all diggers and residents of Ballarat to a mass rally on Bakery Hill on 29 November, calling for 'the immediate abolition of the licence fee and the speedy attainment of the other objects of the Ballarat Reform League'.[10]

At that rally, more than 10,000 people watch as a new flag is raised – a white cross with a star at each corner and another in the centre, representing the Southern Cross, on a dark blue field. The designer of the Eureka Flag – an Australian icon in the true sense of the word – is 27-year-old Henry Ross, captain of a group of well-armed Canadians fresh from the California goldfields and spoiling for a fight.

As diggers march from Bakery Hill to a hastily built wooden stockade on the Eureka Lead, Ross carries the flag before them, and raises the standard on a flagpole at the stockade. There, entreated by Peter Lalor, a thousand voices declare: 'We swear by the Southern Cross to stand truly by each other and fight to defend our rights and liberties,' punctuated by a thunderous, 'Amen!'[11]

A fight is surely coming, but as the waiting game drags on, discipline slackens off and diggers come and go. Of those who stay at their posts, some, such as Henry Ross's Canadians, are equipped with rifles and pistols, but many have only picks and shovels – and all of them are on edge, nervously awaiting the inevitable attack.

Then, at about 4 pm on Saturday, a large company of men is spotted advancing towards the stockade. Miners' leader Fred Vern cries out, 'Here they are coming, boys! Now I will lead you to death or victory!'[12]

Vern's battle cry is somewhat premature. The advancing company is the Independent California Rangers Revolver Brigade, a group of ex-Californian gold-rush diggers led by a 21-year-old

Bostonian named James McGill. Many are hardened veterans of the Mexican War, and certainly look the part.

One of Peter Lalor's captains, the flamboyant Italian poet and adventurer Raffaello Carboni, who is calmly frying a steak on a campfire when the rangers enter the stockade, later recalls, 'I should say they numbered a couple of hundred, looking Californian enough, armed with a Colt's revolver of large size, and many had a Mexican knife at the hip.'[13]

'James McGill is of the breed on the other side of the Pacific,' Carboni writes. 'He is thought to have been educated in a military academy, and certainly he has the manners of a young gentleman of our days. He is rather short, not so much healthy-looking as wide-awake. "What's up?" is his motto.

'This colony will sober him down, and then he will attend more to "What's to be done?" His complexion bears the stamp of one born of a good family, but you can read in the whites of his eyes, in the colouring of his cheeks, in the paleness of his lips, that his heart is for violence.'[14]

On Sunday morning, just before dawn, the diggers awake to a barrage of gunfire and the sound of a bugle. As men rush to the barricades there comes a second fusillade from redcoats and police advancing up the gully west of the stockade.

The battle is only minutes old and the diggers, awaiting orders from Lalor or his captains, have yet to fire a shot.

One man does not wait, however. Robert Burnette, of the California Rangers, steps forward, raises his rifle, takes aim and fires the first shot of the Eureka Rebellion. His bullet finds its mark, fatally wounding a redcoat officer.

With that, the soldiers and police charge the stockade in a fog of musketry. Defending companies of diggers, including Ross's Canadians, Vern's riflemen and the Californian Revolver Brigade, return fire but are soon surrounded and overwhelmed.

Henry Ross is among the first to fall. Defending the flag he created, sword in hand, he is shot in the groin and lies dying at the foot of the flagpole. It will all be over in 15 minutes, with Peter Lalor wounded, the flag torn down and jubilant soldiers shooting and bayoneting diggers even after they surrender. The day is lost.

'The wounded on the ground behind must have numbered a dozen,' Carboni writes. 'There was, however, a brave American officer, who had the command of the rifle pit men. He fought like a tiger, was shot in his thigh at the very onset, and yet, though hopping all the while, stuck to Captain Ross like a man.'[15]

Unfortunately, Carboni was unable to learn the name of that brave American officer, so we may never know who it was. However, we know for certain who it was not. It was not James McGill, leader of the Independent California Rangers Revolver Brigade.

On the eve of the battle, after being delivered a message by an American doctor suspected by Carboni of being an agent for US Consul Tarleton, McGill left the stockade, taking two-thirds of his brigade with him, claiming he planned to intercept redcoat reinforcements on their way to Ballarat from Melbourne.

That left only 150 men, including the remaining Californians, to oppose a force of 276 soldiers and police. Some have since speculated that if the entire Revolver Brigade had stayed to fight the outcome of the battle might have been different.

Curiously, McGill did not head east towards Melbourne but north towards the mining town of Creswick, 20 kilometres from

Ballarat. At Creswick, a Mrs Sarah Hanmer of his acquaintance gave him access to her wardrobe. Dressed as a woman, McGill boarded a Cobb and Co coach bound for Melbourne, passing the troops bound for Ballarat on the way. Apparently, he was so convincing as a female that a young gentleman travelling on the same coach proposed marriage. In Melbourne, McGill went into hiding until pardoned by Governor Hotham, ostensibly because of his youth.

James McGill, condemned by veterans of the battle as a traitor to the cause, will never shake off the taint. He returns to Ballarat, makes a small fortune in mining interests, loses his fortune through poor business decisions, takes to the bottle and leaves Ballarat a ruined man.

On his death in 1883, his obituary in the *Ballarat Courier* states, 'Like too many others of his class, he sought consolation for his misfortune in the "flowing bowl", and his face gradually got to be as familiar in the hotels of Melbourne as it had once been in the main road of the Golden City. Recently he had been living at Sandridge [now Port Melbourne] where he died on Sunday last, his end having probably been somewhat accelerated by the habits of "nipping" which had unfortunately taken possession of him.'[16]

On 4 December, the day after the battle at the Eureka Stockade, James Tarleton sent Governor Hotham the following note: 'I have no hesitation in saying that there are not any Americans engaged in this affair, and they all know my sentiments.'[17]

The same day, the governor's private secretary dashed off a poisonously polite reply: 'The Lieutenant-Governor desires me to say he is sorry to inform you that the leader of this movement is a young American. He has seen a person who is just arrived from Ballarat, who was in the insurgents' camp. He saw this person, and says he is their most active leader.

'His Excellency regrets to be compelled to give you this information.'[18]

So who was this young American leader? It's doubtful that it was the brave young Ranger whom Carboni spoke of. If he had been an active leader, surely Carboni would have known him.

It might have been James McGill, who unlike Lalor, Carboni and others, did not hope for a peaceful solution, and was among the loudest sabre-rattlers at the stockade. That is, before he fled the fight.

And perhaps it was Charlie Ferguson, the man McGill left in command of the Rangers. Ferguson, who fought courageously in the battle, and led the Californians in a desperate counterattack, was a San Franciscan forty-niner with a shady past, who arrived in Australia in 1852 aboard the *Don Juan*. Ferguson was not the only shady character on the *Don Juan*'s voyage from San Francisco. His fellow passengers included Australians deported by the Vigilance Committee.

'All, or nearly all, had been "old residents" of Van Diemen's Land – a few doubly convicted at that,' Ferguson writes in his memoir, *The Experiences of a Forty-Niner*.

'They had escaped from Van Diemen's Land upon the gold rush to California, but were now going back to the Victorian diggings for the reason that San Francisco was too hot for them. Besides, they were wise enough not to disregard the polite notice of the Vigilance Committee to leave the coast.

'Terrific were the threats they showered down upon us, our country, California, San Francisco and the Vigilance Committee, but we looked upon them with the contempt they deserved.'[19]

At about the same time Charlie Ferguson and the Australian deportees arrived in Sydney, news filtered through from California that two men, believed to be former Sydney Coves, had been lynched at Stockton, and that a Sydney man named Henry George, set to stand trial for forgery, had been dragged from his gaol cell and hanged.

These men would not be the last Australian outlaws to die violently in California. The last would go down in a blaze of glory, although the glory would not be their own.

Chapter 38

The man in the white hat

On a lonely trail through Rocky Canyon, in the Sierra Nevada foothills, on 19 December 1854, a band of desperadoes waits in ambush. Just yesterday, the outlaws bushwhacked four American miners, who they robbed and killed, and the day before that they murdered six Chinese miners. And they intend to do the same today, whenever some hapless travellers pass through the canyon and into their trap.

There are 14 men in this outlaw band – a Frenchman, two Americans, two Englishmen, four Mexicans and five Australians. The Australians are former members of the Sydney Coves, still on the run three years after the gang's reign in San Francisco ended, and still armed and dangerous.

The outlaws don't have long to wait until their patience is rewarded. Three men are walking along the trail towards them. Their intended victims are gold prospectors Dr Bolivar Sparks of Mississippi, James McDonald of Alabama, and a man in a distinctive white hat, Captain Jonathan Davis of South Carolina.

The three men – all close friends – are on their way to work Sparks' claim some 40 kilometres to the north.

At a given signal the outlaws dash out of the brush, guns blazing. James McDonald is shot dead before he can even draw his revolver, and Dr Sparks manages to get off two shots before he falls, badly wounded. That leaves just one man, Jonathan Davis, against 13 – hopeless odds.

What is about to happen puts the legendary fight at the OK Corral, in Tombstone, Arizona, in the shade. Captain Davis is armed with a pair of Colt revolvers and a bowie knife, and he knows how to use them. A veteran of the Mexican War, and an expert marksman and swordsman, he fought in many of the bloodiest battles, often in desperate hand-to-hand encounters, was twice wounded in action, and had seen many friends fall around him. Not this time.

In 'a fever of excitement'[1] as he will later state, he draws his pistols and rapidly returns fire. The outlaws' bullets strike him twice and rip through his clothes and his hat, but within seconds seven of them lie dead or dying on the ground, each shot in the head.

Davis's wounds are only minor but his guns are now empty, and four of the remaining outlaws are closing in on him with knives and a sword.

Warding off their blows, he stabs one to death and disarms another by knocking the knife out of his hand, slicing off the man's nose and a finger during the struggle.

Two more, already wounded by Davis, come at him. He later recalls, 'They came up with the rest, making warlike demonstrations by raising their knives in a striking posture, and I acted accordingly. I noticed that they handled them with very bad grace, but attributed it altogether to fright or natural awkwardness.'[2] With his bowie knife, he kills them both, and the remaining three flee for their lives.

Davis then removes his shirt and tears strips from it to bandage Sparks' wound and those of the outlaws. Sadly, his friend Bolivar Sparks, fatally wounded, will die a week later.

If true, what happened in Rocky Canyon is possibly the most remarkable gunfight in American history, yet to many the story seems far-fetched; a romanticised tale typical of the Wild West dime novels that have popularised the myth of the American gunfighter.

The sceptics are unimpressed even by the persuasive eyewitness account of three diggers from a nearby mining camp – John Webster, Isaac Hart and Peter Robertson.

In a letter to the Placerville County Surveyor, John Webster writes:

'Yesterday we had quite an exciting scene to happen within a mile of our tents. While two of my partners and myself were taking a hunt over the hills, we heard the report of guns below us, and saw two small parties shooting at each other. Convinced they were all strangers, we hesitated for a moment before we ventured down to them. A feeling of duty, however, soon prompted us to hasten down.

'On approaching, we saw two of a little party of three, who we had noticed following the trail unobserved, some half hour previous, fall in the fight, and the remaining one, a man somewhat above the medium height, who we could readily distinguish from all the rest by his white hat, fighting bravely for his life.

'Approaching still nearer, we were surprised at the sight of 11 men lying stretched upon the ground, seven of them dead, belonging, as they afterwards proved, to a party of robbers, and one only of the party of three so suddenly fired upon from the bushes by the robbers.

'Three of the wounded robbers having died last night, we had 10 of them to bury. One survives who will probably recover. He is marked however, for life, having lost his nose in toto, and the forefinger of his right hand. Seven of them were shot through the head.

'The surviving one, who seems to be but little hurt, says that their band was composed of two Americans, one Frenchman, five Sydney men and four Mexicans, and they had just commenced operations, having killed six Chinamen three days ago, and four Americans the day before yesterday.

'Although we counted 28 bullet holes in Captain Davis's hat and clothes, 19 through his hat, 11 through his coat and shirt, he received only two very slight flesh wounds.'[3]

Four days after the fight, the Placerville *Mountain Democrat* presents further confirmation of the veracity of Davis's story:

'We received the following startling intelligence last night after our paper had been worked off,' the newspaper reports. 'Rocky Canyon, the place of the tragedy, is a deep and almost inaccessible canyon, about 40 miles north of this place, near Todd's Valley, and uninhabited.'[4]

The report, from miners in the nearby camp, states, 'No officer having been within a convenient distance to attend to a case of emergency that has just happened near our isolated camp here, the undersigned constituted themselves a coroner's jury and held an inquest over the bodies of 12 men that were killed within a mile of our camp.

'Three of the undersigned [Webster, Hart and Robertson] were eye-witnesses of the whole scene, though too far off to give aid in any way, and the rest of us can readily vouch for their veracity.'[5]

The report goes on to describe the fight as seen by the three miners, who were out hunting on the side of a mountain above the canyon, confirming that Davis single-handedly killed seven of the outlaws and seriously wounded three.

'On examination of the persons of the deceased of those that commenced the attack on Captain Davis and party, we discovered papers, carefully concealed in their pockets, purporting to be a copy of laws and by-laws by which they were governed.

'The last of this band has just died. His wound he thought but slight and seemed in a fair way of recovery until within the last hour; had corroborated all the evidence proven by the papers in his pockets.'[6]

There is cause to wonder what kind of papers an outlaw might carry. Australian ex-convicts often carried parole or conditional pardon documents to prove they were free men or women, but the miners' report is frustratingly vague; neither does it identify any of the dead men, even though any papers they carried would surely have included their names.

The report concludes, 'We deem it due to state that from all the evidence before us, Captain Davis and his party acted solely in self defence.'[7] The report is signed by 17 miners from the camp.

Still, when the *Sacramento Daily Union* runs the story it prefaces it with an editor's note suggesting it is probably a fantasy, and, in an editorial titled 'The Eldorado slaughter', cannot resist a polite jibe at San Francisco's *Daily Alta California*:

'The *Alta*, in speculating upon the truthfulness of the rumour regarding the heroic exploits of Captain Davis at Rocky Canyon, says "the Sacramento papers give the story credence". Now, if the *Alta* includes this journal in the number, we respectfully inform it that abundant evidence to the contrary is furnished in our prefatory remarks to the detailed particulars of the transaction. It is not the first time that the Sacramento papers have indiscriminately been obliged to bear the onus of misstatements or erroneous opinions, which properly attach to a single journal.'[8]

Other newspapers are equally sceptical, prompting Jonathan Davis himself to attempt to settle the matter. In a letter to the editor of the *Mountain Democrat*, he writes:

'Though scarcely able to leave a bed of sickness, it may not be amiss that I should say a word or two relative to our fight with the robbers the other day. Hitherto, I have said as little of the matter as possible, lest any veracity should be doubted. And besides, it is a matter of indifference to me whether the world is inclined to believe it or not.

'Your paper of last Saturday has just been shown to me, and I see your remark that I "still persist in saying that every word of it is true". Of course I meant the general facts as published. Since then, the "white hat" has been sent down to me, and, after a more minute examination, I find that the party who published an account of it have erred in the number of bullet holes that passed through it. They must have counted all the holes where the balls came out of it, in their passage through the crown and brim of it, as well as where they entered. The miners have disfigured it very much by poking their fingers through the holes and tearing it, so that it is somewhat difficult to decide upon the number. I do not believe that over one-half of that number touched it. Having been in a fever of excitement at the time I did not examine it carefully, and took it for granted that they were right.'

In closing, he says in all modesty, 'I did only what hundreds of others might have done under similar circumstances, and attach no particular credit to myself for it.'[9]

The *Los Angeles Star* reprints Captain Davis's letter but adds an opinion piece dripping in vitriol, referring to Davis as 'the hero of the 27-bullet-and-11-men-slain story', and comparing him to the fictional Baron Munchausen, whose risible tales of his exploits included riding on a cannonball and flying to the Moon.

'If the whole affair be a humbug, a "sell", as fast people would call it, or a "lie" as slow folk would name it, the redoubtable Captain is pleased to persist in his statements,' sniffs the *Star*.

'There is nothing like sticking to a thing. Right or wrong – stick to it. Thus consistency and the admiration of others are gained. The *Democrat* says that Baron Munch . . . Captain Davis, we mean, has requested it to state that if there are any persons still sceptical, he, the Captain, stands prepared to take them to the spot where the fight took place and show them the graves of the robbers, as well as those of his unfortunate companions, Dr Sparks and Mr McDonald.'[10]

Much is made of the fact that the supposed eyewitnesses to the incident seem to have conveniently disappeared, and suspicious minds sense a hoax. However, the miners Webster, Hart and Robertson had left their camp to go prospecting deeper into the mountains. Out of contact with other diggers, they are unaware of the controversy until Bolivar Sparks' brother-in-law, after searching for several weeks, tracks them down. He tells them their account has been discredited and asks them to return to Placerville and confirm their story. They agree without hesitation.

And so, on 20 March 1855, the three miners are reunited with Jonathan Davis outside the office of the *Mountain Democrat* in Placerville. Invited within, they appear before the editor, a judge and a delegation of prominent citizens, and their declaration is unequivocal:

'In a word, we assert that every word we published in our statement of the fight, in your extra of the 23rd of December last, and the private letter published with it, written to Mr Henderson by one of the undersigned, is strictly true. Our sole object then was to state nothing but the simple truth, and we will ever be ready to verify it, even on our death beds.'[11]

At last the voices of doubt are silenced. Even the *Sacramento Daily Union* runs the story without comment. Captain Jonathan Davis, the fastest but humblest gun in the west, has been vindicated.

For all that, a mystery remains unsolved. There are no markers on the graves of those desperadoes buried without ceremony by the diggers at the mining camp. So who were they? Who were the Americans, the Mexicans, the Englishmen and the Frenchman? And the names of the five Australians – the last of the Sydney Coves to fall – can only be guessed at. Was Jimmy from Town one of them, his luck finally having run out, or Old Jack, Jimmy Briggs, Johnny Edwards, or any number of the Coves who disappeared without trace?

And if the wounded survivor was an Australian, it's likely that if ever he made his way back home he would have been a recognisable character for the rest of his life – the man with no nose.

Chapter 39

Unlucky last

The last Australian known to have been lynched by vigilantes in California is not a gangster, career criminal or ex-convict. Edward Crane Griffiths, a sailor, married with one child, has killed a man with an axe – a crime of passion according to Griffiths himself, but in the opinion of others a brutal, premeditated murder.

And, just a month after the gunfight at Rocky Canyon, one of the men who will decide Griffiths' fate is the man in the white hat, Captain Jonathan Davis.

On 21 January 1855, the *Daily Alta California* reports:

'The most diabolical murder which has ever come under our notice was perpetuated in Sonora last Thursday night, about 9 o'clock. Mr Joseph Heslep, Treasurer of Tuolumne County [in Sonora], was found weltering in blood on the floor of his office, situated on Hospital Street. Mr McBurney has been sleeping in the office of late at the request of Mr Heslep, who was alone.

'About 9 o'clock, Mr McBurney entered the building, and, finding no light, he called the name of Mr Heslep two or three times. Receiving no answer, he struck a light and found Mr Heslep lying on the floor all bloody, with life not yet entirely extinct.

'He immediately ran out and alarmed all the neighbours. As soon as the news spread, crowds gathered in the vicinity of the office, and consternation was depicted on every countenance. The feeling was that when so estimable a man as Mr Heslep became the victim of murderers, no-one in the community was safe.

'It was soon ascertained that the object of whoever perpetrated the deed was robbery – the safe in the office having been opened and emptied of its contents. The first impulse of the people was to hold a meeting, which accordingly took place, the result being the immediate dispatch of riders to all the ferries in Tuolumne, off to stop the egress from the county of any suspicious character.'[1]

A coroner's jury is convened to examine witnesses and gather information that might provide some clue as to the identity or whereabouts of the killer. Under the direction of a judge, the jury consists of 13 men, including Jonathan Davis.

The first witness called is the doctor who examined Joseph Heslep's body. He tells the jury: 'Eight wounds were found on the head of the deceased, done with an axe. The skull was broken on the crown and some of the brains were scattered on the door, and a blow had been inflicted on the left temple and another on the right temple, either of which was sufficient to have caused death.

'The face of the deceased was badly disfigured with wounds and the nose was broken. Not only was the head thus mangled, but more horrible still, the mouth, throat and nostrils were stuffed with paper – the very refinement of hardened villainy. This was done to prevent the deceased from making any noise.'[2]

One of the witnesses examined is the last person seen in the company of Joseph Heslep before his death, Edward Crane Griffiths. Griffiths, a 31-year-old seaman, arrived in San Francisco from Australia the previous November, and had come to Sonora bearing a letter of introduction to Joseph Heslep from Heslep's brother Augustus, a judge in San Francisco.

The judge, a charitable man, found Griffiths and his family destitute and had taken them into his home. Unable to find Griffiths a job, he sent him to see Joseph, hoping he might be able to help. Joseph, too, had befriended Griffiths, who has often been seen lately visiting the county treasurer's office.

The jury questions Griffiths, then calls him back twice more, and each time grows more suspicious of him. And when a search of his room at a boarding house finds in a carpet bag $6000 in gold and a pair of blood-stained trousers, he admits his guilt and makes a full confession.

'I first conceived of the murder last night,' Griffiths says. 'I asked Mr Heslep to loan me some money. He had a bag of money in his hand containing gold and silver, which he had taken from a partition in his desk.

'When I asked the deceased to loan me the money he refused. I then placed my hand upon the bag, with no intention of taking it, upon which he arose and struck me in the breast.

'My blood became aroused. I immediately picked up the axe and struck the deceased upon the temple, then struck him again two or three times while he was down. He continued to make a noise, and then I put the paper in his nostrils and mouth. I then took the bag and the key which he had in his hands, unlocked the safe and took the gold out of it. I replaced the key of the safe upon the table, blew out the light and left the house.'[3]

Griffiths insists he did not go to Heslep's office with murder in mind, or even robbery. 'When I placed my hand upon the bag I had no intention to take the money, but did it in more of a joke than anything else,' he says. 'I said to Mr Heslep, "You might as well lend me this."

'When I saw that I had killed him, I took the money, for then I thought that I could make the matter no worse. The paper which I put in his mouth I got from the table. Five minutes before doing it I had no idea of committing the act.'[4]

Edward Crane Griffiths is charged with murder and committed for trial, but within minutes of news of his arrest reaching the streets a mob of enraged citizens has gathered outside the building where the inquest is being held. In what has become a familiar scene in California, the crowd resolves to hang the accused man at daybreak the next morning, and a group of men volunteer to surround the building and keep watch throughout the night, just in case Sheriff Solomon tries to spirit the prisoner away to the safety of the town gaol. There are no dissenting voices.

During the night, Edward Griffiths writes a letter to his wife Mary Anne:

Sonora, January 19th, 1855.
My dearest wife,
Let not my fate shock or disturb you, for I die under a just sentence, and although the blow was struck in a moment of passion, I am nevertheless the more guilty, but ever loving husband,
E.C.G.[5]

As daylight approaches, he writes again:

Sonora, Friday, 6 A.M.

My dearest wife,

One hour more and I will cease to be as if I never was, but, thank God, I feel happy under my present circumstances, in firm reliance on that God who has so long protected me. I little thought, when last we parted, that it was forever, but my hopes are firm in our meeting again in another and a better world.

If my dying could but return my victim to life, what a source of happiness it would be! Pray for me, my dear Mary Anne, and strive to forget this dreadful affair. But you may depend that though black and bad looking, it was not premeditated.

The crowd are impatiently waiting for daylight and me, so forever farewell in this world, and that you may be happy is the last wish of your unfortunate and dying husband,

E.C.G.[6]

With the first streaks of daylight, the lynch mob returns in even greater numbers. Sheriff Perrin 'King' Solomon appeals to the crowd to observe law and order but he is wasting his breath. Solomon is an old soldier and not short of grit, but when he and his deputies attempt to escort Griffiths to the gaol, the mob surges and seizes the prisoner with little difficulty. If the man in the white hat had come to the sheriff's aid, given his reputation, it might have made a difference. But maybe Jonathan Davis simply wasn't there, or perhaps he was there but wasn't inclined to help.

And so, the inevitable happens. Edward Griffiths, surrounded by armed vigilantes, is marched to the edge of town and hanged from a tree.

The moral of the story, according to the murdered man's

brother, Judge Augustus Heslep, is that extending the hand of charity to a stranger is not worth the candle.

In California, still obsessed with the gunfight at Rocky Canyon, the lynching hardly rates a mention. The Australian press makes the appropriate clucking noises about yet another instance of American contempt for the rule of law.

And nobody gives a damn about Mary Anne.

Notes

Introduction: *Dos Eldorados*

1 *Holy Bible*, New International Version, 1 Kings 9:28

2 De Silva, J., *Letter to Urban VIII, 1623*, quoted in Estensen, M., *Discovery: the quest for the Great South Land*, Allen & Unwin, Sydney 1998, p. 88

3 Montalvo, *The Adventures of Esplandian*, quoted in Haslam, G. (ed.), *Many Californias: Literature from the Golden State*, second edition, University of Nevada Press, Reno and Las Vegas, 1999, pp. 131–33

4 Marshall, J. W., *Account of the discovery of gold in California*, quoted in *Hutchings' California Magazine*, vol. 2, 1858, p. 200

5 Ibid., p. 201

6 Trobits, M., *Antebellum and Civil War San Francisco*, The History Press, Charleston, 2014, p. 48

7 Hargraves, E. H., *Australia and its Goldfields*, H. Ingram and Co, London, 1855, p. 116

Chapter 1: A kind of mania

1 Russell, R., *A Dissertation Concerning the Use of Sea Water in Diseases of the Glands Etc.*, James Fletcher, Oxford, 1753, p. 7
2 Ibid., pp. 7–8

Chapter 2: 'What a great misfortune'

1 Sutter, J., 'The Discovery of Gold in California', *Hutchings' California Magazine*, Vol. 2, No. 17, November 1857, Hutchings and Rosenfield, San Francisco, p. 194
2 Ibid.
3 Ibid., p. 195
4 Ibid.
5 Ibid., p. 196
6 Ibid., p. 196
7 Sherman, W. T., *Personal Memoirs of General William Tecumseh Sherman*, 3rd ed., vol. 1, Charles I Webster & Company, New York, 1890, p. 69
8 Trobits, M., *Antebellum and Civil War San Francisco*, The History Press, Charleston, 2014, p. 48
9 Sutter, J., 'The Discovery of Gold in California', *Hutchings' California Magazine*, Vol. 2, No. 17, November 1857, Hutchings and Rosenfield, San Francisco, p. 196
10 Ibid., p. 197
11 Ibid., p. 198

Chapter 3: The veneration of Saint Barbara

1 *Sydney Morning Herald*, 23 December 1848, p. 2
2 Ibid.
3 Ibid.

4   *California Star*, 3 June 1848, p. 2, reprinted in the *Sydney Morning Herald*, 23 December 1848, p. 2

5   *Punch Magazine*, vol. 16, Bradbury & Evens, London, 1849, p. 64

6   *Colonial Times and Tasmanian* (Hobart), 14 August 1849, p. 1

7   Ibid.

8   Ibid.

9   Foster, S., 'Oh, Susanna!', W. C. Peters & Co, Cincinnati, 1848

10 The Maritime Heritage Project – San Francisco 1800–1899, *Ship's Passengers – Sea Captains*, maritimeheritage.org/vips/nichols.html

11 Coyne, J. S., *Cockneys in California: a Piece of Golden Opportunity*, M. Douglas, New York, 1851, p. 19

12 Bracken, T., *Why, Captain Jackson Barry*, quoted in Jones, J. R., *Writers in Residence: A Journey with Pioneer New Zealand Writers*, Auckland University Press, Auckland, 2004, p. 218

13 *Southland Times*, 6 September 1892, p. 2

14 Lobl, P., *Perilous Gate*, phyllobl.net

Chapter 4: From the ends of the Earth

1   *Daily Telegraph* (Sydney) online, dailytelegraph.com.au/news, 3 July 2014

2   Galloway, T., *Medical and Surgical Journal of His Majesty's hired ship Henry Porcher for 8 August 1834 to 21 January 1835*, National Archives, Kew, UK

3   Backhouse, J., *Letters*, vol. 1 part 4, Harvey & Dalton, London 1842, p. 26

4 *Australian* (Sydney), 2 January 1835, p. 2

5 Ibid.

6 Ibid.

7 Ibid.

8 *Sydney Gazette*, 1 January 1835, p. 2

9 *Sydney Monitor*, 3 January 1835, p. 2

10 European Aeronautical Society, *A Full and Correct Description of this Extraordinary Machine, the First Aerial Ship, The Eagle*, J. Thompson, Lambeth, UK, 1835

Chapter 5: Oranges and leg-irons

1 Wilson, J., *Medical and Surgical Journal of His Majesty's Convict Ship Lady Kennaway for 21 April to 21 October 1836*, National Archives, Kew, 1836

2 Ibid.

3 Ibid.

4 *Sydney Gazette*, 10 November 1836, p. 3

5 King, C. A., *The Life, Hardships and Dreadful Sufferings of Charles Adolphus King*, Birt's Wholesale Song and Book Warehouse, London, 1840

6 *Liverpool Mercury*, 20 April 1847, quoted in Morton, J., *Maximum Security*, Macmillan, 2011, intro

Chapter 6: A red-letter day

1 *Daily Alta California*, 31 October 1850, p. 1

2 Ibid.

3 Ibid.

4 Ibid.

5 Ibid.

6 Ibid.

7 Ibid.
8 Fassin, A. G., 'Yuka Legends', *Overland Monthly and Out West Magazine*, vol. 3, issue 6, June 1884

Chapter 7: Oliver is in town
1 *Colac Herald*, 30 October 1885, p. 2
2 Asbury, H., *The Barbary Coast: An Informal History of the San Francisco Underworld*, A. A. Knopf, New York, 1933, p. 98
3 Muller, K., *Malachi Fallon: San Francisco's First Chief of Police*, California Historical Society, vol. 62, No. 2, 1983, p. 100
4 de Russailh, A. B., *Last Adventure – San Francisco in 1851.* Translated from the original journal by Clarkson Crane, The Westgate Press, San Francisco, 1931, p. 47
5 *San Francisco Herald*, quoted in Asbury, H., *The Barbary Coast: An Informal History of the San Francisco Underworld*, A. A. Knopf, New York, 1933, p. 51
6 Federal Writers Project, *San Francisco in the 1930s: Landmarks of the Old Town*, University of California Press, Berkeley, 2011

Chapter 8: No luck with pick and shovel
1 *Sydney Morning Herald*, 7 September 1850, p. 2
2 *Sydney Morning Herald*, 21 January 1851, p. 2
3 Hargraves, E., Letter to S. Peek, 5 March 1851
4 Davison, S., *The Discovery and Geognosy of Gold Deposits in Australia*, Longman, Green, Longman and Roberts, London, 1860, p. 52
5 Ibid.

Chapter 9: Sainted women and painted ladies

1 Twain, M., et al, *Mark Twain's Travels with Mr Brown*, Knopf, New York, 1940, p. 41
2 Christman, E., Letter to Peebles Prizer, 9 August 1851
3 *Daily Alta California*, 4 October 1849, p. 2
4 Levy, J., *They Saw the Elephant: Women in the California Gold Rush*, University of Oklahoma Press, Norman, 1992, pp. 173–74
5 *Daily Alta California*, 4 October 1851, p. 2
6 Levy, J., *They Saw the Elephant: Women in the California Gold Rush*, University of Oklahoma Press, Norman, 1992, p. 176

Chapter 10: Latter-Day Sam

1 Sherman, W. T., *Personal Memoirs of General William Tecumseh Sherman*, 3rd ed., vol. 1, Charles I Webster & Company, New York, 1890, p. 74
2 Ibid.
3 Ibid., p. 75
4 Ibid.
5 Ibid., p. 80
6 Ibid., p. 81
7 *Daily Alta California*, 27 October 1850, p. 2
8 *Daily Alta California*, 27 October 1850, p. 2
9 *Daily Alta California*, 20 February 1851, p. 2

Chapter 11: Kangaroo courts

1 *San Francisco Daily Herald*, 18 July 1851, p. 2
2 Monaghan, J., *Australians and the Gold Rush*, University of California Press, Berkeley, 1966, p. 182

3 *Sydney Morning Herald*, 12 May 1851, p. 2

4 *Sydney Morning Herald*, 23 July 1851, p. 2

Chapter 12: Who killed Charlie Moore?

1 *Marysville Herald*, 13 December 1850, p. 2

2 *Marysville Herald*, 25 March 1851, p. 2

3 Ibid.

4 *Sacramento Transcript*, 14 December 1850, p. 2

5 *Sacramento Transcript*, 16 December 1850, p. 2

6 *Sacramento Transcript*, 19 December 1850, p. 2

7 Latham, M. S., *Sacramento Transcript*, 18 December 1850, p. 2

Chapter 13: Fanning the flames

1 *San Francisco Daily Herald*, 16 December 1850, p. 2

2 *Sacramento Transcript*, 19 December 1850, p. 2

3 Ibid.

Chapter 14: 'Fie upon your laws!'

1 *Bell's Life in Sydney*, 10 May 1851, p. 2

2 Ibid.

3 Ibid.

4 Ibid.

5 Ibid.

6 *Daily Alta California*, 23 February 1851, p. 2

7 Ibid.

8 Ibid.

9 Ibid.

10 Ibid.

11 *Bell's Life in Sydney*, 17 May 1851, p. 1

12 Ibid.

Chapter 15: 'One vast sheet of flame'

1 Marryat, F., *Mountains and Molehills*, Longman, Brown, Green and Longman, London, 1855, p. 183

2 Thanos, C., and Arentzen, W. (eds.), *Schliemann and the California Gold Rush, 1850–1852*, Sidestone Press, Leiden, 2014, pp. 164–65

3 Ibid.

Chapter 16: 'Something must be done'

1 *California Courier*, 10 June 1851, p. 2

2 Ibid.

3 Williams, M., *History of the San Francisco Committee of Vigilance of 1851*, University of California Press, Berkeley, 1921, p. 205

4 Ibid.

5 Ibid.

6 Ibid.

7 *California Courier*, 10 June 1851, p. 2

8 San Francisco Committee of Vigilance order no. 67, 5 July 1851

9 *Papers of the San Francisco Committee of Vigilance*, 28 June 1851

10 Ibid.

11 Ibid.

Chapter 17: Comings and goings

1 Sullivan, T. D., et al, *Speeches from the Dock, or Protests of Irish Patriotism*, Henry McElroy, Murphy and McCartney, Providence, Rhode Island, 1878, p. 148

2 *Daily Alta California*, 9 June 1851, p. 2

Chapter 18: 'Speedy and terrible vengeance'

1 Williams, M., *History of the San Francisco Committee of Vigilance*, University of California Press, Berkeley, p. 210
2 *Sydney Morning Herald*, 21 August 1851, p. 3, reprinted from the *Daily Alta California*
3 *Papers of the San Francisco Committee of Vigilance*, 12 June 1851
4 Williams, M., *History of the San Francisco Committee of Vigilance*, University of California Press, Berkeley, p. 215
5 Ibid.
6 Ibid.
7 Ibid.
8 *San Francisco Daily Herald*, 12 June 1851, p. 2
9 Ibid., p. 217
10 *California Courier*, 14 June 1851, p. 2
11 *California Local History*, Bluman, E. (ed.), Stanford University Press, Stanford, 1850, p. 26

Chapter 19: The grocer's apologia

1 *California Courier*, 8 July 1851, p. 2
2 Ibid.
3 Ibid.
4 Forbes, F., *Report from the Select Committee on Transportation*, House of Commons, London, 14 July 1837, p. 23
5 Ibid.
6 Ibid.

Chapter 20: The wrong man

1 Pineo, O., *Report to Sir William Burnett, Physician to the Navy*, 20 October 1835

Chapter 21: The Night Watch

1 *Committee of Vigilance Night Watch Report*, 14 June 1851
2 Ibid., 16 June 1851
3 Ibid.
4 Ibid.
5 Ibid., 17 June 1851
6 Ibid., 16 June 1851
7 Ibid., 17 June 1851
8 Ibid.
9 Ibid.
10 Ibid., 20 June 1851
11 Ibid.
12 Ibid.
13 Ibid.
14 Ibid.
15 *Sydney Morning Herald*, 23 August 1851, p. 4

Chapter 22: *Ecce homo*

1 Letter to James Stuart, assumed to be from Sam Whitaker, *Papers of the San Francisco Committee of Vigilance*, 1851
2 *Papers of the San Francisco Committee of Vigilance*, 2 July 1851
3 Ibid.
4 Williams, M., *History of the San Francisco Committee of Vigilance*, University of California Press, 1921, p. 257
5 Ibid.
6 Ibid., p. 260
7 Ibid.
8 Ibid.

Chapter 23: Deeper and deeper

1 *Confession of James Stuart, alias English Jim, alias James Campbell, alias William Stevens, alias James Carlisle,* Committee of Vigilance Papers, 8 July 1851
2 Ibid.
3 Ibid.
4 Ibid.
5 Ibid.
6 Ibid.
7 Ibid.
8 Ibid.
9 Ibid.
10 Ibid.
11 Ibid.
12 Ibid.
13 Ibid.
14 Ibid.

Chapter 24: Law and disorder

1 Confession of James Stuart, alias English Jim, alias James Campbell, alias William Stevens, alias James Carlisle, *Committee of Vigilance Papers*, 8 July 1851
2 Ibid.
3 Ibid.
4 Ibid.
5 Ibid.
6 Ibid.
7 Ibid.
8 Ibid.
9 Ibid.

10 Ibid.
11 Ibid.

Chapter 25: A 'quiet and orderly' occasion

1 *Papers of the San Francisco Committee of Vigilance*, 9 July 1851
2 *San Francisco Herald*, 12 July 1851, p. 2
3 Ibid.
4 Ibid.
5 *Daily Alta California*, 12 July 1851, p. 2
6 Ibid.
7 Ibid.
8 *San Francisco Herald*, 12 July 1851, p. 2
9. Ibid.
10 *Daily Alta California*, 13 July 1851, p. 2
11 Proclamation by Mayor C. J. Brenham, 11 July 1851, *Daily Alta California*, 14 July 1851

Chapter 26: The hangman's banner

1 Walker, F., and Dane, G. (eds.), *Mark Twain's Travels with Mr Brown: sketches written for the Alta California in 1866 and 1867*, entry for 27 February 1867, Knopf, New York, 1940
2 Ibid.
3 Ibid., entry for 6 September 1868
4 Twain, M., *Roughing It*, Harper Bros, New York, 1872, chapter 50
5 Ibid.
6 Ibid.
7 *Daily Alta California*, 27 July 1851, p. 2

8   *Daily Alta California*, 5 October 1851, p. 2

9   Ibid.

10 *San Francisco Herald*, 12 August 1852, p. 1

11 *Sydney Morning Herald*, 20 May 1853, p. 2

12 Ibid.

Chapter 27: Close but no cigar

1   *Empire* (Sydney), 22 September 1851, p. 3

2   Ibid.

3   Ibid., p. 2

4   Ibid.

5   *Empire* (Sydney), 22 September 1851, p. 4

6   Ibid., p. 4

7   Ibid.

8   Ibid.

9   Ibid.

10 Ibid.

11 Ibid.

12 Ibid.

13 Ibid.

14 *Empire* (Sydney), 22 September 1851, p. 4

15 *Empire* (Sydney), 24 September 1851, p. 3

16 *Empire* (Sydney), 25 September 1851, p. 3

17 *Sydney Morning Herald*, 8 November 1851, p. 3

18 Ibid.

19 Ibid.

20. Ibid.

21 Ibid.

22 *Maitland Mercury*, 23 July 1851, p. 2

23 Ibid.

Chapter 28: Pillars of propriety

1 Williams, M., *History of the San Francisco Committee of Vigilance of 1851*, University of California Press, Berkeley, 1921, p. 192
2 Coleman, W. T., 'The San Francisco Vigilance Committees', *Century Magazine*, November 1891 issue
3 Ibid.
4 *Hobart Town Courier*, 29 November 1851, p. 3

Chapter 29: Chasing the wily Cove

1 *Daily Alta California*, 29 July 1851, p. 2
2 Ibid.
3 *San Francisco Daily Herald*, 21 July 1851, p. 2
4 *Colonial Times* (Hobart), 24 October 1851, p. 3

Chapter 30: Never a kind word

1 *Daily Alta California*, 18 August 1851, p. 2
2 Ibid.
3 Ibid.
4 Ibid.
5 Ibid.
6 Ibid.
7 Ibid.
8 Ibid.
9 Ibid.
10 Ibid.
11 Ibid.
12 Ibid.
13 Ibid.
14 Ibid.

15 Ibid.
16 Ibid.

Chapter 31: Flash and counter-flash

1 Williams, M., *History of the San Francisco Committee of Vigilance*, University of California Press, Berkeley, 1921, pp. 296–97
2 Ibid., p. 297
3 Ibid., p. 298
4 Ibid., p. 299
5 Ibid., p. 298
6 Ibid.
7 Ibid.

Chapter 32: Osiris rising

1 Lynch, J., *A Senator of the Fifties*, Robertson, San Francisco, 1911, p. 101
2 Williams, M., *History of the San Francisco Committee of Vigilance*, University of California Press, Berkeley, 1921, p. 303
3 *Sydney Morning Herald*, 20 October 1851, p. 2
4 Ibid.
5 *California Courier*, 24 September 1851, p. 1

Chapter 33: Better angels

1 Williams, M., *History of the San Francisco Committee of Vigilance*, University of California Press, Berkeley, 1921, p. 318
2 Translation of Holinski, A., *La Californie*, Labroue & Co, Brussels, 1853, p. 119

Chapter 34: A scattering of Coves

1 Kay, T. B., Letter to San Francisco Committee of Vigilance, 13 July 1851

2 Boesenecker, J. (ed.), *Against the Vigilantes: The Recollections of Dutch Charley Duane*, University of Oklahoma Press, Norman, 1999, quoted in *Encyclopedia of San Francisco*, sfhistoryencyclopedia.com/articles/d/duane/Charles.html

3 *Molong Argus*, 18 January 1901, p. 3

4 *Windsor and Richmond Gazette*, 26 January 1901, p. 9

5 Ibid.

6 Ibid.

Chapter 35: What goes around . . .

1 Miller, R., *The Lost Frontier*, Rowman & Littlefield, Lanham, Maryland, 2015, p. 79

2 *Daily Alta California*, 4 December 1872, p. 2

3 *Daily Alta California*, 14 December 1872, p. 3

4 *San Francisco Call*, 12 August 1895, p. 2

5 Stanley, G., 'Frank Pixley and the Heathen Chinese', *Phylon Magazine*, vol. 40 no. 3, Clark Atlanta University, 1979, p. 224

Chapter 36: Showgirls and charlatans

1 Collyer, R., Letter to the *Broadway Journal*, 27 December 1845

2 *Boston Weekly Magazine*, vol. 1, Ela and Hall, Boston, 1838–39, p. 120

3 Collyer, R., *Invitation to a lecture on 'The Anatomy of Crime'*, 9 September 1851

Chapter 37: Turnabout

1 *Sydney Morning Herald*, 23 September 1851, p. 2
2 Ibid.
3 Ibid.
4 Ibid.
5 Ibid.
6 *Empire* (Sydney), 22 October 1851, p. 2
7 Ibid.
8 *Sydney Morning Herald*, 18 November 1851, p. 3
9 *Age* (Melbourne), 14 March 1855, p. 5
10 Hill, D., *Gold!*, Random House Australia, Sydney, 2010, p. 175
11 *Argus* (Melbourne), 5 December 1854, p. 2
12 Carboni, R., *The Eureka Stockade*, J. P. Atkinson & Co, Melbourne, 1855, p. 62
13 Ibid.
14 Ibid., p. 63
15 Ibid., p. 71
16 *Ballarat Courier*, 13 December 1883, p. 3
17 *Age* (Melbourne), 14 March 1855, p. 5
18 Ibid.
19 Ferguson, C. D., *The Experiences of a Forty-Niner, During Thirty-Four Years Residence in California and Australia*, Williams Publishing Co., Cleveland, 1888, p. 218

Chapter 38: The man in the white hat

1 Davis, J., Letter to the editor of the *Mountain Democrat*, 4 January 1855
2 Kulczyk, D., *California Justice: Shootouts, Lynching and Assassinations in the Golden State*, Word Dancer Press, Sanger, California, 2008, p. 9

3 Webster, J., Letter to William Henderson, *Placerville County Surveyor*, 20 December 1854

4 *Mountain Democrat*, 23 December 1854, relayed in the *Daily Alta California*, 24 December 1824, p. 2

5 Ibid.

6 Ibid.

7 Ibid.

8 *Sacramento Daily Union*, 27 December 1854, p. 2

9 Davis, J., Letter to the editor of the *Mountain Democrat*, 4 January 1855, p. 2

10 *Los Angeles Star*, 27 January 1855, p. 2

11 *Mountain Democrat*, 20 March 1855, reprinted in the *Daily Alta California*, 26 March 1855, p. 2

Chapter 39: Unlucky last

1 *Daily Alta California*, 21 January 1855, p. 2

2 Ibid.

3 *Adelaide Observer*, 21 April 1855, p. 4

4 Ibid.

5 *Launceston Examiner*, 14 April 1855, p. 2

6 Ibid.

References

Anonymous, *The miners came in forty-nine*, old San Francisco doggerel

Asbury, H., *The Barbary Coast: An Informal History of the San Francisco Underworld*, A. A. Knopf, New York, 1933

Bell's Life in Sydney

Bluman, E. (ed.), *California Local History*, Stanford University Press, Stanford, 1850

Boessenecker, J., *Lawman: The Life and Times of Harry Morse 1835–1912*, University of Oklahoma Press, Norman, 1998

Boesenecker, J. (ed.), *Against the Vigilantes: The Recollections of Dutch Charley Duane*, University of Oklahoma Press, Norman, 1999, quoted in *Encyclopedia of San Francisco*, sfhistoryencyclopedia.com/articles/d/duane/Charles.html

Bracken, T., *Why, Captain Jackson Barry*, quoted in Jones, J. R., *Writers in Residence: a Journey with Pioneer New Zealand Writers*, Auckland University Press, Auckland, 2004

Carboni, R., *The Eureka Stockade*, J. P. Atkinson & Co, Melbourne, 1855

Christman, E., *Letter to Peebles Prizer*, 9 August 1851

Coleman, W. T., 'The San Francisco Vigilance Committees', *The Century Magazine*, November 1891 issue

Collyer, R., Letter to *The Broadway Journal*, 27 December 1845

Collyer, R., *Invitation to a lecture on 'The Anatomy of Crime'*, 9 September 1851

Committee of Vigilance Night Watch Reports, June 1851

Confession of James Stuart, alias English Jim, alias James Campbell, alias William Stevens, alias James Carlisle, *Committee of Vigilance Papers*, 8 July 1851

Coyne, J. S., *Cockneys in California: a Piece of Golden Opportunity*, M. Douglas, New York, 1851

Davison, S., *The Discovery and Geognosy of Gold Deposits in Australia*, Longman, Green, Longman and Roberts, London, 1860

De Russailh, A. B., *Last Adventure – San Francisco in 1851*. Translated from the original journal by Clarkson Crane, The Westgate Press, San Francisco, 1931

De Silva, J., *Letter to Urban VIII*, 1623, quoted in Estensen, M., *Discovery: the quest for the Great South Land*, Allen & Unwin, Sydney, 1998

Estensen, M., *Discovery: The Quest for the Great South Land*, Allen & Unwin, Sydney, 1998

European Aeronautical Society, *A Full and Correct Description of this Extraordinary Machine, the First Aerial Ship, The Eagle*, J. Thompson, Lambeth, UK, 1835

Fassin, A. G., 'Yuka Legends', *Overland Monthly and Out West Magazine*, vol. 3, issue 6, June 1884

Federal Writers Project, *San Francisco in the 1930s: Landmarks of the Old Town*, University of California Press, Berkeley, 2011

Ferguson, C.D., *The Experiences of a Forty-Niner, During Thirty-Four Years Residence in California and Australia*, Williams Publishing Co., Cleveland, Ohio 1888

Galloway, T., *Medical and Surgical Journal of His Majesty's hired ship Henry Porcher for 8 August 1834 to 21 January 1835*, National Archives, Kew, UK

Hill, D., *Gold!*, Random House Australia, Sydney, 2010

Holy Bible, New International Version

King, C. A., *The Life, Hardships and Dreadful Sufferings of Charles Adolphus King*, Birt's Wholesale Song and Book Warehouse, London, 1840

Letter to James Stuart, assumed to be from Sam Whitaker, *Papers of the San Francisco Committee of Vigilance*, 1851

Levy, J., *They Saw the Elephant: Women in the California Gold Rush*, University of Oklahoma Press, Norman, 1992

Lynch, J., *A Senator of the Fifties*, Robertson, San Francisco, 1911

Monaghan, J., *Australians and the Gold Rush*, University of California Press, Berkeley, 1966

Montalvo, *The Adventures of Esplandian*, quoted in Haslam, G. (ed.), *Many Californias: Literature from the Golden State*, second edition, University of Nevada Press, Reno and Las Vegas, 1999

Hargraves, E. H., *Australia and its Goldfields*, H. Ingram and Co, London, 1855

Kulczyk, D., *California Justice: Shootouts, Lynching and Assassinations in the Golden State*, Word Dancer Press, Sanger, California, 2008

Marryat, F., *Mountains and Molehills*, Longman, Brown, Green and Longman, London, 1855

Marshall, J. W., *Account of the discovery of gold in California*, quoted in *Hutchings' California Magazine*, vol. 2, 1858

Miller, R., *The Lost Frontier*, Rowman & Littlefield, Lanham, Maryland, 2015

Proclamation by Mayor C. J. Brenham, 11 July 1851

Punch Magazine, vol. 16, Bradbury & Evens, London, 1849

Russell, R., *A Dissertation Concerning the Use of Sea Water in Diseases of the Glands Etc.*, James Fletcher, Oxford, 1753

Secrest, W., *California Desperadoes*, Word Dancer Press, Clovis, California, 2000

Sherman, W. T., *Personal Memoirs of General William Tecumseh Sherman*, 3rd ed., vol. 1, Charles I Webster & Company, New York, 1890

Ship's Passengers: 1846–1899 – Sea Captains, maritimeheritage. org/vips/nichols.html

Sutter, J., *The Discovery of Gold in California*, Hutchings' California Magazine, Vol. 2, No. 17, November 1857, Hutchings and Rosenfield, San Francisco

Thanos, C., and Arentzen, W. (eds.), *Schliemann and the California Gold Rush, 1850–1852*, Sidestone Press, Leiden, 2014

The Adelaide Observer

The Age (Melbourne)

The Argus (Melbourne)

The Australian (Sydney)

The Ballarat Courier

The Boston Weekly Magazine, vol. 1, Ela and Hall, Boston, 1838–39

The Broadway Journal

The California Courier

The California Star

The Colonial Times and Tasmanian (Hobart)

The Daily Alta California

The Hobart Town Courier

The Launceston Examiner

The Los Angeles Star

The Liverpool Mercury

The Marysville Herald

The Molong Argus

The Mountain Democrat

The Sacramento Daily Union

The Sacramento Transcript

The San Francisco Call

The San Francisco Daily Herald

The Southland Times

The Sydney Gazette

The Sydney Monitor

The Windsor and Richmond Gazette

Translation of Holinski, A., *La Californie*, Labroue & Co, Brussels, 1853

Trobits, M., *Antebellum and Civil War San Francisco*, The History Press, Charleston, 2014

Twain, M., et al, *Mark Twain's Travels with Mr Brown*, Knopf, New York, 1940

Twain, M., *Roughing It*, Harper Bros, New York, 1872

Twain, M., Letter to the *Daily Alta California*, 4 December 1851

Walker, F., and Dane, G. (eds.), Mark Twain's Travels with Mr Brown: sketches written for the Alta California in 1866 and 1867, Knopf, New York, 1940

Webster, J., Letter to William Henderson, *Placerville County Surveyor*, 20 December 1854

Williams, M., *Papers of the San Francisco Committee of Vigilance of 1851*, University of California Press, Berkeley, 1919

Wilson, J., *Medical and Surgical Journal of His Majesty's Convict Ship Lady Kennaway for 21 April to 21 October 1836*, National Archives, Kew, 1836

Acknowledgements

This story owes much to a throwaway remark in a Sydney pub, made by an American whose name sadly escapes me – an acquaintance of a friend of a friend. When the conversation turned to rebellion in Australia, and the Eureka Stockade in particular, he made a point of mentioning the vital part played in that rebellion by diggers from California, adding, 'We did more for Australia in the gold rush days than Australia did for us.'

Asked what he meant by that, he said, 'Did you know that Australian outlaws were the scourge of California, and that they burnt San Francisco to the ground?'

I had to admit that, no, I didn't know that, and resolved to find out more. Researching the inglorious history of the Sydney Coves was made possible through resource material in the United States, Australia and Britain, including the Papers of the San Francisco Committee of Vigilance of 1851, the State Library of New South Wales, the Trove collection of the National Library of Australia, the UK National Archives, the US Federal Writers

Project, and the archives of 19th-century newspapers and magazines in the US, Australia and the UK.

Sincere thanks are due to my publisher, Alison Urquhart; to managing editor, Brandon VanOver; to my eagle-eyed editor, Virginia Grant; and to my friend and guide in San Francisco, Ian McKinnon.

Index

TERRY SMYTH

AUSTRALIAN
CONFEDERATES

HOW 42 AUSTRALIANS JOINED
THE REBEL CAUSE AND FIRED THE
LAST SHOT IN THE AMERICAN CIVIL WAR

AUSTRALIAN CONFEDERATES

Summer, 1865. The colony of Victoria is thriving.

When the notorious Confederate warship *Shenandoah* sails into bustling Port Phillip Bay, Melburnians' curiosity overcomes any squeamishness about the support of slavery. For more than three weeks, the Americans are fêted enthusiastically.

When the sleek black raider steams back through the heads on 19 February, on board are 42 Australians who have secretly enlisted to fight for the South in the American Civil War. So much for the law against foreign warships recruiting in a neutral port.

Under the command of the enigmatic Captain James Waddell, the raider proceeds to wipe out almost the entire New England whaling fleet. The *Shenandoah* fires the last shot of the war, having captured, burned and ransomed 38 Union ships and taken more than 1,000 prisoners.

Award-winning journalist Terry Smyth paints a broad canvas in the telling of this electric piece of history. He brings to life the 42 Australians who sailed off to adventure and controversy, among them the last man to die in the service of the Confederacy.

DENNY DAY

THE LIFE AND TIMES OF AUSTRALIA'S GREATEST LAWMAN

THE FORGOTTEN HERO OF THE MYALL CREEK MASSACRE

TERRY SMYTH

AUTHOR OF *AUSTRALIAN CONFEDERATES*

DENNY DAY

Captain Edward Denny Day – the only law 'from the Big River to the sea' – was Australia's greatest lawman. This is his story.

Once there was a wilderness: Australia's frontier, a dangerous and unforgiving place where outlaws ruled the roads and killers were hailed as heroes. It was here, in 1838, that one man's uncompromising sense of justice changed history and shocked the world.

Denny Day was a vicar's son from Ireland. A member of the Anglo-Irish ruling class, Day joined the British Army before resigning to seek his fortune in New South Wales. There he accepted the most challenging role in the young colony: keeping the peace on the frontier.

Denny Day's abiding legacy is the capture of the perpetrators of the Myall Creek Massacre – the most infamous mass-murder in Australian history and the first time white men were convicted of the murder of Aborigines. Yet Day won no praise for bringing to justice the killers of 28 innocent men, women and children. Rather, he was scorned and shunned, fiercely attacked by the press, powerful landowners and the general public.

The 11 men tracked down and arrested by Day faced two sensational trials, and seven of them were eventually found guilty of murder and hanged. The case sparked an international outcry, resulting in stricter government policies protecting the rights of Indigenous peoples.

Denny Day's story is a brilliant slice of Australian History, with many colourful characters, heroes and villains: inspirational frontier women; outlaws; brave Aboriginal resistance leaders; gormless colonial officials; privileged English nobles and persecuted Irish immigrants; convicts and freemen.